MICROLITERATURES

A volume in the series

Medieval Societies, Religions, and Cultures

Edited by M. Cecilia Gaposchkin and Anne E. Lester

A list of titles in this series is available at cornellpress.cornell.edu.

MICROLITERATURES

THE PRODUCTION OF THE MARGIN IN MEDIEVAL AND EARLY MODERN IBERIAN BOOKS

Jesús R. Velasco

Translated by Consuelo López-Morillas

Foreword by M. Cecilia Gaposchkin and Anne E. Lester

CORNELL UNIVERSITY PRESS
Ithaca and London

Originally published as *Microliteraturas*

Copyright © Jesús Rodríguez-Velasco, 2022

Copyright © Grupo Anaya, S.A.
(Ediciones Cátedra), 2022

English translation and series editors' foreword copyright © 2025 Cornell University

All rights reserved. Except for brief quotations in a review, this book, or parts thereof, must not be reproduced in any form without permission in writing from the publisher. For information, address Cornell University Press, Sage House, 512 East State Street, Ithaca, New York 14850. Visit our website at cornellpress.cornell.edu.

First published 2025 by Cornell University Press

Library of Congress Cataloging-in-Publication Data

Names: Rodríguez Velasco, Jesús D. author. | López-Morillas, Consuelo, translator. | Gaposchkin, M. Cecilia (Marianne Cecilia), 1970– writer of foreword. | Lester, Anne E., 1974– writer of foreword.
Title: Microliteratures : the production of the margin in medieval and early modern Iberian books / Jesús R. Velasco, translated by Consuelo López-Morillas, foreword by M. Cecilia Gaposchkin and Anne E. Lester.
Other titles: Microliteraturas. English
Description: Ithaca : Cornell University Press, 2025. | Includes bibliographical references and index.
Identifiers: LCCN 2024059237 (print) | LCCN 2024059238 (ebook) | ISBN 9781501782374 (hardcover) | ISBN 9781501782381 (paperback) | ISBN 9781501782404 (epub) | ISBN 9781501782398 (pdf)
Subjects: LCSH: Literature—Philosophy. | Marginalia. | Literature, Medieval—History and criticism. | Literature, Modern—15th and 16th centuries—History and criticism. | Iberian Peninsula—Literatures—History and criticism—Theory, etc.
Classification: LCC PN49 .R634 2025 (print) | LCC PN49 (ebook) | DDC 860.9/003—dc23/eng/20250209
LC record available at https://lccn.loc.gov/2024059237
LC ebook record available at https://lccn.loc.gov/2024059238

*This book is dedicated to Aurélie Vialette,
Miguel Velasco Vialette, and Simone Velasco Vialette*

Contents

Series Editors' Foreword   ix
Preface: In Prison   xiii

Introduction	1
1. Order and Discipline	19
2. The Production of the Margin	52
3. Centripetal Glosses	77
4. Activism	102
5. Assemblage, Subject	137
6. A Vernacular Society	164
Epilogue	184

Acknowledgments   189
Bibliography   193
Index   219

Series Editors' Foreword

Microlituratures, first published in Spanish in 2022, is a tour-de-force, a close reading of what Jesús Velasco has identified as "micro" writings done along the margins of pages in medieval manuscripts and early modern text editions. Eschewing the term marginal, implying that they were of little value or meaning, Velasco embraces the notion of micro and argues that the kinds of texts and writing done in the small spaces of a page's margins show the process of *thinking with* the text. In turn, by noticing and giving renewed attention to these microliteratures we are better able to witness the ideas, conversations, and thought-worlds of premodern writers, thinkers, copyists, glossers, students, and readers unfold in practice. Velasco then invites us into a process of thought in the works.

We are delighted to include this rich and masterful English translation of *Microliteratures*, rendered beautifully by Consuelo López-Morillas, in the Medieval Societies, Religions, and Cultures Series. Jesús Velasco's scholarship is wide-ranging and creative. A professor of Spanish and Portuguese and comparative literature at Yale University, Velasco has written about textual traditions, literary methodologies, citizenship, and legal genealogies with great precision and elegance. A capacious and creative thinker, Velasco's writing in Spanish and English is likewise lively and engaging. Beginning from his own first-person experiences and observations, Velasco invites the reader on an intellectual journey that ranges over vast territories and temporalities. In *Microliteratures*, we are guided through a carefully curated set of texts that reveal a series of fascinating readings linked not so much by a shared theme or historical context, but by a core humanistic practice, that of reading, reflection, and writing. This is a recursive intellectual journey that travels from the reader to the "tutor text" at the center, to comment and commentary text along the graphic margins, and returns to the reader again, now changed by this process.

Eschewing the dichotomy of center and periphery, Velasco implores us to see the intellectual work of conversation and interpretation constantly at present in the micro-spaces of the margins. It is the intellectual process that holds center stage here. What is more, Velasco shows how personally transformative and politically upending the thought-work of the margins could be. His decentering of the text is both an exciting new exploration of the long overlooked and a call to recognize new presences and voices that have been undervalued and unheeded, especially those of women. The ideas, opinions, and voices of these microliteratures articulate forms of written activism, political commentary, subjectivity, and vernacular discourse that questioned and pushed against a dominant center, framing, interpreting, and changing that centered text in turn.

Through such writing we see the dialogues that readers had with previous authors. We likewise see medieval and early modern readers inviting other authors into this dialogic process and thus can follow through the development of ideas, of criticism, and of political and ethical frameworks that ranged widely in time and space. Not as formal as medieval glosses, microliteratures—written sometimes in haste or abbreviated form—are encapsulations of thoughts at work, taking shape in a smaller but nevertheless vitally important juncture. As Velasco shows, they are critical for understanding how reader and text worked together, engaging ideas and sometimes questioning establishing interpretations. They offer another entry point into well-known texts and serve as a barometer for how canonical texts were received. Modern printed critical editions of central text are typically shorn of the manuscripts' comments and notes. This creates a falsely sanitized version of canonical texts. By returning to the manuscripts at the heart of this project, Velasco resuscitates these microliteratures and emphasizes writing and reading as a process and practice rather than the final product. In this sense, the microliteratures that hold our attention here are part of a deeply humanistic endeavor. Simultaneously intimate and private, once copied and printed microliteratures become public texts that are integral to future textual traditions, commentaries, and interpretations, especially in the legal tradition.

Over time, the fact that a text would receive comments in the form of both glosses and notes required the very materiality of the text space, of the page itself, to change to accommodate an ever-growing set of comments and dialogues with ever more interlocutors. Thus, margins were made wider, leaving ample room for noted thoughts and comparative texts and ideas to take shape. Ripe for such commentary and mental engagement, as Velasco shows, were legal texts and the textual traditions folded into the study of the law. From there, he turns to the treatment of texts on the religious life, commentaries on chivalry, and a complaint about the nature of government. Turning then to treaties of political philosophy and ending with volumes that address the self and space. In this way, microliteratures become a way of philosophizing about the intellect and the self.

Velasco's innovative book invites a wide array of readers to take part in this process. Drawing on his expertise in fields ranging from comparative literature, political philosophy, and legal theory, to language, textual, and manuscript studies, he exposes a space of cross-pollination and asks that us to engage in this ongoing conversation. For those interested in scholastic, intellectual, material, and conceptual history as well as philosophies of knowledge, *Microliteratures* reaches across disciplines and throughout the later Middle Ages and into the early modern world in its treatment of authors and textual traditions. There were and are intellectual and political consequences for such forms of thinking beyond the center. This translation is a welcome tutorial for navigating and engaging with microliteratures that have and had outsized and long-lasting consequences.

M. Cecilia Gaposchkin
Anne E. Lester

Preface: In Prison

          The island is a prison complex that covers more than four hundred acres. Thanks to the graphic artist, professor, and activist M. R., I was able to offer a short series of seminars there with her, as part of the social justice program of Columbia University, where I was teaching at the time.[1] We discussed the circumstances in which the seminar would take place. M. R. knew the ins and outs of this prison well: although we had twenty female prisoners enrolled in the class, they could not always attend. Because of some act of violence, or simply from neglect, or as retribution by the prison officers, some of our students might not be allowed to come to class, or no one would remember to bring them; as for them, they couldn't move without being escorted by a guard. Sometimes we even might, and did, have a guard posted inside our classroom. It wasn't easy for us to enter, either. One day the prison officer at the entrance hadn't been told about the schedule; on another, there was no one to run the metal detector and the scanner. Sometimes we were grilled about materials we were bringing in, like tablets and even books.

    I decided that one seminar would be devoted to Christine de Pizan, the French writer of Venetian origin who was active from the late fourteenth to the early fifteenth century. I would speak briefly about one of her manuscripts, the *Book of the Queen*, which contains her complete works in a version that she organized and corrected with her own hand.[2] It is a very well-known manuscript in medievalist circles, and I had had the pleasure of working with it directly in the British Library during one of my visits there. Because the library has a digitized version, I was

---

    1. At M. R.'s request I have concealed both her name and the prison's. The prison has activated an automatic internet search that informs them about what people say about the institution itself; this may threaten the continuation of the program.

    2. Made for the queen of France, Isabelle of Bavaria-Ingolstadt, between 1410 and 1414, it bears the signature Harley 4431 of the British Library. See its catalogue entry and a link to digitized materials at http://searcharchives.bl.uk/IAMS_VU2:IAMS040-002050268.

able to take away a few printed images and hold a little workshop with them for the imprisoned women, because in the prison there is no internet available for this sort of activity.

I decided on a few pages from the *Epistre Othea* (letter of Othea): Othea is a goddess of prudence, invented by Christine, who is explaining to the Trojan hero Hector everything he needs to know about chivalry—the ultimate expression of masculinity. It is divided into one hundred tales, each of which has four parts: a miniature, a fragment of the matter of Troy called a *texte*, and two explanations or interpretations, one labeled *alegorie* and the other *glose*.[3] The structure is highly dynamic: the text occupies just a handful of verses, usually fewer than ten, and neither the allegory nor the gloss is very long, so that a page can be read very quickly. The editorial history of the work gives proof of its enormous popularity.[4]

Each session at the prison has to be self-contained. The students who come one day may not be there the next, so everything must have a beginning and an end, a Genesis and an Apocalypse, within the allotted time. Therefore, the plan for the class was to study the manuscript as an object of art, and then *do something*. It's essential to do something with what you study in prison. It's not enough to gain a more or less abstract or immaterial sense of it; you have to hold it right in your hands and collect not only the facts but your emotions.

M. R. and I had also brought in the materials needed for the workshop: sets of colored pencils and markers, together with sheets of size A3 paper (42 × 29.7 cm) reminiscent of the paper in the *Book of the Queen*, which is a thick, heavy parchment in folio volume (36.5 × 28.5 cm). Library catalogues do not list the weights of manuscripts, as far as I know, but I can assure you that this one is extremely heavy.[5] In our workshop we would ask our students to create their own manuscripts.

Their assignment was to recall two things: an image and a poem. The imprisoned women are not allowed to bring personal objects with

---

3. The general page layout can be seen in this British Library link, showing folio 98r of the *Book of the Queen*. The manuscript's two volumes are reproduced online at: http://www/bl.uk/manuscripts/Viewer.aspx?ref=harley_ms_4431_f098r.

4. The ARLIMA (Archive de Littérature du Moyen Âge) lists forty-eight medieval manuscripts and four sixteenth-century printed editions of the work: see the link at https://www.arlima.net/ad/christine_de_pizan.html#oth.

5. A request to libraries: tell us the weight of your books. That would give us an idea of whether a book was portable, or if it was a space to travel into rather than an object that could be carried from place to place.

them, so in order to make even a simple sketch and write three or four meaningful verses of a poem they had to search in the immaterial world of their minds. Their images were invariably related to their families: many of our students had children or other relatives that they hadn't seen for a long time. Almost all of them, though, thought they didn't know any poems by heart, until they realized that they called them songs. Perhaps the ones they quoted most were Beyoncé's, because her album *Lemonade* had just come out. Her lyrics soon appeared on the lips, in the cadences, and in the laughter of the students, who were fascinated by the thought that this could be a poem, a piece of literature, something that they had never studied but was embedded in their memory. Finally, in imitation of Christine, each student had to write an allegory and a gloss. For the allegory they had to travel mentally outside the prison, to a world in which the image and the poem meant something very different from the life they were locked into now. For the gloss they had to take an internal trip—to study their own feelings, the intimate meaning of those remembered images and texts.

At the end of that afternoon, with the students exhausted and weepy—like the prison officer, who had spent all those hours with us—we mounted an exhibit. We hung up all the manuscript pages, each with its image, text, allegory, and gloss, and then strolled around to look at them. We were sharing a moment of microliterary intensity in which these women who had suffered violence in the streets, violence at home, violence in prison, found a space of creation and collaboration, and also a small space of activism and redemption. There in that place of state-sponsored violence, they were claiming their right to compose and express their ideas about public and private matters, including the systemic racism that, in certain communities, beats a sinister path from school to prison.[6] We all knew that when the class was over those papers on the wall would go straight to the recycling bin. Neither their authors nor M. R. nor I could keep them or photograph them—that was forbidden in jail. Only the memory of twenty lost manuscripts would remain, the memory of a moment of emotion.

But also the memory of a moment of freedom. Not escape, not liberation, not a brief forgetting of life behind bars. A moment of creative freedom, of thinking for oneself, of projecting a wish, an allegory, a spiritual and personal interpretation of something that was held in

---

6. See, for example, Oluo, *So You Want to Talk*, 121–33.

memory and that meant something. A moment of searching for that meaning.

Commentators, glossers, writers, and artists for a day. Microliterary artists. I owe those women my inspiration for finishing this book, and I write it now to express my respect for them. I don't know their names, I don't know if they're still in jail. But I remember them, their voices, their accents, their way of mixing languages, their writing, and above all their laughter. To all of you, wherever you are, I hope you are well, and many thanks.

Introduction

Margins are helpful when, opening a book, you don't want to cover any of the text with your fingers.[1] And also for taking notes. Edgar Allan Poe liked to buy books with very wide ones, to give free rein to his obsessive reading and note-taking. No width was enough for him, so the little literary texts that he would compose at the edge of the page and then copy out for his public readings might need more space, to add details or to work out a debate. Poe remarked that sometimes he had to add more margin to the margin by pasting on a slip of paper with gum tragacanth (an ancestor of the Post-it) to give more scope to his pencil.[2] The available space may be limited, but the microliterary impulse is not threatened by that trivial circumstance.

---

1. NB: Throughout this book I use the singular "they/them" pronouns when I have no idea about the possible gender of the persons I refer to, and the masculine or feminine ones when I know. I may have been inconsistent in this use, but my intention is always to be inclusive.

2. Gum tragacanth derives from a botanical species, native mainly to Iran, that was introduced to the United States in the nineteenth century (Gentry et al., "Introduction of Chia," 252-56). Poe began publishing his "Marginalia" in the November 1844 issue of the *Democratic Review* and continued to publish examples of these marginal writings until 1849, both in that journal and in *Godey's Lady's Book*, the most popular magazine for women at the time (while it published some female writers, most of its authors were well-known literary men). Others appeared in *Graham's* and the *Southern Literary Messenger*, on both of whose editorial boards

While the space may be minimal, it must be exploited to the maximum. You can't always stick a slip of paper onto the book you're reading with tragacanth gum. Even if you can, your handwriting gets smaller and you abbreviate words; those idiotachigraphic signs invade the narrow white space like a troop of illegible soldiers. Robert Walser, in his own microscripts, used whatever surface came to hand to satisfy his unquenchable thirst for annotation.[3] A card, a matchbox, the back of a calendar page. His microscripts use a traditional system of handwriting, common in German until the mid-twentieth century, called *Kurrent*, but in miniature; it has caused many a migraine, including, I am sure, for his splendid American translator Susan Bernofsky. Writing very small is not only a physical necessity, it's a challenge. One could choose not to write between the lines of a Bible, or to leave the space between two columns on a page blank.[4] Any of us might decide not to write in the narrow margins of a volume issued by a stingy publisher—but we do it anyway. The microliterary urge wins out, institutionalized by the magic of small handwriting.

Marginal writing is expansive and increases the size of something that is already large. It does not accept the imposing presence of the main text centered on the page. And the gloss is a huge presence not only physically, but conceptually; marginal writing subscribes to the notion that glosses can provide food for thought. Microliterature arises from the realization that what this particular book I have in my hands says, and conveys, can be excavated and studied. If I make a mark at this point, the text begins to expand outward in several directions: it might be an asterisk, a dagger, a simple underlining, a letter, or other fairly conventional signs that suggest that there is more here, that this in particular needs expanding, needs exploring more deeply.[5] "There is more

---

Poe served. His theory of marginalia appeared in the November 1844 issue of the *Democratic Review*.

3. Susan Bernofsky offers a full history of this system of microwriting, the "horror of the pen" that came over Walser even before he was diagnosed with schizophrenia (in 1929, twenty-seven years before his death in 1956). In 1927 Walser wrote to his intellectual mentor Max Rychner that microwriting had taught him "patience, such that I now have mastered the art of being patient." Walser, *Microscripts*, 12.

4. On the assertion about the Bible, see chapter 1. Shortly after 1419 an expert in Hebrew philology, philosophy, and theology, who knew the various versions of Maimonides's *Guide to the Perplexed* in that language, began to read its Spanish translation by Pedro de Toledo, based on the Hebrew versions by Samuel ben Jehudah ibn Tibbon and Yehuda al-Harizi. Pedro de Toledo worked in the library of Gómez Suárez de Figueroa, lord of Zafra. See chapter 2.

5. The conventional signs used to indicate a marginal note, or another place for a commentary, are many; while generally stable they can differ from manuscript to manuscript,

here" does not mean that there is less in the master text, to be replaced or completed by this "more."⁶ Rather, the thought process does not have a single destination, it doesn't end once and for all. Sometimes "there is more here" represents a lateral move, a digression, a bringing up to date. In any event, it always seems that the comment orbits like a satellite around that great planet, which at once attracts and repels the act of creation. Marginal writing may be expansive, but it is adjacent to something already given, in relation to which it constitutes a microliterature.

The central text is a spotlight that emits its authority throughout its history of presences and translations—it is the very canon of great male and female writers, speaking from the middle of the page. Sometimes its difficulty resists commentary. Occasionally, as with certain legal texts, it forbids it: the *Siete Partidas* tried to do so, with little success.⁷

---

copyist to copyist, century to century, textual tradition to textual tradition, and so on. The most common ones can usually be identified with Latin paleography and are covered in basic manuals. See, for example, Adolfo Tura, "Essai sur les *marginalia*," esp. 273–76, devoted to signalectic notes (technical signs that draw attention to a comment). Evina Steinová's *Notam Superponere* is a systematic examination of manuscripts from the years 400 CE to 900 CE; she offers a (manuscript) table of those technical signs, available on her website (in the future, will people wonder what happened to all those websites cited in footnotes, in spite of their many permalinks? Or will the permalink have become the new permafrost?): the pdf can be found at www.homomodernus.net and https://f-origin.hypotheses.org/wp-content/blogs.dir/1137/files/2019/07/Steinova-Most-Common-Western-Annotation-Symbols-in-the-Early-Middle-Ages_colour_2019-07-19.pdf.

6. Dagenais (*The Ethics of Reading*, 38–39), like many of his readers, believes that the tutor text's *deficiency* is what generates the gloss, which would offer an enhancement, a *surplus*. Medieval commentators subscribed to this idea: Marie de France, in the prologue to her *Lais*, writes: "Custume fu as ancïens / ceo testimoine Prescïens, / es livres que jadis faiseient / assez oscurement diseient / our ceux que a venir esteient / et ki aprendre les deveient, / que peüssent gloser la lettre / et de lur sen le surplus metre" (22, vv. 9–16). The central issue here is that, according to Marie, who followed Priscian, authors of antiquity wrote obscurely so that their future readers might both literally gloss them and add new items of knowledge. This "surplus" is not a failing of the ancient text, but a positive asset in the future. It is a *past future* (a concept of Reinhart Koselleck's, *vergangene Zukunft*): one of the ways in which the past imagines and speaks of the future, endowing historical time with meaning. It is tempting to bring in here Jacques Derrida's notion of the *supplément* (or *logique supplémentaire*, as he explains in *De la grammatologie*)—a way for marginal thinkers to establish their opposition to something without actually contradicting it. My impression is that this logic is not operating here as a necessary element or generalized structure; rather, while it occurs especially in self-glosses or marginal comments by an author on his or her own text, it does not constitute a specific logic in itself.

7. I cite Alfonso X's *Las Siete Partidas* (a legal codification originating in thirteenth-century Castile) in the 1555 edition (unless otherwise noted), in the following format: *Partidas* [number of *Partida*].[title].[law] (for example, *Partidas* 7.33.4), or [ordinal number of *Partida*].[title]. [law] (for example, seventh *Partida* 33.4). *Partidas* 7.33.4 establishes that "no one should, or

4   INTRODUCTION

In certain cases commentary is made physically impossible, as when a manuscript's composers turn its margins into a series of pits that would swallow the ink. That happened to a fourteenth-century Book of Hours now in the Walters Art Museum in Baltimore: the blank edges that surround the central text and images have been cut out with architectural shapes that the museum's manuscript curator, Lynley Anne Herbert, is studying in comparison to the ornamental motifs of Gothic churches. The authority of the center has to be conquered, because it does not surrender easily to a siege. The marginal commentary seems irrelevantly local by comparison; as Poe said of his marginalia, they were a mere whim, and as such inferior in authority to the center.[8] However, it is microliterature that usually wins the battle.

Beside a full, solid, and continuous text that fills the center of the page with its large letters—sometimes in inks of different colors, or gorgeously illuminated, or simply written clearly so as to be read and studied—the margin expands in a constellation of commentaries. The *Corpus Iuris Civilis*, in the version championed by Francesco Accursio, has around one hundred thousand glosses, but who's counting?[9] The *Sátira de Infelice e Felice vida* by Pedro de Portugal is supposed to have exactly one hundred—one for each eye of Argus—but wouldn't you know, it has 105.[10] In certain manuscripts of Juan de Mena's *Las Trescientas* (or *Laberinto de Fortuna*), conscientious binders and restorers have washed off the marginal glosses with bleach.[11] In many manuscripts of *De Re militari* by the Latin author Flavius Renatus Vegetius (translated, with spiritual glosses, by Alonso de San Cristóbal in the fifteenth century), the glosses have either disappeared, or else the structure of the

---

can, explicate or declare [what] the laws [say]" (Espaladinar nin declarar non debe ninguno nin puede las leyes). A similar stricture occurs also in *Partidas* 1.1.

8. Book of Hours shelf number W 93, Walters Art Museum, Baltimore, MD. Laura Fernández Fernández reminds me that "it is in these 'local' details that the relevant information resides. They are often what reveals the identity of the makers, the doers, the context, those who illuminate the scene beyond what is evident" (personal communication to author, November 2, 2020).

9. Dingledy, "*Corpus*," 231–55, offers a brief history of how the *Corpus Iuris Civilis* was used. The bibliography it includes can give only a slight idea of the creative depth of the work's glossers, whose epitome is Accursio. A complete bibliography of the project cannot be given here, but "Taking Inventory" by Dolezalek, one of the greatest experts in the subject, will be helpful.

10. There are two manuscripts of this work, one in Spain's Biblioteca Nacional, MSS/4023. The other is in the jealous hands of a private collector in Barcelona; there is a digital copy, but the equally jealous philologists who are studying it have refused to let me see it.

11. This is the case of the one in the Hispanic Society of America in New York, HC 397/703.

work—which had been well designed by Fray Alonso de San Cristóbal, a master in theology—has been altered so as to avoid all marginal writing.[12] In many of the manuscripts of Giles of Rome's *Glosa castellana al Regimiento de príncipes* the gloss has been joined in an indissoluble manner to the center of the page.[13] The order and presence of marginal comments are optional and sometimes so excessive that they have been erased, summarized, abbreviated, turned into compendia, or forgotten. If still alive they are fragile, in a minority state that we may call microliterary.

Those who write glosses do so in the shadow of another entity with which they seek to be related, a larger object that they confront in their minor key as microliterary writers. All too often, what they are facing is themselves. Both male and female authors of microliterature can be self-glossers: Christine de Pizan (1364–ca. 1430) is the capstone to the whole vault of self-glossing women, since she is the expert constructor and organizer of her manuscripts, in which text, allegory, gloss, image, and page layout work together with the coherence of a multimedia creation.[14] Next to her, self-glossers such as Enrique de Villena (1384–1434) and Diego de Valera (1412–88), both in Cuenca, look like mere amateurs—or, as Juan de Valdés called the latter, chatterboxes and fantasists.[15]

Microliterature, then, is a form of production within written culture; microliterature is also a materiality of communication and an activity performed by those who produce it—a feverish, somewhat crazed activity. The study of microliterature involves studying objects, material aspects, circles of production, and ways of creating communication networks. When we look at microliterature we see its most prominent activity: *thinking with*. Thinking something, anything, in relation to

---

12. For this work, see chapter 2.

13. I have written about all these cases elsewhere: see Rodríguez Velasco, *El debate*; "La 'Bibliotheca,'" 119–34; "La producción," 249–72; and *Plebeyos márgenes*. See also Gille Levenson, "L'évolution," 137–40; Fradejas-Rueda et al., "La transmisión textual," 31–38; Díez Garretas et al., "Las versiones A y B," 227–33; and Díez Garretas, "Recursos estructurales," 151–96.

14. See Desmond and Sheingorn, *Myth, Montage, and Visuality*.

15. Of course I do not share the humanist's opinion of Diego de Valera, whom I admire so much that I wrote my doctoral dissertation about him back in the Middle Pleistocene. But here are his words: "And you must know that I call Mosén Diego a chatterbox [*hablistán*] because, being so fond of talking, he puts into his writing some improper things that he could just as well do without; and I call him a fantasist [*parabolano*] because he mixes facts together with so many things that never existed, wanting to convince you that they are true, that he makes you doubt all the rest." Valdés, *Diálogo de la lengua*, 253–54.

what is open to reading and criticism. Thinking with expressions, concepts, ideas, images, metaphors; thinking with, not only interpreting.

Make Haste Slowly

This book intends not to be exhaustive.[16] The great gift of microliterature is the challenge of *thinking with*, that is, critical thought. In contributing to critical thought, we must do so slowly and in detail, enlarging in a legible way. In the humanities, exhaustiveness does not necessarily add to critical thought; it tends to impose typologies, hierarchies, teleologies, and even fads and tendencies, rather than giving voice to the individual impulses that, painstakingly, construct the products of intellectual labor and its material manifestation.

Academic writing tends toward a certain degree of confidentiality. Sometimes this is necessary; it is not easy to speak of complex matters in a simple way. Often one must use the technical jargon of a given discipline, obscuring the surface of the text. An academic text should be written so as to think along with it, and sometimes that requires elaborate concepts, concision, or a rigorous use of technical terms. But confidentiality and obscurity can prove unsatisfying as well. It would be ideal if, even within the limited world of academia, we could know or learn how to share with our contemporaries the kind of knowledge that goes with our mysterious, specialized research. But this does not imply diluting that knowledge to the point of simplifying it.

Therefore, this book proposes a thesis of which it should also be an example: that microliterature is a humanistic activity performed in the public sphere. In this sense, microliteratures are abundant and enduring manifestations of the essay genre, and thus belong to the literary world. This book, though academically based, seeks to share that familiarity with the essay, so as to show that certain intellectual activities and concerns that we have assimilated almost to the point of

---

16. Julian Weiss has cataloged glossed manuscripts, both of translations and of works written in the vernacular, covering most of the surviving examples: "Comentarios y glosas vernáculas," 199-243, and "Vernacular Commentaries and Glosses," 237-71. There are no truly comprehensive studies, and I have decided not to write one, which would be overwhelmingly descriptive. Therefore, in the present work, I do not discuss certain manuscripts and works by the authors most obvious to those with some knowledge of the subject, such as Enrique de Villena and Juan de Mena. Should anyone point out that I have not mentioned their theories or practices I can only say that they are entirely correct, and that I simply did not wish to do so.

forgetting them are still active, and still underlie our ethical, political, and juridical actions by means of cultural production and its material manifestations.

Microliterary insertions and their presence in manuscripts and printed books are not necessarily rhetorical exercises for preaching to a choir—often made up of an elite that is conscious of being so, and of possessing a certain social and cultural capital. It is also true, however, that "the choir has to rehearse, too . . . [and] learn its parts," and therefore needs constant reminding.[17] Writers and readers produce their microliterary spaces carefully, to act as a fulcrum with which to modify the ethical and political conditions of their contemporary world. Microliterary glosses are constructed within books intended to be seen in certain semiprivate or semipublic libraries, like that of Íñigo López de Mendoza (1398–1458), in which some fifteenth-century Castilian intellectuals worked. Other nobles and aristocrats shared their libraries and collections: Pedro Fernández de Velasco, count of Haro, whose double library was kept in Haro and the Hospital de la Vera Cruz; Gómez Suárez de Figueroa, lord of Zafra, and many others.[18] From there, and from the court of John II of Castile, from Charles II of Navarre, from the workshop of Christine de Pizan, books emerged ready to be copied with their glosses. Enrique de Villena's translation of, and glosses on, the *Aeneid* bear strict instructions to the scribe to copy the glosses along with the text. Not to copy the glosses, Villena admonishes, is a clear sign of Satanic possession, of obeying the orders of a malignant demon.[19]

---

17. This observation arises from the conversation between Noel King and Michael Eric Dyson about the latter's book *Long Time Coming*. "DYSON: Well, the thing is, of course, the right white people are the ones who are going to read the book. The ones who won't stand a chance of being convinced or changed probably won't. Yeah, maybe it's a self-selective audience. Maybe it's preaching to the choir. But the choir has to rehearse, too. The choir has to learn its parts. It's got to get the altos different from the sopranos, who are not the same as the baritones, who aren't the same as the bass." Michael Eric Dyson, interviewed by Noel King, *Morning Edition*, NPR, December 1, 2020, link at https://www.npr.org/2020/12/01/940418711/dysons-book-long-time-coming-aims-to-help-america-reckon-with-race.

18. The most important work on medieval Iberian libraries, using innovative methodologies, is Marta Vírseda Bravo's doctoral dissertation, "La biblioteca de los Velasco en el hospital de la Vera Cruz." See also Faulhaber, *Libros y bibliotecas*.

19. I have consulted the manuscripts directly. The image from Biblioteca Nacional de España MSS/17975 contains the text with its glosses, proving that the copyist was not in the grip of any devil. The text in the left margin reads, in part: "A todos los quel presente libro querran & faran trasladar plega delo escrevir con glosas segund aqui esta complida mente [. . .] & sean ciertos que si les verna a boluntad ho deseo delo traslador syn las glosas que les viene por temptaçion & subgeçion diabolica . . ." (To all who are willing and able to make a copy of this book, I beg them to copy it with the entire apparatus of glosses, as it is here,

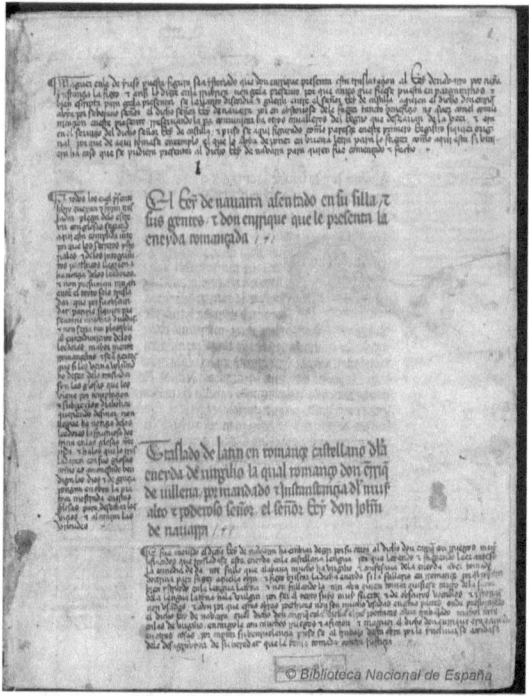

FIGURE 0.1. Enrique de Villena, *La Eneida* de Virgilio, MSS/17975, fol. 1r. Image from the collections of the Biblioteca Nacional de España, licensed under a Creative Commons CC-BY license.

From that universe in which the private action and the public availability of glosses are joined in solidarity, microliteratures are a way of producing the contemporary. That means the ability to make present in public debate those aspects that, irrespective of their historical age, help us to understand, and to better resolve, problems related to social justice in the broadest sense. Involvement with the contemporary presumes a commitment to burning questions that affect the social and political integrity of our common existence. The *contemporary*, then, does not necessarily reside in the *now*, in simultaneous time periods, in coetaneity.

---

and know that if they want to copy it without the glosses, this is because they are subjects to diabolical temptation. . .)

There is an edition by Pedro Cátedra (also including the glosses, so we presume that the editor is not possessed by Lucifer or any of his ilk): *Enrique de Villena*. There was still no possession a few years later, when Cátedra published the work and its glosses in Villena, *Obras*. We make no assumptions about Ramón Santiago Lacuesta, who did not transcribe the glosses in his edition (Villena, *La primera versión*).

Coetaneity is a value held by Western civilization, whose administration was criticized by the anthropologist Johannes Fabian as a colonial artifact.[20] Fabian explains how dominant structures of power establish the calendar of modernity, while excluding or denying that modernity to entire societies. That is why coetaneity—the fact of being simultaneous in the calendar of modernity—is not useful when we speak of the contemporary. Perhaps, as Giorgio Agamben points out, if we wish to be in greater harmony with the most urgent problems of our own time we should stand somewhat outside the limits of coetaneity.[21]

In this book, being someone's contemporary resides in one's capacity to engage with things that require close examination, because our individual and collective ability to face inequality in an active manner depends on those same things. As we are about to see, it is contemporary female and male writers who prove able to observe and criticize some forms of systematic dominance and oppression in their own societies.

This idea is also the stricture I impose on myself in this research: I do not analyze *everything* available, only those expressions that I call microliteratures because they demonstrate the will to think critically about issues related to social and political strife, or issues of social justice in general. That is how, in some way, they push back against systemic structures of power, the kind that perpetuate inherited modes of action. By my definition here, microliteratures are those that do not accept the weight of those modes of action but would prefer to affect them. To operate this voluntary affect (an art of voluntary inservitude, as Michel Foucault put it),[22] they set in motion material forms of communication that, in employing the margins, seek to connect with forms of scientific production, such as the tradition of marginal glossing in the transmission and application of civil law, ecclesiastical law, and theology.

More importantly, a critical shake-up such as the one I speak of also operates by using spaces of individual reflection and thought, an intimacy with the object of study, in a form external to the institution. In many cases, these marginal notes related to emerging political conflicts form the basis for creating networks of intellectual exchange around contemporary issues that belong to no particular age, but they develop

---

20. Fabian, *Time and the Other*; the second chapter concerns the theory of time in anthropology and the ways in which coetaneity ("coevalness") is established or denied.
21. Agamben, "What Is the Contemporary," 39–54.
22. Foucault, *Qu'est-ce que la critique?*, 39.

and in some way structure historical time and what is capable of being narrated within it.

Let Christine de Pizan, once again, be the concrete example of what I have just stated in an abstract or general way. Her work is an enormous experiment in the construction and balancing of her manuscripts. At the same time, each manuscript administers and establishes a rhythm among the various central and marginal elements it contains; illuminations and quotations come accompanied by allegories and glosses, all sharing a single page. In these manuscripts, intended for the levels of society that wielded sovereign power—kings, queens, princesses, regents—Christine critiques cultural models and political positions to argue in favor of a peaceful civil society. In her works, as someone who had to become a man to match her own view of her role in the world, she addresses peace and the processes of peacemaking, denounces violence, and asserts that female voices are capable of assessing political history and constructing civil society.[23] It is fundamental for Christine de Pizan to create a form of politics in which theories elaborated by women can break the monopoly of masculinity and its discourses—including the use of violence and distinction that characterize the prevailing codes of chivalry, which she proposes to change.

Therefore, one more element in the central premise of *Microliteratures* is that there is a direct relationship between public humanities—through microliterary actions and artifacts—and the problems of contemporary life. This direct relationship is not always easy to see, however, and must be revealed through historical research that combines the interpretation of texts with the history of the book.

Each section of this book is, in its way, an overgrown gloss. Of my own volition, I travel into the past in order to think about its microliterary activities for a while. I depend on a word, a gesture, a notion, or

---

23. Christine states in her *Livre de la Mutation de Fortune* that she became a man. In a well-known passage near the beginning of the work, she explains how "de femelle deuins masle" (from a female I became a male) because fortune wished it so: fortune changed both her body and her face until she turned into an "homme naturel parfait" (a perfect natural man), so that one who had been a woman was now a man. "Verite es ce que ie dis / Mais ie diray par fiction / Le fait de la mutation / comment de femme devins homme" (What I say is the truth / But I will say it like fiction / the fact of transformation / how from a woman I became a man). This mutation is only one of Christine's many metamorphoses. Becoming a man allows her to create a history of literature and its political and ethical touchstones based on masculinity. But it is still Christine who speaks, in a play of true pronouncements that can function only through distance and through the epistemological experiment that is fiction. I quote from the manuscript that was made for Baron Pierre Balzac in the early sixteenth century, now in the Bibliothèque de l'Arsenal, Ms-3172, fol. 4r (corresponding to vv. 139–53).

on how microliteratures connect the points of light within a constellation of ways of thinking and of expressing one's thoughts. I presuppose that the authors with whom I will think had to make an enormous effort to write what they did: paper, pens, time, light, health, life's circumstances, pain, loneliness, illness, concentration, cannot be taken for granted. Writing was very difficult in the Middle Ages, for these and other reasons. But as with Walser, who learned patience by writing with tiny letters in pencil, these microliterary products are also conditioned by the slowness and patience that went into them. To write is difficult in any age, and to carry it out one must also summon the force of will to change something. This is a microliterary attitude.

The glossers and commentators who make up the world that I myself am going to gloss enjoy a special relationship to history. Since they are dealing with contemporary—therefore ageless—events, they feel no overwhelming need to create chronologies; instead, they deploy forms of synchronization that begin in their own time zones. Whatever they intend by and through their glosses, they feel free to bring the past into the present so as to make it no longer past—so that the past may become the present material on which the past will perform its work. In a way, glossers invert the work of professional historians who insist on separating the past from the present, walling off the latter with a cordon sanitaire. Glossers and commentators overcome the physical difficulty of writing so as to present, within their intellectual, sociopolitical, and cultural networks, conclusions that result from non-chronological research. They do not seem interested in offering a cause-and-effect narrative based on the calendar's order of events; instead, they consider in synchronic fashion ideas, authors, moral personalities, and concepts that have the potential to be analyzed theoretically.

My own role in the present study is more traditionally historical, but its chapters cannot obey a chronological order of events. This is because not all the microliterary artifacts I will read here have a single genealogy, nor do they exist in the same time frames or share traditional models of historical periodization.[24] Like the River Guadiana, they appear

---

24. One of my favorite literary characters is Billy Pilgrim, the hero of Kurt Vonnegut's novel *Slaughterhouse-Five, or The Children's Crusade*. The book, published in 1969, has repeatedly been condemned, removed from libraries, excised from school reading lists, et cetera. All that makes Billy Pilgrim even more interesting to me—he doesn't even exist, but he's still a hero of censorship. Billy can jump around in time, move from the European past to the present on another planet, without being tied to any chronological sequence; he wants to narrate his past accurately, conscious of the gaps that exist in the transmission of history as he experienced it.

and then disappear; they flow over level ground and then plunge into a rocky canyon. A single example will suffice. The extensive gloss about war that Gregorio López added to the thirteenth-century *Siete Partidas* in 1555 is intimately connected to an editorial history that began with Alfonso X the Wise (perhaps earlier), and which still flourishes theoretically and historically to this day. Other commentaries and glosses, in contrast, experience long periods—even centuries—of silence, only to reappear in the present and invite us to formulate new questions, as has happened with the work of Teresa de Cartagena.

Chapters of This Book

In undertaking this project I have discarded most of the materials that I had been amassing, reading, and forgetting over a period of years. I want to travel light. Further, although I wish to be consistent in my attention to intellectual networks, political conflict, and social justice in these microliterary glosses and comments, I have decided not to offer an overarching interpretative framework, because I believe that there isn't one. Microliterary activity should be observed close up, and not as a kind of puzzle piece to be fitted into a larger possible context of a culture in its history. Microliterary activities may show us that the context is, above all, a model to be assembled.

Just because there is a model to be built, each chapter may be read independently, even though together they present different facets of the book's central premise. Read in the order given, I hold that they offer a polyhedric but coherent perspective on my ultimate thesis: how certain intellectuals of the middle and early modern ages conquered the margin as a way of claiming an affective space for reading and study. This affective space offers the pleasures of a multifocal, strabismic, polyphonic page, together with the challenge of a more difficult and effortful reading. Microliterary authors, once they control this affective space, can draw on the juridical values and cognitive advantages offered by glossing as an industry and institution within their scholarly and academic milieu; this can launch them into other intellectual networks and fields of knowledge that, while not academic, hold enormous sway in constructing a public sphere that has political impact.

The opening two chapters deal with the production of the margin from two different points of view. Chapter 1, "Order and Discipline," speaks of the very industry that underlies the creation of ordinary glosses and how it is organized around certain disciplinary requirements. Out of these I choose certain examples most relevant for my research: a method of reading I call "strabismic," the *figura* as a theory of history, typology as a way of introducing ethical value, and finally the action of the juridical in the disciplinary order of the gloss. This chapter proposes that microliterary authors understand the epistemological and affective space of the glossed page as well as its legal potential.

Chapter 2 addresses the production of the margin from a cognitive point of view. The margin is the written space used for criticizing central features of contemporary culture. The production of the margin in vernacular media implies discovering and adapting techniques suited to the academic and intellectual sphere, such as the marginal gloss and its ordinary versions in the science of law and in biblical and theological studies. The production of the margin claims the right to participate in this institution of the gloss and its possible conditions, within a non-academic medium that nonetheless requires deploying pedagogical and cognitive effects in the act of marginal writing and its techniques of commentary. This chapter also interrogates the material aspects of this type of communication: what is the intellectual and pedagogical impact of working on books that contain several levels and modes of writing? Why would one submit to a strabismic form of reading?

In chapter 3, the editorial history of Alfonso X's *Siete Partidas*, with its marginal comments, leads us to a specific gloss supplied by Gregorio López, the jurist and member of the Council of the Indies. In 1555 López published his profusely glossed edition of the *Siete Partidas*. In the section on war (the twenty-third title of the *Segunda Partida*), he includes an immensely long gloss—ten pages of two columns each—in which he makes a decision (a very difficult one, by his own confession), or in other words issues a legal opinion, related to the political debate about the conquest of America. Though the gloss was written around 1553, it draws on debates contemporary with the *Partidas* themselves or even earlier, and projects them into the future. Because the *Partidas* published in 1555 were revived in the nineteenth century as an authentic text of codified law after a gap of some fifty years, that future lasted for centuries; it even accompanied the *Partidas* up to their reprinting with an accompanying law in the *Boletín Oficial del Estado* beginning in 1969.

Activism is a topic not often discussed in the medieval context, but I make it the subject of chapter 4 in the persons of Diego de Valera and Pero Díaz de Toledo, two intellectuals of converso origin. Valera was a microliterary activist and champion of causes such as the peaceful resolution of civil strife, and the need to research women's history rather than perpetuate misogynist forms of expression. Díaz de Toledo demonstrates the direct link between poetry and political activism through his gloss on a living poet who was critical of the régime in Toledo. Activism is not very easy to find, nor homogeneous, and of course it does not resemble modern forms of activism; yet research into microliterature affords us ways of perceiving critical discourses even when, as often happens, they emerge from those who seem to belong to the same system of power they are criticizing.

The Portuguese prince Pedro de Avis, the subject of chapter 5, wrote little, experimenting with the presentation of his texts in manuscript form. His manuscripts, as I explain, are epistemological artifacts. Through them we study one of the central issues of social and political criticism: the construction of the subject in the face of a body of knowledge that is articulated in the margins. This body of knowledge constitutes a system of cultural oversight based on tradition and its political capital. A reading of two of Pedro's manuscript works will allow us to explore this way of creating a subjectivity at a time of fragmentation in the personal, political, and intellectual realms.

In my final chapter, "A Vernacular Society," I try to situate philosophy in the ambience of the city and the home, a space that emerges in certain fifteenth-century glosses on philosophical texts. This notion allows us to explore the construction of a renewed civil society through works by Christine de Pizan and Teresa de Cartagena. Both women set down in writing their plans for building a civil society that would involve not only new voices and discourses but also new forms of governance. The volume ends with an epilogue, a bibliography, and my acknowledgments.

Some Incomplete Notes on Research

Marginal writing is not a new object of interest in any field of the humanities. In 1972 Jacques Derrida published *Marges*. The book's subtitle is *De la philosophie*, and since there is no punctuation between title and subtitle, we wonder if he meant to speak of the margins of philosophy (*marges de la philosophie*), or of philosophy from the viewpoint of the concept of margins (*marges: de la philosophie*). Or perhaps both—that is the challenge of arranging any text on the page with the orthotypographical conventions of a given time.[25] The first chapter, "Tympan,"

---

25. Derrida, *Marges de la philosophie*.

offers two texts: one in the center of the page that was signed by Derrida in Prinsengracht, the longest and outermost of Amsterdam's four canals; the other from *Biffures* by Michel Leiris, a text about the assemblage of Leiris's "I," a creative autoethnography (which I can't call an autobiography).[26] In the French edition, by Éditions de Minuit, the material differences between the two texts are clear: Leiris's words are in a slightly larger type than the central text's, and both the letter spacing and the justification on the page are irregular, so that the eye feels a little disconcerted on reading the two passages in parallel. Even though Derrida's words occupy most of the page, the relevance of Leiris's contribution is made clear through this typographic arrangement: one senses that Derrida's text is only a canal that flows through a major city, with its bridges, its locks, and its interrupted navigation. "If there are margins, is there still a philosophy, is there still philosophy?"[27]

This question (one of postmodernity, which was emerging at that very moment only to retreat in recent decades) has nourished, explicitly or implicitly, scholarly work on marginal glosses, beginning with the article that Lawrence Lipking published in 1977.[28] That piece starts with Paul Valéry's reversal of Poe's theory of marginality, and goes on to study Samuel Taylor Coleridge's "Rime of the Ancient Mariner" and other marginal glosses of the eighteenth and nineteenth centuries. Lipking's original and elegant study, which contains its own glosses, lingers over the distinction between the beauty of a fleeting thought as represented by marginalia and the "marginal gloss": "Unlike marginalia, therefore, the marginal gloss frequently serves to affirm the relation of the part to the whole."[29]

Inspired by Poe's ideas about "whim" and "nonsense" (the latter used to signal that marginalia add no new, strictly necessary meaning), Lipking invites his readers to concentrate on what the glossed page does rather than what it says.[30] He distinguishes (as Anthony Grafton had done in his scholarly book on footnotes) between a footnote and a gloss, saying, "We come late in time, as scholars: we cannot do without glossing. Yet the question remains: is the footnote, that method popularized in the eighteenth century, still adequate to our needs?"[31]

---

26. Leiris, *Biffures*.
27. Derrida, *Marges de la philosophie*, xvi.
28. Lipking, "The Marginal Gloss," 609–55.
29. Lipking, "The Marginal Gloss," 612.
30. Lipking, "The Marginal Gloss," 633.
31. Grafton, *The Footnote*; Lipking, "The Marginal Gloss," 638.

He goes on to say that the long hegemony of the footnote may be jeopardized for another reason. Fewer and fewer literary critics, these days, would accept the philosophical model of discourse on which the relation between text and note was founded: the clear division between certain knowledge, brought to light in the text, and conjectural or historical evidence, cited below. He concludes that "footnotes, as everyone knows, are defensive . . . The marginal gloss is more embattled. Originally, as I have said, such glosses responded to the need for a total interpretation, the fitting of the part to the whole. But the notions of what interpretation might be, of what a whole might be, have not remained stable."[32]

If footnotes are defensive, it is easy to admit that glosses are not only more aggressive but clearly offensive, in the vanguard of how to express certain ideas and theses that may not fit into the central text. In fact, Lipking works not on medieval texts but on texts and authors who already make up that public-sphere institution that we call literature. Those marginal glosses do not interfere with the texts they comment on; they help to form networks and "topics of conversation" that find their way into the public square. This is what seems most important to me: the besieged gloss, with the flow of thought it represents, is also the result of a negotiation within a cultural network; it produces the complex of ideas and themes that can be distilled from texts that make up the institution of literature and can play a role in public debate.

Robert Hauptman, in his book *Documentation*, takes on the Derridean influence on the criticism and creation of glosses: he thinks that they are unnecessarily confusing and that, like other contemporary glosses (he cites Luc Boltanski and Laurent Thévenot), they "seem to serve no necessary purpose."[33] He mentions that reading glosses no longer forms part of most readers' habits, although it is far superior to the technology of hypertext. This connection between the marginal gloss and hypertext has also been explored by David Salomon in *An Introduction to the "Glossa Ordinaria" as Medieval Hypertext*.[34] Both authors think of the gloss as a way of opening oneself to an experience of reading based on the impulse to abandon the central text in pursuit of other intellectual interests—these are left behind by the links that open when we press our fingertip onto a sensitive surface.

---

32. Lipking, "The Marginal Gloss," 639.
33. Hauptman, "Marginalia," in *Documentation*, 71–111, esp. 77.
34. Salomon, *An Introduction*.

Glosses do not work that way, however. They are not hypertextual. Like the central text, they were designed to be ever-present. This does not mean that they are always present (although the *Glossa ordinaria* would be a poor example of this): there are works in which the text and the glosses were copied into two different volumes to make them easier to consult in a library. One such case is Enrique de Villena's *Traducción y glosas de la Eneida*. MSS/10111 of Spain's Biblioteca Nacional is a volume containing only Villena's glosses on his translation of the *Aeneid*, boasting all sorts of elements that make it useful for study (and marks that show that it was, in fact, studied), including an alphabetical list of the glosses. A separate manuscript contains the translation itself (M-102, Biblioteca Menéndez Pelayo, Santander, Spain). This is an unusual situation, however, and as we shall see in chapter 1, it is not readers' preferred method of working with a text and its glosses—whenever possible, they prefer to see both on the same page.

Recent critical approaches to the gloss have been consistently seduced by the gloss's ambition to place itself in the center—to replace what we know with what we are now exploring. This is an essential aspect of the humanities. The margin, in some way, is always besieging the center, and sometimes managing to deactivate it. This has been happening in the field of law ever since Accursio compiled his *Magna Glossa* in the mid-thirteenth century. In later commentaries on civil law we often find the legal text that traditionally occupied the center reduced to allusions and abbreviations within the commentary. When Bartolo da Sassoferrato developed his geometrical and trigonometrical theory about islands (in both rivers and the sea), he studied specific laws from the *Corpus Iuris Civilis*, especially from the Digest ("De Adeo," C 41, 1, 7, 1-6). But he did not confine himself to its margins: he flooded and colonized it with his own commentary, turning the Roman-law text into mere references. The center was broken down into a series of floating islets that include even the gloss compiled by Accursio.[35]

I have explored other areas of the bibliography in earlier publications, and I will not repeat myself here. As I have said, in the present work I do not aim to be exhaustive but rather to achieve a certain level of analysis. The gloss and the commentary are invasive, threatening the rhetorical and intellectual power held by the center; they are

---

35. There are hundreds of manuscript and printed versions of Bartolo's work, including a Spanish translation: Bartolo da Sassoferrato, *De insula*. See also, on the trigonometry (and for pleasant reading), Boureau, *Le Feu des manuscrits*, 65-72.

ever-present, depending only on the will of the one who participates in the act of glossing or commenting; they are the fruit not of necessity or of argumentation but of desire. They are there; they do not need to be there. But in fact they are there, and therefore they are a challenge. Because there are margins, there is philosophy—the will to know.

Chapter 1

Order and Discipline

Every book has multiple beginnings—one per chapter at least, sometimes more. The chapter opens, and there is the promise of an idea. Will this beginning fulfill its promise? Or will what looked like an idea lead into a blind alley? This first chapter is one of the entry points into this book; the next chapter will be another. Each of these two doors leads to a different genealogy: one related to the creation and development of academic disciplines, and the other (from a material perspective) to the cognitive and pedagogical features of glosses and marginal writing.

In the Middle Ages, certain branches of scientific and professional knowledge were constructed on the basis of marginal thoughts. These marginal thoughts reflect the scope and content of the fields under study, but brought up to date and converted into scientific, academic, intellectual, and professional approaches that were acceptable in the political, juridical, and theological circumstances of the time. In the following pages I will focus on aspects of the emergence and development of a disciplinary order in areas related to law. This disciplinary order comprises the evaluation and explication of, as well as the commentary on scientific and academic disciplines that are connected, directly or indirectly, to legal thought. Here I am concerned with every branch of law; I am also interested in theology and biblical studies, but only insofar as they are related to law, so I deal with them here solely from that perspective.

A Strange Thing

The central thesis of this chapter may be expressed as follows: reading the margins, whether from a legal standpoint or not, is a difficult task. It asks us to become familiar with the labyrinthine nature of the glossed page, a way of reading that we shall call "strabismic." Reading the margins of legal texts requires a specific ability to reconnect the different parts of the page with the central, or master, text, both literally (which part matches up with which other part) and in the critical and temporal terms of the discipline (how to make present what was written in the past). The reader cannot lose sight of the central text, no matter how strongly the physical form of the manuscript text tempts the eye to zigzag and wander. Nor can the reader ignore the margins in an attempt to relate a critical model that is used today to textual instruments inherited from the past.

Glosses are "strange things."[1] Reading the Bible, a legal text (for example, Justinian's compilation), or the corpus of Aristotle's philosophy, among others, proves a constant source of distraction or interrupted perception.[2] Words, concepts, institutions, references, translations, ideas, theories, and other novelties in the master texts

---

1. The French lexicographer Félix Gaffiot defines the gloss as "mot rare, terme peu usité (qui a besoin d'une explication)" (A word that is rare and seldom used [and that requires an explanation]): *Dictionnaire*, under "*glose*." Lewis and Short call it "an obsolete or foreign word that requires explanation" (*A Latin Dictionary*, under "*glossa*"). The *Diccionario de Autoridades* (Real Academia Española, online) offers four definitions of the word, of which the first is the most important: "La explicación, interpretación o comento de alguna proposición o sentencia obscúra, o de dificultosa inteligéncia" (The explanation, interpretation, or comment of some proposition or obscure sentence or that cannot be easily understood). This dictionary already thinks of the gloss as a literary genre, whereas the lexicographers of Latin hew to the relatively ironic sense of the Greek term in its Latin usage. A gloss, the clarification of a rare term, is often written between the lines and also in Latin: that is to say that in this case, a gloss is an interlinear, intralinguistic translation. This method, whether intra- or interlinguistic, is employed in many manuscripts of different texts, not only in the Bible. An example of how an ordinary biblical gloss (on the Song of Songs, in this case) is placed on the page can be found in MS Marston 2, Beinecke Library, Yale University, accessed November 22, 2024, https://brbl-zoom.library.yale.edu/viewer/11377808, which shows folio 1r. The renowned Spanish *Glosas Silenses* and *Glosas Emilianenses* are based on the same method of interlinear glossing, with occasional glosses in the margin. I could include more cases, but I do not wish to prolong this footnoted gloss.

2. Shklovsky, "El arte como artificio," 122–46.

draw the readers' attention and invite them to intervene: the "strange thing" that pricks their curiosity becomes a launchpad for a critical thought or a mere explication, whether between the lines of the text or in some other space that allows for more writing—in the margin, for instance, but also on small waxed tablets where one could make notes before transferring them to a more permanent material.³

Many interlinear glosses are lexical ones: as Quintilian said, they call for "interpretatio linguae secretioris" (an interpretation of the most hidden or secret aspects of language), "quas Graeci γλώσσας vocant" (which the Greeks call glosses).⁴ To engage with them one must form part of a certain sociopolitical order, to have reached a certain level of education, a special status. To the extent that these interlinear linguistic thoughts merge with the text and become inseparable from it, they grow ordinary; what would be strange would be not to find them between the lines. Ordinariness is an institution in itself.

It is also an institution that expands. A gloss is like a form of vegetation that propagates not only through pollination but also through a connected root system that is hidden from our sight. The institution of the gloss is not confined to the narrow space between one line of writing and another; the margins continue their critical work in many different ways. Perhaps the interlinear gloss is the most typically linguistic one, a kind of translation, but every translation suggests an equivalence that is problematic in itself. Decisions made in the twelfth century about how to interpret the beloved in the Song of Songs led to her recasting as the institution of the synagogue and then her transformation into the church. This change is radically juridical. The gloss, therefore, not only translates or interprets; it is a metamorphic agent, it alters everything it touches.

Interconnected in the underground layers of tradition, marginal glosses spread out their complicated theoretical nets. Undoubtedly, they present as forms of agreement or argument. They also offer themselves as models of reference, as handbooks for solving certain problems, for serving the various needs of an attorney, a judge, a preacher, a theologian. They appear as analogies, as plausible explanations, as models of behavior, imitation, reproduction, as precedents for something. They are intimately influenced by *figura* and by typology. The *figura* is

---

3. Roger Chartier analyzes Baudri de Bourgueil's poems to his waxed tablets in *Inscrire et éffacer*, 17-31.
4. Quintilian, *Instituto Oratoria*, 1, 1.35.

a rhetorical artifact that reveals the hidden connections between one thing and another, the second being a sublimation and perfection of the first. Typology is a system of fractal analogies (also, in some sense, infinite) that allows something—a narrative, a character, an event—to be reproduced in the tale and in its moral.

Ordinary as they are, many of these glosses continue to be "strange things" to most people. Only after the Second Vatican Council, held from 1962 to 1965, was individual Bible study in one's native language approved as a fundamental activity in the layperson's daily religious practice. This decision affirmed the conclusions of Leo XIII in *Providentissimus Deus* (1893), on Christian education, and Pius XII in *Divino Afflante Spiritu* (1943), on producing Bibles in the vernacular. However, it says nothing about glosses or their translation.

Perhaps glosses and their interpretive weight are so ordinary that they have even invaded the spoken word. Are they not useful in the preparation of sermons? Are not the ordinary glosses of the law, compiled in the great law-code manuals, an essential source for arguing cases and bringing suits in the space where justice is dispensed?

Legal and biblical glosses are not mere academic instruments, even though the disciplinary order might make us think otherwise—that they were designed for use only inside the ivory tower. But that is the trick played by strange things: they seem to belong to a world exclusive to just a few people who subject them to intellectual analysis and debate, but they actually perform a public role. Through channels that do not enjoy the stamp of academia, such as the pulpit, the courtroom, the royal court, the city, and many other public spaces, the margins are made ordinary in a different way: they penetrate into our normal habit of speaking about things that had previously been strange.

Something Ordinary

First, let us explore this "ordinary" character. A gloss or comment, whether marginal or not, aspires to be indispensable. A rare word may be replaced by its explication or translation, may be endowed with a new meaning from a different semantic field. That rare word is in some sense relegated to the past, while its gloss points toward the present day, offers a new framework for debate, opens doors to a fresh interpretation of a body of knowledge. It is also the fulcrum for institutional creativity.

Something ordinary is something usual, that can be used, that is often used. It falls within the order of things, it is normal. Nothing to see here—you can go on your way as if nothing special has happened. The ordinary causes no surprise. If you hadn't noticed it before and notice it now, it is not because the ordinary thing wasn't there but because you hadn't been paying attention. Ordinary things belong to daily life: they have a before and after, a regular appearance, a time, a space. This is the ordinary—it almost seems extraordinary.

We understand how things occur in a certain order. That too is ordinary, since it is already ordered. If the order changes, things in themselves can change and become hard to understand, more obscure. The order in which we turn the pages of a book lets us read the word order in its syntactic construction (ordered, but also constitutional).[5] All this, too, is ordinary.

The ordinary is also one of the pillars of the *ordo disciplinae*. According to Alain de Libera, an expert in medieval philosophy and theology, the *ordo disciplinae* is the search for the "mot d'ordre de tous ceux que vont essayer d'organiser le savoir théologique" (the watchword of all those who will try to organize theological knowledge). It is the very order of the discipline not as regards its original content, but as it incorporates modern thought, that is, the scientific, scholastic, logical, and philosophical thought of the medieval thinkers who considered themselves the "moderni."[6]

The movement of ordinariness calls for displaying a full range of contemporary analysis. Neither theologians nor jurists are interested

---

5. Syntax is the subfield of linguistics that studies word order in language; the word comes from the Greek noun *syntagma* (order). In Modern Greek *syntagma* means primarily "constitution," as in Syntagma Square in Athens. That was where, in 1843, an uprising forced the king to accept the Greek constitution, and since 2012 it has also been the site of many political protests.

6. Libera, *L'Archéologie philosophique*, 57; Chenu, *Introduction à l'étude*, 258-59. Ordo disciplinae: "C'est ce qui explique que l'on va remettre en ordre le corpus d'Aristote mais aussi y ajouter ce que n'y est pas et qui manque à la discipline, pour en faire non plus un corpus mais véritablement une science qu'on expose, développe et construit sur des bases nouvelles" (This explains that it is necessary to set Aristotle's corpus in order, but also add whatever is missing in it and what is necessary to the discipline in order to turn it from a corpus truly into a science that we can explain, develop, and build on new foundations). Libera, 57. As I have suggested, the notion of something "lacking" in this case (*qui manque*) does not satisfy me; I prefer the idea of surplus I have mentioned in an earlier note in the introduction. See Libera, 68-69n11, on how Albertus Magnus's *scientia perfecta* competes for the construction of a science "par refonte, suture et retextualisation du corpus aristotélicien" (by means of recasting, suturing, and retextualizing the Aristotelian corpus) (68). The rest of the note is equally important, with a fresh perspective on the work of many intellectuals who transformed disciplines in different ways in the course of the thirteenth century, among them Alfonso X and Ramon Llull.

in simply reconstructing a paradigm of knowledge in order to place it under glass in a museum and explain how things were at some point in the past. Rather, the ordinary is the process of liberating bodies of knowledge from the time they seem to occupy, so as to apply them to a discipline that is emerging or constantly being renewed. From the twelfth to the fifteenth centuries, canon law, civil law, theology, and biblical studies (the two latter closely linked to the two former) formed the vanguard of disciplinary renewal and invention by appropriating the theories and practices of philosophical thought, including logic and rhetoric, ethics and politics, metaphysics and psychology.[7]

The affinity between the disciplinary order and the thing ordered can be seen most clearly in the production of ordinary glosses. This process takes place in several fields or disciplines, but it is most evident in the corpus of biblical studies and the corpus of legal studies. The two disciplines also stand in a relationship of affinity to each other.

The search for the ordinary is in itself a strategy of normalization. The so-called *glossa ordinaria* of legal texts or the Bible establish a canon of thought against which any critical departures can be defined.[8] It is, so to speak, the foundational fiction of the normal. In the case of the ordinary glosses on civil law that arose in the mid-thirteenth century, the one hundred thousand glosses that surround the text make up the corpus of modernization, judicial experience, and theoretical debate of the previous two hundred years of reading and teaching Roman civil law. At the same time, they are the zero-grade form of what would become the deep process of commentary and discussion on legal matters in the independent commentaries of writers like Bartolo da Sassoferrato and Baldo de Ubaldis: in their comments the intellectual referent is ordinary thought, with and through which they critically renew legal studies and heuristics. It is through that normality, that ordinariness, that Bartolo introduces new elements, such as mathematical sciences, particularly trigonometry, as a system of argument for determining

---

7. Libera, *Penser au Moyen Âge*. There are several fascinating recent publications on how disciplines were organized and debated in the universities, especially König-Pralong and Imbach, *Le Défi laïque*; and König-Pralong, *Le bon usage des savoirs*. See also Marmursztejn, *L'Autorité des maîtres*, and the four-part study by Boureau, *La Raison scolastique*. Boureau performs virtual detective work on the intellectual structures that, for a century and with implications in the present, sustained the modes of thought and interpretation of scholastic reasoning: the forms of casuistry, distinction, and other rational procedures.

8. I have not seen this precise notion of a reference point for critical departures anywhere in the literature, but it arises from my reading of Boureau's *La Raison scolastique*. I am not certain that Boureau would agree with it, however.

the properties of islands that emerge suddenly from a river or a sea, a topic that had concerned the glossators of the relevant section of the *Codex Iustiniani*.⁹ Likewise, Bartolo leans on the disciplinary order of the gloss to develop a new definition of nobility, making a fundamental distinction between theological nobility (that explains the birth of noble lineages) and political nobility.¹⁰

With the latter concept Bartolo introduces something extraordinary, something absent from the ordinary glosses but which successive manuscripts and printed editions of the *Corpus Iuris Civilis* could not avoid including as a supplement to the ordinary glosses. The *Siete Partidas*, a law code that submits to sustained criticism the body of legal knowledge contained in the ordinary glosses, make specific decisions that, in this case, result in a body of legislation. For example, their titles devoted to the theme of *tabula picta*, or painted panel, discussed in the third *Partida*, propose definitive legislation that overrides the stage of ordinary debates contained in the glosses of the *Corpus Iuris Civilis*.

The ordinary glosses—ordinariness itself—are characterized, however, by their perpendicular nature, their breakdown of linearity. There are no ordinary glosses without an additional strange element, which I call here a strabismic order.

Strabismus as a Virtue in Reading

Until the early twentieth century, scholars had attributed the *glossa ordinaria* on the Bible to an eighth-century writer called Walafrid Strabo ("strabo" means "the Squint-Eyed").¹¹ Those *Glossa* present the canonical sacred text on the page, with interlinear notes and marginal glosses taken chiefly from the doctors and fathers of the church; they are the result of intensive, open-pit textual mining. Like a handbook, manuscripts of the Bible with *glossa ordinaria* (which differ greatly from each other, in any case) present the central order of the books, chapters, and verses of the text of texts together with the labyrinthine universe of pertinent commentaries, explications, translations, and interpretations, carefully selected from the most trustworthy canonical authors who

---

9. I have already mentioned Sassoferrato's *De insula*, where some of these scientific and disciplinary operations are demonstrated.

10. He addresses these themes in the treatises *De insigniis et armis* and *De dignitatibus*. Bartolo, *De insigniis et armis*; Bartolo, "Sobre las enseñas," 52–70; Rodríguez Velasco, "El *Tractatus de insigniis*," 52–70; Bartolo, *De dignitatibus*. See also Rodríguez Velasco, *Plebeyos márgenes*.

11. See his biography in Wesseling, "Walafrid Strabo," 13:169–76.

had been elevated to fathers and doctors of the church. The presence of this apparatus made it impossible to read the Bible line by line, verse by verse, chapter by chapter, book by book. Instead, one's eyes had to roam over the page, finding the central text interrupted by interlinear and marginal observations. The reader had to grow cross-eyed, like the mythical compiler of the *glossa*; the new method of reading the Bible was strabismic.

It is unfortunate that Walafrid Strabo was not actually the mind behind the creation of this book, which initiated a manner of reading the Bible that became the norm for theologians and other scholars over the centuries. The more pedestrian name of John the Teutonic is the one attached to the creation of a text whose handwritten mobility and multidirectionality were temporarily fixed in the printed edition of 1480–81.[12] That edition, however, launched an editorial history of its own that is no less interesting than that of the manuscripts.[13]

The *glossa ordinaria* not only included texts that filled up the margins of biblical manuscripts; they also excluded texts, hundreds and thousands of them, that never achieved the status of canonical interpretations of the Bible. Texts not deemed worthy as normative sources were left out on purpose or by accident, and were no longer there—the space in the margins was limited. The ordinary gave way to the extraordinary, what had lain outside the disciplinary order as the *glossa ordinaria* had come to define it. The texts that had been naturalized, had become the interpretative norm, and until then were considered ordinary and ordered, could in effect inhabit the same body that was occupied by the Bible. They might have immigrated from other texts and treatises, but they were documented immigrants.[14]

This movement implied a transformation in the market for manuscript versions of the Bible, and, from the late fifteenth century onward, for printed versions.[15] In the eleventh and twelfth centuries, the production of Bibles had led to ever more complicated and artistic examples for individual clients: miniature Bibles, illuminated Bibles, and so

---

12. Froehlich and Gibson, *Biblia Latina*.
13. See Morard et al., *Glossa ordinaria*; also Smith, *The "Glossa Ordinaria."* For the production of Bibles containing *glossa ordinaria* and the book trade, see De Hamel, *Glossed Books*.
14. A provisional inventory of biblical manuscripts containing *glossa ordinaria*, still under construction, contains over four thousand entries. See https://gloss-e.irht.cnrs.fr.
15. See De Hamel, *Glossed Books*; Froehlich and Gibson, *Biblia Latina*.

on.¹⁶ But the ordinary glosses were directed to an audience of scholars who sought to keep abreast of advances in theology as a university discipline, with a growing presence in the intellectual world of European institutions of higher learning.¹⁷

In other words, Bibles were also becoming commodities, produced by specialized scribes in specific workshops, most of them located in monasteries. From them emerged Gospels, Pentateuchs, and other sequences of books made for different types of clients. They were simultaneously forms of reading the Bible, forms of meditating on and feeling the Bible, and forms of appreciating the Bible as an aesthetic object. This object, as we see with many illuminated Bibles, may contain other objects, images meant for meditation and interpretation, and may even require physical contortions for reading especially very large or truly small Bibles.

But these Bibles are too luxurious. If they are commodities, it is because they also speak to the wealth of their owners and principals, and to the complex paths by which those individuals came to possess them, arrange them, pay for them, or have someone else pay in their name (as a gift, or in exchange for a gift of a different kind). What, then, are Bibles that contain the *glossa ordinaria*?

Perhaps they are a type of "uncommodity." I know that the word does not exist in the sense I wish to give it, a pun that loses its point once it is explained (commodity/uncommodity, or merchandise/unmerchandise). I'll simply invent the word. An uncommodity is, in fact, a piece of merchandise in the sense of belonging to a capitalist economy that implies value, use, spectralization, and all the rest. Nonetheless, uncommodities are specific pieces of merchandise belonging to intellectual history, the history of the intellectual world and especially of the academic world. Like a *commoditas* (commodity), an *incommoditas* is also something, a thing, an artifact that is useful and opportune, that has value and can be immediately used and scrutinized. But as its

---

16. On the uses, practices, study, production, and interchange of Bibles in the Middle Ages, see Smalley, *The Study of the Bible*; Boynton and Reilly, *The Practice of the Bible*; Riché and Lobrichon, *Le Moyen Âge et la Bible*; Ruzzier and Hermand, *Comment le Livre*; Dahan, *Lire la Bible*; Nelson and Kempf, *Reading the Bible*. For illumination, see Cahn, *Romanesque Bible Illumination*. Of course there are many works for the general reader on the production and illumination of medieval Bibles, including Fingernagel and Gastgeber, *The Most Beautiful Bibles* (National Library of Austria).

17. The history of the formation and transformation of the medieval Bible is much more complicated than this, as Van Liere shows in *An Introduction to the Medieval Bible*.

in- prefix suggests, it implies a degree of inconvenience and inadequacy: it overwhelms the shelves of a professional library, concealing other books, excluding them wholly or in part, making them extraordinary. But let us not linger too long over the name, so as to concentrate on the definition.

The ordinary gloss opens up a different way of producing and receiving the Bible, and this is what makes the movement of "ordinarization" so important. In effect, this "ordinarization," this form of production and reception so essential to intellectual history, implies the development of an industry that achieves two goals at once: the very process of normalizing the marginal and interlinear texts that proliferated within the biblical one, and the manual reproduction of objects so like one another that they seemed to be exact copies of the original.

Normalization and reproduction are the two key elements of the *ordo disciplinae*. On the one hand, they establish the procedures and theories of the discipline itself and how it works. On the other, they permit the coherent distribution of the objects, texts, theories, ideas, concepts, and methods that make up the discipline itself.

The discipline forms part of the business as well. Ordinariness is the business itself, the industry. Francesco Accursio (the jurist and businessman who invented the *glossa ordinaria* of the *Corpus Iuris Civilis*), John the Teutonic (who did the same with the Bible), and others, thought they were producing ordinary glosses that belonged to the order of the discipline, sanctioned by the authorities who signed each gloss with their initials or full names—and all while making money with them. Perhaps they did not imagine that they were creating the institution called *glossa ordinaria*. This means that they knew how to manage the terms in which the *ordo disciplinae* comes to represent the entire business. The ordinary gloss is not only a form of scientific capital, it is also the industry that controls the economic and social life of these disciplines. Without this affinity between the disciplines of the *ordo* and the industry, there would be no corporations of theologians or corporations of lawyers—the same ones that gave the universities their growing power in the cities of the Western hemisphere.[18]

---

18. In Latin, *universitas* means "corporation"; they are one and the same. See Gilli et al., *Les Universités et la ville*; Verger, *Les Universités au Moyen "Âge"*; Verger, *Les Gens de savoir*. The history of universities is a very broad field; since Rashdall published his monumental work in 1895 (*The Universities of Europe in the Middle Ages*), historians of the university have dealt with every aspect of university life, including strikes, socio-intellectual movements, et cetera, as in the works of Catherine König-Pralong and Ian Wei.

An industry based on a strabismic technique of reading—as we have said, it is something ordinary and also doubly strange, while being tremendously useful at the same time. Within the industry devoted to the creation of ordinary glosses, the strabismic order guarantees the material representation (or perhaps the foundational fiction) of two basic aspects of a disciplinary order that administers bodies of knowledge from the past: it synchronizes them on the page, and it subjects them to various modes of translation, interpretation, and contemporary criticism. The first aspect is a stratigraphy of knowledge: central text, interlinear notes, layers of marginal glosses, titles, abstract marks—paragraph signs, daggers, letters—all these make visible strata of knowledge that, through letter shape, position, and of course content, require different types of attention. The second aspect is the temporality that, in turn, also presents on the page, and determines the order among its elements beyond the actual age of the things that appear before one's eyes. It is a temporality and not a chronological order, because the page forbids us to consign certain items to the past and others to the present; at the same time, however, it establishes that the order of reading, no matter how strabismic, is still an order that belongs in a sequence of scientific and textual events.

Several procedures reveal the intellectual stratigraphy, and the temporality, that lie within ordinary glosses and their disciplinary order. Three of them seem to me especially significant, because they are also the most enduring in any microliterary essay such as those we will explore in this book. The first procedure is the most common and consists of the exegetical techniques that define the disciplinary order. The second procedure, the *figura*, is a theory of history. The third, typology, is closely related to the other two, draws on them, and furthermore displays an ethics (therefore also a politics), while revealing jurisprudential relationships within the texts that are commented on by this method.

Exegesis

We are thoroughly acquainted with exegetical procedures. Cardinal Henri de Lubac studied the four senses of scripture in his monumental work from the late 1950s and early 1960s, the indispensable reference for every study of medieval exegesis.[19] De Lubac did not merely wish to

---

19. De Lubac, *Exégèse médiévale*.

understand medieval exegesis. He sought to comprehend the relevance of the four senses of the sacred page from the viewpoint of a Jesuit priest who had lived through one of the most violent periods in history, who had joined the Resistance during World War II. After the Holocaust, was there any way to imagine a spiritual reading of the Bible?

The more recent work of Frans van Liere, of a scientific and technical bent, is a splendid manual of the theory and practice of exegesis in the central Middle Ages.[20] The volume edited by Ineke van 't Spijker collects cases that form the basis for new theories.[21] Gilbert Dahan's research is fascinating for other reasons: while the other studies focus on Christian exegesis, Dahan is concerned with the simultaneous production of exegetical models and practices of Christian, Jewish, and Muslim commentary in a shared intellectual milieu.[22]

All of these works present us with the debates about the exegetical arts. Exegesis moves between two poles: historical or literal reading, and spiritual or allegorical reading. Either pole may give rise either to ethical or political interpretations that employ tropological techniques of commentary, or to transcendent interpretations that employ anagogical ones. There is persistent ambivalence about literal interpretation, which is sometimes not even classed as a form of exegesis; but influential medieval thinkers such as Hugh of Saint-Victor declared that literal or historical interpretation was primary.[23] The questions that arise in this millennia-long debate are crucial, and emerge in the Christianity of Saint Paul, above all in the dichotomy between the letter that "killeth" and the spirit that "giveth life."[24] What is the spiritual? How does a spiritual interpretation give life? Is tropology, or moral and political interpretation, to be placed on the same footing as anagogy, or transcendent interpretation? Are all those forms of interpretation obligatory, or are they optional? Are they arranged in an exegetical hierarchy, or are they not in any necessary order? These questions have been approached and studied for a long time, and the scholars mentioned above treat them in their works.

---

20. Van Liere and Harkins, *Interpretation of Scripture*; Harkins and Van Liere, *Interpretation of Scripture*.
21. Spijker, *The Multiple Meaning of Scripture*.
22. Dahan, *Lire la Bible*; *L'Occident médiéval*; *Études d'exégèse médiévale*.
23. Saint-Victor, *Hugonis de Sancto Victore* (English: Saint-Victor, *Didascalicon*); Illich, *In the Vineyard of the Text*.
24. 2 Corinthians 3:6 (King James Version).

Perhaps the most visible aspect of medieval exegesis is the distance between, on the one hand, the theoretical need to create a complete, complex intellective structure that accounts for the whole exegetical process and its internal and external order, and on the other, a practical resistance to achieving, or perfecting, this theoretical structure. In theory the structure exists without interruptions, while allowing us to grasp the various epistemological processes that characterize each stage of interpretation: knowledge of the literal and knowledge of the ethical should be clearly distinguished. Some of those who benefit from this theoretical perfection are also the microliterary authors who appear, or could appear, in this book. For instance, when Enrique de Villena sets out to gloss the psalm "Quoniam videbo," or even the *Aeneid*, he does so by also establishing the four-part exegetical structure that had already become traditional in scholastic theology.[25] But these are practices of theory: they play simultaneously with the coherence of the structure and the institutional nature of the intellectual work they perform. The practice of glossing is not always adaptable to this type of overarching theory; rather, it leaves more space for the needs or the exceptional nature of the commentary and forces us to think of exegesis not only as a mode of interpretation but also as an affective space.[26]

The exegetical work appears in front of our eyes: it is on the surface of the page, along the margins, between the lines. Two questions arise

---

25. Other examples might include *Los doze trabajos de Hércules*, also by Villena. We have already cited his translation of, and glosses on, the *Aeneid*; see also Cátedra, *Exégesis, ciencia, literatura*.

26. In one form or another, the notion of *affective space* has been around for a while. In my view, it keeps its notional, intuitive character: I define it as a physical space so loaded with emotions that they take over the whole experience. Architects and sociologists have more recently been preoccupied with this idea to better understand the emotional universe of the subjects—because subjects are at the center of both architectural and sociological ideas of the affective space. See Matteis, *Affective Spaces*. Matteis does a beautiful job of defining the affective space, and the emotional states of people, based on architectural practices and urban design. In other words, Matteis's affective space is an analysis of the production of physical spaces. I think this is enormously productive for other kinds of work, including the one I suggest here. See also Gherardi, "The Fluid Affective Space." Gherardi defines the affective space as a concept (which I don't think it is):

> The concept of "affective space" focuses on affect as spatialized and space as affective and draws attention to those ephemeral elements which have the power of holding all the practice elements together and giving a qualitative tone to what is accomplished in practising. This approach entails a rethinking of space as processual, performative, multiple, affective and fluid. Consonant with the turn to practice, the turn to space and the turn to affect, I focus on the everyday spatial becoming of different organizing practices in order to raise the methodological question of how to conduct empirical research on affective spacing as an ephemeral and fluid phenomenon, that I name "fluid affective spacing."

immediately: first, how do exegetical theories and practices transform the text, both in its form and in its content? Second, do glosses limit themselves to provide the interpretation of a given text by submitting it to a well-crafted exegesis according to identifiable theories, practices, and techniques? I would rather suggest that the experience of reading the content of the various ordinary glosses is not simply an experience of interpreting the central text (and feeling the peace of mind derived from understanding the exegetical work and its tenets). Although such an interpretation exists, we should ask ourselves if interpretation is the chief effect that glosses have on those who use them.

Glosses, in effect, establish an affective relationship with the central text: they belong to its margins, they embrace and interrupt it, they are even confused and intertwined with the central text. And even then, they do their own thing: they create their own pact of reading in which they interact with the reader in a kind of imaginary dialogue. The experience of reading glosses is a constant back-and-forth between what interpreters want to emphasize and what they believe will move their readers to perplexity, revealing the reader's astonishments, their fears, perhaps their desires.

Exegesis does not merely impose a necessary technical superstructure; rather, it makes possible an affective space, created by the gloss. The page is an aesthetic experience, and this aesthetic experience allows interpretation—exegesis itself—to be disorderly or partial, since it is part of the imagined dialogue between texts and their readers.

It has been suggested that there exist interpretive communities: spaces in which models and modes of interpreting texts, or even dreams, form an ordered, stable, serial, and predictable structure.[27] The interpretive community is a fictional construct that allows control of the creative capacity inside the affective space in which the aesthetic experience of the gloss and commentary is manifested. But the interpretive community functions only at the moment when a *community* is suggested, a homogenous grouping around a chapter with definite rules. Outside this homogeneous group, a community cannot be said to exist. We can imagine, however, an unpredictable complex of networks, and the interactions that take place inside those networks. The networks may freely confront the affective experience of the gloss and of exegesis

---

27. Stock, *The Implications of Literacy*; on dreams, see Schmitt, *La Conversion*.

itself. This is what we will find in grossly overgrown form in the texts that we will examine in chapters 3 through 6.

Figura

One might think that a concept like *figura*, an interpretation that "establishes a connection between two events or persons, the first of which signifies not only itself, but also the second, while the second encompasses or fulfills the first," and the typological thought that accompanies it, would have little to do with the social dynamics within what David Nirenberg has called "communities of violence."[28] These are urban spaces in which the dominant community is defined by its violent practices toward other communities with minority status; these communities of violence correspond essentially to those that Robert I. Moore places within the sights of a "persecuting society."[29] As Nirenberg explains, discourses of misinformation and manipulation, emitted through interpretive events such as sermons and harangues, not only initiate an act of attack and violence but also define violence itself as that which establishes relationships between communities. Within those communities, then, it is violence that constitutes the relationship. One would perhaps expect that neighboring faiths (the expression corresponds as well to Nirenberg) and their respective public intellectuals would participate collectively in common, shared intellectual practices and modes of knowledge.[30] But instead the opposite happens; one may say that the interpretative artifact of the *figura* is a powerful device for commentary that unleashes a wave of violence within the legal text, and in particular within the legal-religious body of knowledge.

A pioneering study on *figura* is the article that Erich Auerbach first published in 1938. Avihu Zakai and David Weinstein saw in it Auerbach's rejection of a dominant "Aryan philology."[31] "Figura" was an outstanding article because it reacted against very specific instances of violence. The first occurs at the end of the first third of the article, where the author points to Tertullian as the first Christian thinker to note that the *figura* is the announcement, in the Old Testament, of something that the New Testament will fulfill; Auerbach also comments

---

28. Auerbach, *Figura*, 53; Nirenberg, *Communities of Violence*.
29. Moore, *La formación de una sociedad represora*.
30. Nirenberg, *Neighboring Faiths*; Schmitt, *La Conversion*.
31. Zakai and Weinstein, "Erich Auerbach," 320–38.

on Tertullian's explicit statement that the *figura* does not diminish the historical value of the Old Testament. In other words, the *figura* and its fulfillment, each on its respective side of biblical history, do not exclude each other. Fulfillment does not make the *figura* unnecessary; on the contrary, it affirms and manifests it.[32]

Auerbach tried to do many things with the genealogy of this initially grammatical and rhetorical concept; one of which was to create the terms of affinity between Judaism and Christianity based on a typological device. As Auerbach theorizes it, the *figura* in effect makes it impossible to separate the Jewish and Christian laws, because in the thought of the church fathers, reading the Tanakh and understanding Jewish Law from the Torah and beyond was the way to liberate the legal and political potential of the New Testament. The art of commentary begins at the moment when the *figura* itself is identified and requires genealogical analysis.

Obviously, the meaning of Auerbach's work in the world of Aryan philology is not the meaning it holds for us today. What was presented as a way of establishing affinities between two theological and legal forms of thought is, now, a demonstration of the degree of systemic violence against Judaism in the history of Western thought; it is one of the pillars of antisemitism. The *figura* is one of the procedures that ensures the appropriation of Jewish political, legal, and theological concepts by a Christian history that presents itself as perfect or completed.

The *figura* is an important component of the *ordo disciplinae*. It helps to encapsulate the inner world of the discipline by theorizing and reworking the coherence of the textual system. Like other models of legal-religious commentary, including the Islamic *kalām*, it happens within the boundaries of the legal text.[33] The *figura* works to consolidate those limits: theoretically, historically, and in practice it expresses how ideas, concepts, characters, narratives, and prophesies should be translated and reinterpreted on both sides of the dividing line on the calendar, between one revelation and the other. It greatly resembles the philological narrative of continuity and transformation within a tradition. Possibly the two share the same legal bases: the notion that law is neither created nor destroyed but is transmitted and renewed.

There are many acts of violence involved in this series of procedures that fall within the sphere of the *figura*. The clearest is the one that

---

32. Auerbach, "Figura," 28–53.
33. See Zysow's classic *The Economy of Certainty*; also Gleave, *Islam and Literalism*.

animates rhetorical and typological thought. Jewish Law may constitute an experience of prediction of the law, but at the moment when figurative and figural thinking enters the picture, Jewish Law expires immediately. Its historical content may not cease, but its juridical value does. In this sense, *figura* becomes a supersessionist device.

Here is one example of the *glossa ordinaria* on the Song of Songs, to which I will also devote the last part of this chapter. The first verse, "osculetur me osculo oris sue" (let him kiss me with the kisses of his mouth), displays a series of interlinear glosses: the kiss equals delight, *me* is human nature but also the incarnation of the Son. Here we have an immediate transformation of the paradigm: nothing is what it seems, and while some things are universal (human nature), others announce salvation in the future (the incarnation). On the margin, another gloss inspired by the same verse announces simply that it will speak of the synagogue; in fact, the beloved is the synagogue. The latter, according to the glossator, is an assembly, but only as *lapidum*, inanimate stones; whereas the figurative equivalent is the church, now understood as the "conuocatio, quod rationabilium," that is, the congregation of rational creatures.[34]

The congregation interpreted as stones or uninhabited walls speaks, of course, to the emptiness of the institution, its expiration as a group of humans endowed with rational souls, but it also speaks of its necessity: those walls are the same ones on which the ecclesiastical congregation rests, and they are weighted with the divine majesty that first caused them to be raised. According to Roman law commented on in the Middle Ages, an empty congregation continues to possess its own legal personhood, which devolves onto the building's or the city's walls. This legal personhood will be embodied in the congregation of rational souls that may inhabit it in the future, which will be the present for the new community.[35] It is at that moment that the stones may be freed from their juridical personhood.

---

34. This gloss is attributed to Anselm of Laon; it is edited in Mary Dove, *Glossa Ordinaria*, and with her English translation in *The "Glossa Ordinaria."* These editions are excellent, but of course do not show clearly how the glossed page functions; therefore I provide an illustration from Marston MS 2 of the Beinecke Library, Yale University, folio 1. There is also an online image of the gloss from the incunable edition of the *Glossa Ordinaria*: see, for example, the website of The Lollard Society, https://lollardsociety.org/?page_id=409.

35. On the fiction of the congregation without people and the moral character of the walls, see the magnificent study by Thomas, "L'Extrême de l'ordinaire," 207–37.

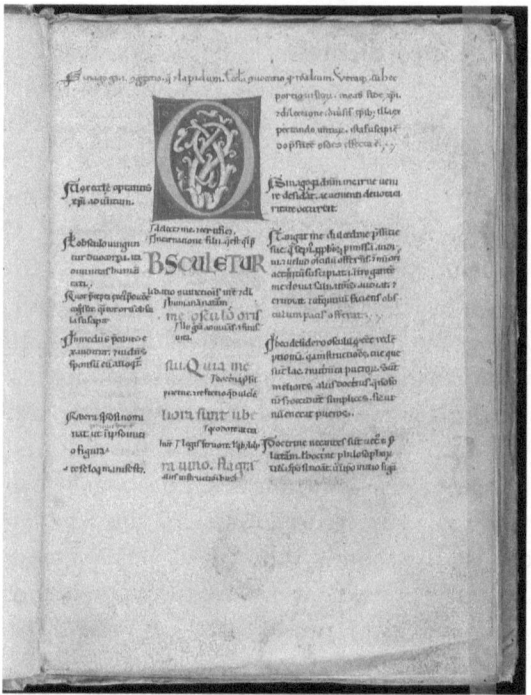

FIGURE 1.1. *Canticum Canticorum, cum Glossa Ordinaria* / Bible. O.T. Song of Solomon, s. XII 4/4 (last quarter of the twelfth century). General Collection, Beinecke Rare Book and Manuscript Library, Yale University. Shailor, B., Marston MS 2, fol. 1r.

The *figura* as a nucleus of interpretation performs a specific task: it changes the thing interpreted in itself, as well as the relationship between the legal subjects and the thing interpreted. To those subjects, the *figura* assigns a specific meaning that describes reality and its agents. It is a hermeneutic device: it explains the rules for interpreting groups of concepts, agents, institutions, or customs, and it limits the field of knowledge in which interpretation takes place. Hermeneutics, here, is a very precise interpretive concept that arises from the theorizing of Aristotle's *Peri Hermeneias* (*On Interpretation*), chapter 1, and the debates that surrounded that text in the central and late Middle Ages. The chapter speaks of words and things, and of the concepts or *noemata* that link those concepts and things. In this sense, the *figura* is a certain logical and semantic approach to a given text with its own logical and semantic networks. Interpretation operates at the level of those networks.

But the *figura* is also a heuristic device. It allows one to discover things and to be overcome by the sensation of surprise and astonishment that comes with discovery. We only need to recall Archimedes, the heurematographer par excellence in the history of Western philosophy, shouting "Eureka!" (from the same root as "heuristic" and "heurematography") and feeling euphoric, beside himself. The *figura* is a device that establishes the rules for discovering things within specific texts. It is also an anxiety-triggering device: it works so well, it helps so much with the consolidation and coherence of discoveries within the legal text, that it expands into other realms even while staying inside the milieu of the legal text. It is a potentiality: it does not tie one to a particular interpretation and the hermeneutic data, but rather allows one to poach (Michel de Certeau's *braconnage*) inside the text, to identify, unfold, and reveal its figurative structures.[36]

The *figura* is a literal device.[37] It works on the level of the physical appearance of the text. Even when it connects different things (like Joshua/Jesus), it does so in order to take history from point A to point B, stressing its continuity. This literal quality functions very well not only for the coherence of the discipline itself but also for the heuristic capabilities of other disciplines.[38]

Above all, the *figura* is an artifact for a theory of history. It allows the glossator to view history's periodization as a reflection on characters and events that announce things, and characters and events that fulfill the things announced. In this sense, it is also an artifact that establishes a genealogy of jurisprudence: what happened in the past as a *figura* points toward similar events in the future. For the glossator, the *figura* is—as Gil Vicente said about love-hunting—like falconry: aspirational, hard, and dangerous. For several of the glossators we will study in the following chapters, this hunt makes it possible to establish figural connections, not between a Jewish calendar and a Christian one but among multiple calendars and the persons or events who live within them. For a glossator like Diego de Valera, for example, ranging

---

36. See what De Certeau says in his *Arts de faire*, chap. 12, on reading as a form of poaching (*braconnage*).

37. It is one of the elements for weaving medieval biblical exegesis that, as Mary Dove has explained, "suppl[ies] it with what continuity it has as a narrative," except in the Song of Songs, which, according to Bede, has "a continuous allegorical sense." Dove, *The "Glossa Ordinaria,"* xvii.

38. Chris Harrison proposes a visualization of the Bible's system of concordances and correspondences. See "Bible Cross-References."

among the Roman, Jewish, and Christian calendars allows him to bring in historical and jurisprudential models of biographies of women, so as to propose ways of perfecting those models and *figura*s. Through the *figura* the disciplinary order is constructed, with its stratigraphy and its temporality, while at the same time it points toward history and its teleologies. Together with typological thought, it forms a basic element of the aesthetic experience of the gloss.

Typologies

The scholars and intellectuals Thomas Aquinas and Giles of Rome are two giants of the Parisian theology of the thirteenth century. Their names do not represent just a person: as Alain Boureau has claimed, they form a *mens*, a workshop.[39] In other words, their modus operandi is that of a co-laboratory (collaboratory). In this co-laboratory the disciplinary order is established by the "author function" (Michel Foucault's concept), by the proper name of the *mens*; after having been treated and discussed, the resulting material could be written down, then copied in dozens of manuscripts for circulation. Thomas and Giles were the origin of their own industry, as in other marginal industries in which compilation and the reproduction of materials call for a well-oiled machinery of copyists and artisans. The Parisian scribes and *stationes* (businesses that produced university books) located along the River Seine, which served the growing needs of both scholars and students, developed the style of book copying known as the *pecia* system, creating the perfect setting for their work.

Thomas modifies somewhat our understanding of the "figured" approach that we spoke of earlier. In his *Sententia Ethicorum*, a non-marginal commentary on Aristotle's *Nichomachean Ethics*, he explains as follows:

> Oportet ostendere veritatem figuraliter, idest verisimilter, et hoc est procedere ex propriis principiis huius scientiae. Nam scientia moralis est de actibus voluntariis: voluntatis autem motivum est, non solum bonum, sed apparens bonum.[40]

---

39. Boureau, "Peut-on parler?," 267–79. See also, for the notion of "author function" mentioned here, Foucault, "Qu'est-ce qu'un auteur?," 73–104.

40. Thomas Aquinas, *Sententia libri Ethicorum*, L. 1, l. 3, n. 4: English translation, accessed November 22, 2024, at https://aquinas.cc/la/en/~Eth, with some minimal modifications. If you have a little over $220,000 you can purchase a gorgeous fifteenth-century manuscript of the

(We should bring out the truth in figural mode—that is, verisimilarly. This is to proceed from the proper principles of this science. Moral science treats the acts of the will, and the thing moving the will is not only the good, but even that which appears to be good.)

Thomas's comment concerns both the content of ethics and the organization and order of the discipline itself. What concerns him above all is how to construct that "moral" science, how to understand its arguments and the form they take. In this sense, Thomas points to a homology between the form and the content of that science: since it concerns not only what is good but also that which appears to be good, its arguments must likewise conform to this dual mission. They must speak while considering the transmission and argumentation of truth to the extent that it is a *figura*, which Thomas considers a synonym of verisimilitude. It is an important displacement, because the *figura* points toward the fulfillment of something (an ethics) in the future, while at the same time it lays down the rules of what is best, what is proper, and therefore what most resembles the truth in that ethical future.

The semantic displacement that grounds the *figuraliter* in the *verisimiliter* is highly relevant, given the role played by the concept of verisimilitude in the rhetorical arts and the art of logic. We already know that for Thomas, truth in ethics should (*oportet*) be presented or exhibited (*ostendere*) not as truth itself but as *figuraliter*, that is, acting as verisimilitude or probability. In Ciceronian rhetoric, such as *De inventione* or the *Rhetorica ad Herennium*, both verisimilitude and truth create a probable

---

Sententia Ethicorum to grace your bedside table. It contains illuminations by Leonardo Bellini or his workshop in Venice, including one of an effigy of Thomas, who is probably in the act of writing in his famous *littera illegibilis*, or unreadable script. If you wish to know the prices of the bestsellers of 1275 in different disciplines, including the books of Aquinas, see Thomas Aquinas, *Corpus Thomisticum*, accessed November 22, 2024, http://www.corpusthomisticum.org/l1275.html. These prices were set by the university's *statio* or bookstore. The changes between 1275 and 1304 are not extreme; in the following list are the differences in price according to discipline, and within disciplines according to author: http://www.corpusthomisticum.org/l1304.html. The number of *peciae* (manuscript sections rented out to students for copying) in each volume determined the final price, but that was only one of the variables. There are certainly details unknown to us, such as the quality of the writing surface and, above all, the type of writing or *littera* used by the scribes; some scripts were more expensive than others. For instance, in legal texts the *littera bononiensis*, or Bolognese script, was one of the costliest. Legislators like Alfonso X attest to this in the *Siete Partidas*, 3.18.75, where he determines the price of the different scripts used in writing documents, with the Bolognese script being the most expensive.

cause.⁴¹ This idea goes back ultimately to Aristotle's *Poetics*, paragraph 1451b. For Aristotle, one reason that poetry is more philosophical than "history" is that the former is more general and speaks of universal truths.⁴² These truths, he claims, are stated in accordance not only with what is necessary but also κατὰ τὸ ἐικός, that is, with what is possible: the Latin and Ciceronian concept of verisimilitude is modeled on this Greek expression. One might say that verisimilitude is the (rhetorical) art of showing the truth without blinding its receivers with too much light; verisimilitude is truth as it can be told, as it can be explained in relation to the necessary, to create an atmosphere or affective space where things can be transmitted and it is possible to philosophize. In a complicated way, verisimilitude is more philosophical than truth, to the extent that, like poetry, it allows us to speak of things as they might have been. Truth, like "history," deals only with particular things as they are and have been. The operation invoked by the adverb *figuraliter* allows the philosopher to work with verisimilitude.

This theoretical operation allows Thomas to enter the terrain of appearances, of actions and intentions that are not only true and good (which are the same thing), but that also appear to be true and good. This is what ethical figurative investigation offers him. It was not easy to accept the existence of a new discipline called "ethics" based on the *Nichomachean Ethics* of Aristotle. It cannot be said that Aristotle's text even existed for Thomas and his contemporaries. It is supposed, or probable, that he accessed it through the translation made by Herman the German in around 1240 of Averroes's Middle Commentary on Aristotle's *Ethics*.⁴³ Therefore Thomas was extracting statements and theories from a commentary in order to comment on them in turn, so

---

41. Cicero, *De Inventione*, 1.7: "Inventio est excogitatio rerum verarum aut veri similium quae causam probabilem reddant" (Invention is the devising of matter, true or plausible, that would make the case convincing). Translation from Cicero, *On Invention*, Loeb Classical Library, accessed November 22, 2024, https://www.loebclassics.com/view/marcus_tullius_cicero-rhetorica_ad_herennium/1954/pb_LCL403.7.xml. The Loeb translation is less than satisfactory because it leaves some elements of technical content to be discussed: *veri similar* is not equivalent to plausible, and *probabilem* does not exactly mean convincing but rather that it is possible to prove the case. For the spread and knowledge of Ciceronian rhetoric in the Middle Ages, see Ward, *Ciceronian Rhetoric*.

42. I place "history" in quotes to indicate that this "history" is not historical narrative; rather, as I read the *Poetics*, it means any type of scientific discourse about actual facts, such as "natural history."

43. For the reception of the *Nichomachean Ethics* it is essential to take the Arabic tradition into account. See Kasoy, "Arabic and Islamic Reception," 85–106; and Woerther, "The Arabic Tradition," 37–64.

that those statements could become the nucleus or the axioms of the new discipline. The activity in itself is figurative in its own theoretical terms.[44]

Giles of Rome, with his *De regimine principum*, became one of the inventors of political science. He completed the work sometime around 1265–70 and dedicated it to Philip IV the Fair, king of France and Navarre. At the beginning of this work Giles writes:

> Cum enim doctrina de regimine principum sit de actibus humanis, et comprehendatur sub morali negocio, quia materia moralis (ut dictum est) non patitur perscrutationem subtilem, sed est de negociis singularibus: quae (ut declarari habet 2. Ethicorum) propter sui variabilitatem, magnam incertitudinem habent. Quia ergo sic est, ipsa acta singularia, quae sunt materia huis operis, ostendunt incedendum esse figuraliter et typo.[45]

> (The doctrine that touches the governance of princes has to do with human acts, and therefore falls within matters of morality. Moral matters, we have said, do not suffer general theoretical investigation, rather the matters must be considered individually; this is because of the uncertainty that, as is stated in book 2 of Aristotle's *Ethics*, derives from the variability of individual acts. Therefore singular acts themselves, which are this book's object of study, should be presented here figuratively and typologically.)

The procedure is similar to that of Thomas; both are doing things with the same types of words. There is a close relationship between the two treatises that, even from a somewhat restricted viewpoint, may be owed to a single source: both seem to take Albertus Magnus as their model. The latter explains in his *Tractatus I: De Delectatione*, the first chapter of his tenth book on ethics, why he speaks of "delectation" as a part of ethics. His general reflection on this type of investigation is that one should analyze things in a schematic way ("pertranseundo oportet dicere"), represent them in a figurative and typological manner

---

44. The book by Thomas usually known as *Super libri ethycorum* was composed in Paris, and its exemplar (the manuscript authorized for copying and distributing) was also made in Paris: Thomas Aquinas, *Opera fratris Thome*.

45. Aegidius Romanus, *De regimine principum*, pt. 1, chap. 1, p. 3. I quote this work following the 1607 edition, but the division into part and chapter is consistent in other editions and the host of manuscripts that transmit this medieval bestseller.

("figuraliter et typo pingere"), and not require excessively subtle discourses about them ("de nullo requirere subtilem rationem").[46]

For Giles of Rome, as for Albertus Magnus before him, *figuraliter et typo* is a kind of exploration that does not require formal dialectics, because ethics and politics, as disciplines, cannot pose questions that call for yes-or-no answers or any other type of reply involving opposites. They presuppose many variables, just as legal thinking does. Therefore, they demand a discourse that Albertus calls *pertransitum*, a broad perspective that is not, in the end, analytical.

The procedure implied by the work of figuration includes specific ways of approaching the creation and development of new disciplines. Figuration helps to establish what belongs to the sphere of verisimilitude, the sphere of the possible and the probable, one of the forms in which certain disciplines can work with the truth.[47] However, the task of one who operates with the elements of figuration belongs to the realm of singularity, where problems must be stated and modified repeatedly because they are not universal and cannot be answered with a yes or a no; they require a theoretical treatment, a *contemplatio*. It is from these kinds of works that ethical and political disciplines arise. They do not propose to comment on something in order to explain it; rather, they seek with their commentaries to create and debate new questions, new problems, new ideas, all of which respond to the *ordo disciplinae* while urging it toward new horizons.

The perspective of *figuraliter et typo* is very important to us in our construction of microliteratures. In many microliterary texts in the vernacular, truth is masked behind a practice of verisimilitude that sometimes involves specific biographies, as in Diego de Valera; sometimes legal ethics, as in Gregorio López; and sometimes fictions with which to construct a new ethics, as in Christine de Pizan. This analytical perspective is centered on what is individual, on a theory of history that

---

46. Albertus Magnus, *Ethicorum Libri X*, 599: "Rationes enim ethicae necessitatem non habent, sed sub motu liberi arbitrii sunt: quod quamvis fortuiti movetur, eo quod in electione et ratione electionis posita frequenter avertunt. In ipso enim est facere vel non facere, nec cogi potest ad sic vel non, nec agitur a natura nec communiter ratione. Et ideo per liberum arbitrium homo est dominus quorum actuum. Sub forte ergo et non sub necessitate determinare qui de moribus dicuntur: pertranseundo autem oportet dicere et figuraliter et typo pingere, et de nullo requirere subtilem rationem."

47. I am now reading the marvelous book by Jimena Canales, *Bedeviled*. It analyzes the occasions on which scientific, humanistic, and social research, in both the modern and the contemporary periods, uses the Devil as an agent of verisimilitude in order to invoke theoretical constructions.

surfaces in argumentation with examples that are, because of their possible value for jurisprudence, cases or *causae*.

Originalist Textualism: The Glosses on the Song of Songs

Something especially important to me in the present work, as I have indicated, is the specific relationship of the disciplinary order of the gloss or commentary to the general field of law. The law, in turn, maintains a delicate balance between the forces of textual originalism and a spiritual interpretation. The letter of the law says one thing, but was that its spirit? This discussion is as old as the law itself in all its forms, but we have constant proof that it is still alive in our legal culture today. Since I am writing in the United States I hear this debate daily: it marks the division between those who read the Constitution and its amendments (particularly the Bill of Rights) according to their originalist signifier and meaning, and those who approach those foundational texts from the viewpoint of a historical semantics and a spiritual exegesis—purposivists. When we speak of the modes and modalities of interpretation the law immediately presents its theological face to us, even where there is presumed to be a separation between church and state.

In her preface to the English translation of *The "Glossa Ordinaria" on the Song of Songs*, Mary Dove shows little patience for those who have little patience for its allegorical interpretation. For the latter, who include David Aers, the Song of Songs describes nothing other than erotic and carnal love, and Aers seems to assign no importance to what commenters have said and preachers preached.

Dove goes further in her research. It was not only the glossators who insisted on a sustained allegorical commentary on the Song; readers themselves participated as well. For Dove, those readers were "moving much more flexibly than modern readers from one kind of meaning [allegorical] to another [literal]."[48] I might add that, while we view the different meanings of a text as discrete groups of procedures that function in relative isolation from each other, medieval writers saw the several tools of exegesis as a type of superimposed, interdependent device: their approach was paradigmatic, synoptic, and synchronic, as opposed to syntactic, linear, and diachronic.

---

48. Dove, *The "Glossa Ordinaria,"* xxiv.

Perhaps this synoptic character of the glossed page, as well as the synchrony of the exegetical process, are important for understanding how the *glossa ordinaria* were read and employed. We need to envision reading techniques that include not only the linear—the kind we are used to, or were when we still read printed books—but also the strabismic forms of reading to which I have referred.

In fact, the manuscript page (of which there are many examples among the various ordinary glosses) is often filled with illustrations that escape our understanding, or lead us to dream about possible modern, even radically postmodern, meanings. We can imagine that they form parts of complex systems of interpretation, but we do not know exactly which ones. These images arouse speculation, and perhaps they were really speculative in several senses, including the notion that they lie on the other side of the *speculum*, the looking glass. As Dove comments: "To demand of the medieval reader 'are you reading these glosses literally or allegorically?' would be to attempt to do just what Aers argues the church attempted to do, that is, to 'control the interaction between the readers' imagination and the text's diverse potentials' (*Medieval Literature*, 64). If the church had really wanted to exercise this kind of control (and I find no evidence for this), it should have suppressed the *Glossa Ordinaria*."[49]

These words of Dove's seem pregnant with common sense. She also claims that the *Biblia cum Glossa Ordinaria* (*BGO*) was not necessarily conceived as a reference work. These, then, are Dove's three theses about the *BGO*, and about the *Glossa Ordinaria in Canticum Canticorum* in particular: that the gloss is a sustained allegorical interpretation; that such an interpretation is more fluid than anything modern readers can imagine; and, finally, that medieval users of the *BGO* did not necessarily think of it as an intellectual or academic platform on which to draw so as to do something else with its material. (This is, after all, what a "reference work" means to me: a book that is essential to the development of a specific discipline in the hands of the professionals of that discipline or ancillary ones.)

Dove's theses are based both on evidence and on a lack of evidence. There is no problem where evidence exists; but an argument based on a lack of evidence is an *argumentum ex silentio*, which is more problematic. Of course, Dove is refuting other scholars, telling them not that

---

49. Dove, *The "Glossa Ordinaria,"* xxv.

they lack evidence to support their thesis, but that she cannot see such evidence—in other words, that Aers and his like are those who have advanced and defended some form of *argumentum ex silentio*. While this exchange is brief, it still reveals that the two theses are polar opposites.

In the first place, there is actual proof that the *BGO* was used as a tool, as a work of reference. Medieval scholars refer to glosses as a locus of authority. Thomas Aquinas, in his *Quaestio de Magistro*, the ninth part of his *Quaestiones disputable de veritate*, begins with a reference to Matthew 38:8–10 in the *BGO*; it is his reference, his point of departure. Likewise preachers, including Bernard of Clairvaux, nourish their own thinking from the *BGO*, as in his *Sermones super Canticum Canticorum*. There is a mountain of evidence for the use of the *BGO* as a reference. "Ordinariness" and "reference" are the same thing, so naturally allied that one must consult a reference as the launchpad for thinking and writing.

The issue of whether or not the Song of Songs in particular is an erotic poem can be debated. Its literal surface is obviously that of an erotic poem. You would have to be blind to miss its sensuality: the kisses, the embraces, the breasts, the approach of marriage, the delayed consummation of love, the anticipation, the delight. If those are not typical of an erotic poem, someone needs to tell me what an erotic poem is.

But to my mind, a more appropriate question in these circumstances is: When did the allegorical reading begin? Was it before or after the manuscript containing the poem became part of the Bible? In other words, was the Song of Songs an allegorical poem from the time of its creation? Or is it only interpretation that establishes the allegorical system of a poem that cannot be read literally within a biblical text based on the *figura*? Put another way, is there exegesis going on, and can it be called allegorical exegesis? Is the *glossa ordinaria* a sustained allegorical reading of the Song of Songs?

For Jewish readers in the Middle Ages such as Rashi (Shlomo ben Itzak) or Abraham ben Ezra, the Song is full of allegories and cannot possibly be read without them. For Ben Ezra, the language that appropriates erotic love in the biblical and theological medium is the language of the prophets.[50] His commentary on the Song is a way of forging a link between the poem and the prophetic voice. In this it resembles the figural order, but instead of looking toward a goal

---

50. Del Valle, "El comentario," 334; Tarradach and Ferrer, "El comentario de Rashi," 407–39.

established in another legal text (in the New Testament, for instance), it looks forward to a future outside of time, whose goal is promised but has not been realized.

Rabbi Moshé Arragel, in the Bible that he glossed for Luis de Guzmán, master of the Order of Calatrava, claims that "this book of the Songs is so obscure that the glossators are very reluctant to touch it, so many are the figurative glosses that weigh it down."[51] Arragel mentions some of the figural interpretations, chiefly to reject them—for instance, the notion that the beloved and the lover represent, respectively, the Virgin Mary and Jesus—and focuses above all on an Aristotelian reading of the poem. This reading is contrasted with an interpretation of the legal allegories in the Song, such as, for example, the kisses, which are "the affirmative and negative commandments of God, which our Lord revealed to Israel on Mount Sinai."[52]

If we accept that the *glossa ordinaria* on the Song of Songs constitute a sustained allegorical reading of the poem, an important question still remains. What do the *glossa ordinaria* do to the Song as a legal text? To what extent are the *glossa* a legal meditation on the Song of Songs? The question is not without problems, because the Song of Songs belongs to one of the sources of the law (the Bible), but it does not present as a prescriptive text in itself; it contains no specific orders, rights, or obligations. Nor does it form part of the Torah or Pentateuch, the Bible's most clearly juridical text. Do the margins of the Law (the *glossa ordinaria*) affect this text, which seems marginal to the Law?

The prologue to the *Glossa ordinaria* states that while earlier texts (Proverbs and Ecclesiastes) deal with the disciplines of ethics and physics—an audacious claim in itself—the Song of Songs concerns the "theoretical" or contemplative discipline. "Contemplation" is a good translation of "theory," because both have to do with the question of vision and the staging of that vision. This setting of the stage for a vision is a sort of mixture of theory and theater; the words share a common root, *théa* (sight). In other words, it is good to regard this text not from the viewpoint of actions (although that is the concern of the law), or from that of natural philosophy, but from the viewpoint of

---

51. Paz y Melia, *Biblia*, 495. There is a wildly expensive facsimile of this manuscript in Spain's Biblioteca Nacional, under the signatures MSS/622 and MSS/623. I quote from the transcription of the text and glosses made by Antonio Paz y Melia. I wish to express my thanks to Andrés Enrique Arias for his help in accessing several texts and images from the manuscript, since the Biblioteca Nacional's digital copy is of very poor quality and scarcely legible.

52. Paz y Melia, *Biblia*, 498.

theories—general, universal images that seek to fill the mind with a *theatrum*, a representation, in order to encourage meditation.

One vision is that of the reorganization of the community. The allegorical interpretation of the *Glossa ordinaria* turns the beloved into the community of the faithful, those who collectively love the lover. However, there is a figurative transformation that underlies the allegorical interpretation and forces a secondary historical interpretation, or an exegetical moment: while in the Song of Songs the only possible community is the synagogue, in its interpretation as a contemporary artifact the only possible community is the church. The law does not, in fact, possess a time joined to its textuality; it is atemporal, universal, always happening at this very moment.

In this case, the commentary is not centered on the synagogue as the *figura* and the church as its fulfillment; nor does it proceed to an allegorical interpretation of the bride. All of that exists so as to bring forth a tropological interpretation based on these questions: What kind of community is the *ecclesia*, the universal church? And what shapes it politically and legally?

Here a second question arises. The fundamental element of this community is also the concept around which the Song of Songs is built: it is love. The ultimate command of the Christian Bible is simply to love one another. But what is the nature of this love? What is its philosophy? How can it be subsumed into legal and political thinking? To these questions, the Song of Songs offers an excellent response. The challenge resides in understanding this type of love as the political force that cements an alliance—in this case, the alliances of solidarity within the *ecclesia* itself.

Going beyond the practical techniques of biblical exegesis, I would like to pose a question about what exegesis actually does. In other words, what is the capacity of exegesis to do things—its action, what is termed its "performativity"? And therefore, what kinds of things can be done with exegesis? In my view, the most important result of these "acts of exegesis" is the creation of a "lawscape" (I adopt here the concept of Andreas Philippopoulos-Mihalopoulos), that is, a milieu in which all that exists is turned into law, where nothing lies outside the law. It is within this legal landscape or lawscape that particular legal and political operations become possible.

This brief analysis based on the Ordinary Glosses to the Song of Songs brings to the fore the very functioning of the disciplinary order, the limits of exegesis, the function of the *figura*, and its ethical manifestation—whose consequences are, in the last instance, legal and allied with the juridical world.

Apprentice Jurists

Joanot Martorell wrote *Tirant lo Blanch* before Shakespeare had Dick the Butcher tell Jack Cade: "First thing we do, let's kill all the lawyers."[53] Tirant, in his long conversation with a former knight, now a hermit, describes the spectacular celebrations of the king's nuptials at the English court—perhaps those of the same Henry VI of Lancaster against whom Dick and Jack want to rebel. He tells how a violent debate arose between the weavers' guild and the smiths' guild over the protocol and hierarchy to be followed in the procession in honor of the king. The king and the duke of Lancaster decide that those truly responsible for this confrontation are the guilds' respective lawyers, so the duke has three jurists from each side seized and hanged upside down from two sets of gallows, and watches until "agueren tramés les miserables ànimes en infern" (their miserable souls had gone to hell). The king, on learning of this, tells the duke:

> Mon oncle, en lo món no·m podíeu fer major plaer e servir del que fet haveu, per quant aquests hòmens de leys fan richs a si mateyx e destroexen tota Anglaterra e tot lo poble. Per què yo man que stiguen açí en la manera que stan fins a demà, e aprés sien-ne fets quartés e posen-los per los camins.[54]

> (Uncle, you could not have given me greater pleasure nor better service than you have done, for these men of laws enrich themselves and destroy all of England and all the people. Therefore

---

53. *Henry VI, Part II*, act 4, scene 2. Jack approves of Dick's proposal, and adds a note that is directly related to a commentary by Pope Innocent IV on the *Decretals* of Gregory IX. There Innocent asserts that no one should believe "the skin of a dead animal" unless it includes some kind of notarial authentication: "charta animalis mortui non creditur sine adminiculo alio" (Innocent IV, *Super libros quinque Decretalium*, 2.22.15). Gregorio López, the editor of Alfonso X's 1555 *Siete Partidas*, employs a similar formula in his gloss on *Partidas* 3.18, attributing it to Innocent IV, but in fact it is wholly transformed. Perhaps López was consulting an index or compilation where the pope's thought was cited incorrectly. Roger Chartier drew on an intuition by Marta Madero in analyzing this passage of Shakespeare (but without naming Pope Innocent as the original source): "Jack Cade," 77–89; Madero, "Façons de croire," 197–218.

54. Joanot Martorell, *Tirant lo Blanc*, 68 (or at the end of chapter 41, if you are using a different edition).

I order that they remain as they are until tomorrow, and that afterward they be quartered and strewn along the roads.)

This is not the only time that Martorell's text expresses his cruel disdain for jurists. Nor is it the only written example of a growing antagonism toward a profession that, as Patrick Gilli has shown, was transformed into something resembling a social class by seeking and obtaining articles of nobility.[55] This same profession and social class, furthermore, is responsible for a whole verbal system, a language that pervades both public and private modes of expression as well as models of debate within society.[56]

Microliteratures, marginal glosses, are not independent of the specific prestige of the field of law and its professionals. The ocean of glosses collected by Francesco Accursio around 1250 swelled even more with the so-called post-glossators and commentators of the fourteenth and fifteenth centuries; the manuscripts and editions produced in the sixteenth and seventeenth reached almost unimaginable limits, together with indices and other tools of research. The industry of marginal legal commentary, more than any other factor, dominates the European cultural scene of the late Middle Ages. Its language, bibliographic references, abbreviations, methods of argumentation, and other techniques become the essence of the gloss even beyond the legal profession.

The professional jurists who comment in the margins, and write independent commentaries on specific concepts or problems, are not merely vehicles for prestige; above all, they are vehicles for action. The problem presented by the weavers' lawyers and the smiths' lawyers is that their claims change the order of events: they modify the acts that were going to take place, creating the most feared outcome in the judicial world: a blocked trial, a blind alley. Their public and private influence is so great that they can transform things, institutions, and acts, interpreting and arguing in favor of a given application of the law. This is where the true power of glosses resides: they confer on their users a weapon that alters the order of things and actions.

In earlier publications and here, I take as my basic premise that the systematic marginal glosses of the fourteenth and fifteenth centuries stand in direct relation to the writing of legal glosses, to their disciplinary order, and in particular to the aspects of the disciplinary order that

---

55. Gilli, *La Noblesse du Droit*.
56. Rodríguez Velasco, "Political Idiots," 86–112.

I have analyzed in this chapter. The persons who, in the fourteenth and fifteenth centuries, immerse themselves in the marginal glosses on manuscripts in semiprivate bourgeois and noble libraries, and who occupy the greater part of this book, are connected to the authors' need to acquire authority based on the forms of expression used by the legal profession. Just as happens with legal institutions, legislation, and jurisprudence, the capstone of the production of glosses comes from specific cases, actions, and precedents (exempla)—that is, the chief components of all jurisprudence. But what we observe above all in this search for an affinity—an affinity desired, rather than elective—is the chance to transform the context, to bring about actions, to modify the order of things.

I have called this a desired affinity. And in this sense, the affinity does not accept the distinctions that operate, or may operate, within the legal profession. It desires legal action in its entirety, whether spiritual and moral or civil and political. For the professional world of law is not, in fact, homogeneous. Medieval and early modern law is not concerned only with civil life but also with religious life, which combines theological learning, the study of sacred texts, and canon law. The latter, while primarily ecclesiastic, also touches important aspects of people's lives such as baptism, marriage, inheritance, the legal process, and the juridical forms of the Inquisition. In dealing with these matters, canon law also defines who is a legal person, thus creating forms of subjectivity, and how these subjects act before a body of knowledge. The very concept of law, or of juridical thought, permeates every form of existing in the world; types of affinities among disciplines are not accidental, but a complex means of mutual collaboration for establishing the rules of the game for persons who live within the structures of power that we call jurisdictions.

To desire this affinity is to aspire to say what is just, to speak justice. "Saying what is just," from any point on the page, is a triumph of critical thinking. "Speaking justice," when one is not part of the profession or professions that have normally received authority and authorization for establishing the terms of the jurisdiction, is an act of courage, however simple or humble it may be. It is not always possible nor appropriate to "mourir pour les idées" (to die for one's ideas). Foucault's parrhesiast in *Le Courage de la vérité* (a seminar that he taught in person in the last weeks of his life) is not always available.[57] Nonetheless,

---

57. Foucault, *Le Courage de la vérité*.

political activity, political criticism, the questioning of things that seem unjust, call for different levels of courage. This is the courage of both female and male glossators. Not always, sometimes not coherently, sometimes not managing to reach the highest targets of criticism—but in a way that makes one's voice heard, this courage, in the process of legalizing the world, claims the right of male and female citizens to say something (anything, even a little) from inside certain networks through which power circulates.

I believe that putting this theory into practice is best understood by exploring just some of its aspects: those in which we establish the order of the disciplines and the ordinary character that certain glosses seek to achieve; we also need to look into other practices that derive from mandatory methods and have their own, limited flexibility. In particular, as to this last feature, I have concentrated on the power of the *figura* and of the ethical and juridical artifacts that can be set in motion by the idea of the figural and typological. In other words, this practice of the theory is an investigation into how the normal microliterary process operates: what it puts into play, what the disciplinary strategies and rhetorics are that activate marginal commentary. And how many of those who give themselves over to microliterature are, in their own way, apprentice jurists.

Chapter 2

The Production of the Margin

Early in this century, some psychologists and pedagogues conducted a phenomenological and cognitive learning experiment.[1] After selecting appropriate groups of students who performed at different levels in the classroom, they had them read several series of texts. Some were printed so as to fill the page, while others contained glosses of different types and lengths. The experiment aimed to determine whether students learned better from unglossed or glossed texts. The precise results differ from study to study, but the general conclusions can be summarized in four points:

1. The best students, the ones who normally earn an A or a B, do not seem to learn more by studying glossed texts than by studying unglossed ones.
2. Weaker students, however (less motivated, or with poorer study habits), who normally score between C and F, clearly benefit from studying with glossed texts.
3. In every case, glossed texts are retained in long-term memory more securely than unglossed ones.

---

1. Bell and LeBlanc, "The Language of Glosses," 74–285; Ko, "Glosses," 125–43; Stewart and Cross, "A Field Test," 113–39.

4. Among students of every age, grade level, and degree of preparation, 99 percent greatly prefer to study with glossed rather than unglossed texts.

This research demonstrates how the material nature of what is communicated is relevant to cognitive processing. The arrangement of elements on the page, the physical aspect of the learning materials, the relation between the center and the margin, and the reader's interaction with all those features form part of the act of communication. Further, these experiments suggest particular pedagogical strategies: in preparing study materials we must consider not only how to cover the course content (what the page says), but also where to place that content on the viewed object in a way that challenges the student's, reader's, or writer's very body movements (what the page does).[2]

At different times in the Middle Ages and the early modern age, people must have come to a similar conclusion, exerting an undoubted influence on the creation of manuscripts and printed books. The materiality of communication was the object of analysis and research into the practice of reading and the development of bibliographic forms of all kinds, and determined the relationships between the different textual spaces into which content could be organized.[3] Certain industries, such as the production of texts of civil law in *stationes* or workshops from the twelfth century onward, depended on how university professors like

---

2. An eighth-century scribe named Martin gives us a glimpse of those challenges: "O beatissime lector, lava manus tuas et sic librum adprehende, leniter folia turna, longe a littera digito pone. Quia qui nescit scribere putat hoc esse nullum laborem. O quam gravis est scriptura. Oculos gravat, renes frangit simul et omnia membra contristat. Tria digita scribunt; totus corpus laborat. Quia sicut nauta desiderat venire ad proprium portum, ita et scriptor ad ultimum versum. Orate pro Martino, indignum sacerdotem vel scriptorem sed habentem deum protectorem. Amen. Aymohenus inlustrissimus comes fieri iussit" (O blessed reader! Wash your hands and then take up this book; turn the pages slowly and keep your fingers away from the letters. He who does not write thinks that it does not take much work. How hard it is to write! It makes the eyes grow heavy and the kidneys ache, and saddens the other limbs. Three fingers write, but the whole body labors. Just as the sailor longs to reach his home port, so the scribe yearns to reach the last verse. Pray for Martin, this unworthy priest and scribe, even though he has God as his protector. Amen. This was ordered by the most illustrious Count Aymon). Bluhme, *Leges Burgundionum*, S. 589.

3. Mary Carruthers (*The Book of Memory* and *The Craft of Thought*; also Carruthers and Ziolkowski, *Medieval Craft of Memory*) has amply demonstrated the relationship between the making of bibliographic or material objects and their use as "machines for thinking" (in the words of the late lamented Michael Camille). D. F. McKenzie's postulates allow us to include these issues within an analysis of the sociology of texts. Paul K. Saenger (*Space Between Words*; "Lire aux derniers siècles," 147–74) has approached the problem from the perspective of techniques and processes of reading.

Francesco Accursio (who also owned a *statio* or workshop for manuscript production in Bologna) appropriated the margins of books that contained their ordinary glosses. The same happened with many sacred texts: the internal margins of the Torah and the Talmud were devoted to the literal commentary of Rabbi Shlomo ben Itzak (Rashi), from Champagne. His name was also used for the actual typeface and letter shapes in which his commentaries were written and printed.[4]

Our cognitive intuition about the importance of the margin in textual study, now demonstrated empirically by the psychologists and pedagogues in the experiments described above, explains clearly why the margins of books are a sought-after space. It is not enough to occupy that space and set up camp in it. It must also be produced, infused with new life as an epistemological artifact, granted citizenship. The margin must be turned into an institution.

It is not enough, though, for this institution to become an industry, as happens with the *glossa ordinaria* of sacred texts or bodies of laws. The institution is an object desired by individuals who—even if they practice one of the disciplines that participates in the glossing industry—still see a chance to construct this marginal intervention outside that discipline, often in the vernacular tongue.

We will study some of these cognitive and political problems from the viewpoint of the production of space for creating textual glosses in medieval manuscripts. By "production of space" I mean individual movements in which the process of writing and studying takes the form of a multidimensional search for organizing the location and use of cultural products on the surface of the page. Individuals who aspire to become public and intellectual authorities within their own networks do so through intensive use of a pristine white space, the margin. They need to index it as a space from which to enter into dialogue with the system of authorities and with the doctrinal system that allowed the book to be constructed and organized.

Cultural Engineering

Creating a glossed manuscript is a work of engineering. Its forms must be balanced so as to create a self-sufficient product for the reader, while

---

4. Yardeni, *The Book of Hebrew Script*. Of course, Rashi himself was not the source of the name: it was applied in the fifteenth century to a Sephardic font in which a Bible and a Talmud with Rashi's commentary were printed. See Heller's review of the first edition of Yardeni (2002).

including the whole range of meanings that one wishes to convey and establishing all the mnemonic anchors needed for study. The twelfth-century intellectual, author, and teacher Hugh of Saint-Victor (who died in February 1141 at the age of forty-five) devoted a large part of his work to reflecting on forms of commentary and the surfaces of books, as well as their internal organization. His chief concern is precisely the uncertain youth who must often read several books at a time ("si sepius codicem inter legendum mutaverit"), which may make it hard for him to remember everything he reads ("quod legitur memoriae imprimere possit"):

> When we read books, let us study the manner of imprinting on our memory not only the number and order of the verses and sentences, but also their color, their shape, the placing and position of the letters, if we saw such and such a thing written here or there, in what place, at what point on the page we see its positioning (above, middle, below); we are to consider what color was the letter-stroke or the adornment on the surface of the parchment.[5]

In other words, the manuscript's structure has to allow for the hierarchical markings that direct the reader's attention and study to various points on the written surface. Creating the manuscript means appropriating the whole of its written space, while deploying a strategy for the functional division of the elements that make up the page, seen as a cartographic artifact. One needs, then, to separate and specialize each cardinal point of the manuscript leaf; the ways of marking this "map" (with colors, signs, letter shapes) indicate different uses of the material that is carefully distributed over the page.

Controlling the territory of the page is not a merely theoretical or moral concern. Ruy López Dávalos, who was constable of Castile from 1400 to 1423, was particularly interested in reading Boethius's *De consolatione philosophiae*. As he explains, among the available versions he obtained a copy that contained the glosses by Nicholas Trevet (or Trivet) but found the experience extremely frustrating.[6] López Dávalos can

---

5. "Cum libros legimus, non solum numerum et ordinem versuum vel sententiarum, sed etiam ipsum colorem et formam simul et situm positionemque litterarum per imaginationem memoriae imprimere studeamus, ubi illud et ubi illud scriptum vidimus, qua parte, quo loco (supremo, medio, vel imo) constitutum aspeximus, quo colore tractum litterae vel faciem membranae ornatem intuiti sumus" (Hugh of Saint-Victor, *De tribus maximis*, 490).

6. For the Castilian versions of Boethius's *Consolatio* the fundamental work is Doñas Beleña, "Versiones hispánicas," 295–312. Doñas Beleña has also published three installments of his *Bibliographia Boethiana*.

clearly see that the text is a mixture of Boethius and Master Nicholas, making it impossible for him to concentrate on or fully comprehend how all the elements of the text he is reading work together. The problem is that the voices of the Roman poet and politician, the fourteenth-century English Dominican, and the (inevitable) anonymous copyists who have handled the text occupy the center of the page without differentiation. In fact, the glosses are not separated from Boethius's text but incorporated into it, in the form of long parentheses or remarks that force one to interrupt the central reading (as opposed to glancing voluntarily at the margin):

> And although I have read this book translated by the famous Master Nicholas, I have not understood it as I would have wished. I believe this to be from my lack of wit, and I even find it troublesome to have the text mixed with glosses, which causes great obscurity. I would consider it a great favor if you would explain it so that I can understand it better, keeping the words with which the author expresses himself and marking whatever you can in the margin so that I can understand the text without any companion.[7]

The constable expresses very well the purpose behind the book's cultural and pedagogical engineering: it should be understood *without any companion*. Producing the spaces on the page should be enough, sufficient unto itself; or at least it should supply all the *companions* or even *teachers* the reader needs. This is the notion behind Maimonides's *Guide*: a remote teacher who is asynchronous and accompanies in writing the student who cannot be in the master's presence (and in fact, Joseph ben Judah is in Aleppo while his teacher Maimonides is 1500 kilometers away in Fustat, in Egypt). Books like this—for instance, Bobby Fischer's classic chess manual—should form a program in which the book and the student who thinks together with it interact in a partly automatic way.[8]

---

7. Boecio, *Consolación de filosofía*, MSS/10220, fol. 1v, Biblioteca Nacional de España, Madrid. On May 11, 2010, I was consulting another manuscript copy of the work, HC 371/173 of the Hispanic Society of America, which also contains the constable's letter. That same evening two friends came to supper at my house in New York: Gemma Avenzoa (a respected philologist who died on January 22, 2021), and Lourdes Soriano. According to my diary, Gemma told me that "[this manuscript] is scored with a lead point on the folios' recto side. Sephardic scribes used to make their letters hang from the line, rather than sit on it, and in this manuscript they hang that way. That does not necessarily mean that the copyist was a Sephardic Jew, but it is more than possible."

8. "In preparing this book, I did not want to write just an ordinary Chess book—so I used a new method called *programmed instruction*. Instead of merely presenting information that

López Dávalos's correspondent accepts this assignment, incorporating into his work both the constable's letter and his own response in the form of a prologue, which serves as a sort of user's manual for the book:

> And where there is a fiction or story that is not often told, it should be briefly Summarized, not for your instruction, but because you have read widely and so can retell it rather than have to listen to it [again]. It is better for your memory, which being so full of different things, if you forget something it will be the more easily recalled. ¶ If some doubtful Statement is found, an addition will be made of the kind the said teacher has declared, only in relation [4r] to the letter. ¶ And because titles illuminate how to proceed, & so that nothing foreign interrupt the text, at the beginning of each book shall be placed an Account or argument that indicates something of the content of its verses & prose passages.[9]

Preparing the text requires incorporating additions, and above all removing everything "foreign" from within the text, placing it spatially or writing it so as to allow one's senses to distinguish between text and non-text—these are the different levels of addition. Glosses and titles both attract attention in a formal way, freeing up the central text but also having the virtue of isolating what is expressed in other textual forms; this "illuminates how to proceed" and avoids everything that might "interrupt the text."

The manuscript is transparent in separating its textual elements and the relation established among them. Also to be considered are the imaginary lines that connect the text in the center to the one in the margin, through the markings of space that are the tie marks of a gloss. In this particular manuscript the glossed words are underlined in red ink; the glosses themselves reproduce the glossed and underlined words from the center, repeating them in darker and thicker

---

you have to try to understand, this book, called a *program*, actively teaches the material it contains." Fischer, *Bobby Fischer Teaches Chess*, 16.

9. "E donde se tocare fiction o ystoria que no sea muy vsada, Reduzirse ha breuemente, no para vuestra enseñanza, ca aviendo vos grande notiçia de muchas lecturas mejor podes dezirlo que Inclinarvos a lo oyr. Mas seruira a vuestra memoria que Instruyda de cosas diuersas, seyendo de algo oluidada menbrarse ha mas de ligero. ¶E fallando alguna Razon que paresca dubdosa en sentençia, sera le puesta adiçion de las que el nonbrado maestro en su lectura ha declarado solo tocante [4r] a la letra. ¶E por que los titulos son claridad a la via del proçeder & no se entreponga al texto cosa agena, en comienço de cada libro se porna una Relaçion o argumento que señale algo de lo contenido en sus versos & prosas." MSS/10220, fols. 3v–4r.

letters (as if in bold) that are underlined in red and preceded by a red paragraph sign. The book as constructed does not send the reader to a different place but invites them to concentrate all their attention on the internal experience of the written page, and how the forms created on its surface are related to each other. The book's surface is a *system* created for the cognitive archiving of the texts, contexts, and groups of ideas that appear connected on its face, with special attention to those words that, marked off with inks or abstract signs, now form part of a dictionary of concepts, notions, or simply topics of conversation. It is essential to understand these *glossaries*, lexica, conceptual maps, if we are to comprehend a specific cultural project.

Ruy López Dávalos's anonymous correspondent belongs to an intellectual circle that may accept a literal interpretation as a sufficient explanation for the *sentencia* or ultimate meaning of a text. In fact, the correspondent takes the opportunity to add, where that ultimate meaning may be unclear, the glosses that Trevet has "declared" or explained "only in relation to the letter." This is not a comfortable posture, in a working environment in which the chancellor of Castile at the time, Pablo de Santa María, was composing his critical additions to Nicholas of Lyra's literal or historical glosses on the Bible. Pablo de Santa María's additions, as Yoshi Yisraeli has shown, actually criticize the very system of literal commentary known as *peshat*, the usual practice of that influential rabbi from Champagne, Rashi.[10] However, the interlocutor's method also includes summarizing rare or "not often told" stories or fictions, so that the constable may not so much *learn* them as *remember* them. Finally, he recommends including summaries, résumés, or arguments in the form of titles so as to give structural clarity to the whole. The objective is a page in which each section can be distinguished synoptically, directing the reader's attention to each one in a particular way, so that he knows at every moment *who is speaking*.

Scribes and copyists tried to construct manuscript pages on which more or less systematic abstract and concrete signs organized the traffic on the page, while allowing a precise grasp of its contents and functions. In many manuscripts, the glosses establish these relations through tie marks that require certain movements of the eyes if one is to join the concept in the center to the concept on the margin. The only

---

10. Yisraeli, "A Christianized Sephardic Critique," 118–41.

help offered is a graphic marking of those concepts, often an underlining (sometimes in the same ink as the text, sometimes in red), as well as fairly conventional signs like an asterisk, a dagger, or a trigon. A manuscript may exhibit individual marks, the language of its copyist at a given time. The direction of written glosses may also orient the reader: though types vary, many glosses begin at the upper and outer edge. One's perception quickly establishes the hierarchy of these stressed elements: they become a conceptual map of the text, the bases for reading and study, and the interpretative principles that the rest of the text (the unmarked portion) must obey.

The ordering of the material, and the relationship between center and margin, play a fundamental role in the creation of a conceptual map. There is a symbiotic connection between the two aspects. The order is the content—it is not independent of it. Decisions about the book's form are not a mere lattice or framework that artificially separates the materiality of the object and the content of its ideas, as happens in painting.[11] The people who will read the book, aspiring to possess it both intellectually and materially, and who plan to employ it in future political and intellectual projects, seek a pristine space for reading as well as lexical precision, an adaptation to the vernacular of what classical rhetoric called *sermo purus*: a way of codifying language in a sphere in which the use of language and the exercise of power fully coincide. A reader of Pierre d'Ailly's *Imago Mundi* expresses this as follows:

> You wrote to me the other day, among other matters, that [as to] the book *Mapa mundi* or "Image of the world," as it is called, which you were sending me, to the best of my ability I should explain it in clear words from our common Castilian tongue, in the most polished and elegant style possible according to our modern usage, and that I annotate it not in the center (as was done with the treatise that I sent to the bishop of Sigüenza the other day), but in the margin; because it did not seem right to you that the foundations [*fundamentos*] in this book should be mixed with the text [*letra*], because introducing them to men of little learning may make them forget the first thing that they read and make it hard for them to finish reading, as Seneca claims in his letter to Lucilius. For although this book has been rendered into Romance

---

11. The legal issue of the *tabula picta* is discussed in *Partidas* 3.27, among the laws related to property and the possession of objects.

before, the master who translated it, being a native of Galicia, was unable to express properly the words of our pure, polished ordinary Castilian.[12]

The translator is saying that making commentaries within a text is not an uncommon practice, but it is a tedious one. The translator has made this kind of internal commentary before, asides or brief explanations that resemble interlinear glosses in which difficult words are provided with an immediate equivalent or a brief definition. But the practice is insufficient for someone who is requesting a new commentary on the *Imago Mundi*: that person will need to see a clear distinction between the text and the explanation.

The glosser offers us a hint about exegetical intervention and its role within the cognitive program of the manuscript he has before him. If the *letra* is the text of the *Imago* itself, the glosses or annotations are the book's *fundamentos* or foundations. The glosses are the lexical and interpretative bases of the central text, and without them the edifice of the center would collapse like a building without a foundation. This particular manuscript is a defective copy of a longer version, and we must assume that it is lacking many glosses. Manuscript II/215 of the Real Biblioteca del Palacio Real in Madrid also contains fragments of this work in its folios 1r to 12v, but they do not help us to know the full extent of the marginal glosses. Some glosses allow us to compare the Castilian text with the Latin original, while others, especially those toward the end of the copy in Spain's Biblioteca Nacional, include some explanations in which the glosser adds details about Spain that are absent from Pierre d'Ailly. I know of no other manuscripts, and the PhiloBiblon database records only these two. The signs that connect

---

12. "Vuestra merced me escreuió este otro día entre otras cosas que el libro de Mapa mundi o Ymagen del mundo se dize, el qual me enbiaua vuestra merçed, quanto en mi posibilidat fuese declarase por vocablos claros del nuestro ydioma e vulgar castellano e que fuesse del más pulido e elegante stillo que ser pudiesse segun el moderno vso de agora, e lo acotase non por la parte de dentro segund fue acotado el otro tractado que enbié al señor obispo de Çigüença este otro día, mas en el margen porque non le paresçió a vuestra merced conuiniente que los fundamentos en este libro fuesen con la letra inclusos porque la interposiçión dellos a los omnes non mucho letrados es cabsa que se les oluida lo que primero han leydo e non acaban tan bien lo que han de leer, segund dize Séneca en la epistola que enbió a Luçillo, ca avnque este libro ya sea romançado antes de agora, pero el maestro que lo romançó commo era de Galizia natural non supo bien declarar los vocablos del nuestro puro pulido e castellano vulgar." RES/35, fol. 1ra, *Historia de los reyes de España y otras cosas*, Biblioteca Nacional de España, Madrid.

the central text with the glosses are chiefly daggers, and both the glosses and the signs were added after the text was composed. This may be what the correspondent means when recalling that "you" had sent the book to the glosser: here is the text, go ahead, add some glosses in the margins but not in the center, because those will not be understood. It is a strategy for studying a text that was not planned with glossing in mind; rather (as in Flann O'Brien's imaginary industry) the text's owner sends it to someone whose knowledge, and "polished Castilian" style, he trusts.[13]

The patron (or merely client) of this translation introduces this sociolinguistic and rhetorical comment: whoever translated the *Imago Mundi* previously did not know ordinary (*vulgar*) Castilian well. For this client, ordinary Castilian is pure and polished in style. With these two adjectives he refers to the rhetorical standard of a discourse without barbarisms, that is, capable of maintaining a Castilian register without introducing words from other languages, a *sermo purus*; it should also be reworked until it achieves the desired precision. Here I assume he is adapting the act of polishing one's discourse that Horace speaks of in his *Epistula ad Pisones*, and which is fairly common in Provençal poetry like that of Arnaut Daniel and even in Fernando de Rojas, who employs the Occitanism *dolar*, "to polish" (*mis mal doladas razones*), specifically to mark a change of register with respect to the earlier author of his work.[14] He does so with a graphic sign, not a verbal one: "And that you may know where my poorly polished [*mal doladas*] phrases begin and those of the former author end, you will find a cross in the margin; and it comes at the end of the first supper. *Vale*." Here the purity and polish of the style are opposed to the inability of a Galician translator to capture the conceptual richness of Castilian.

---

13. Flann O'Brien imagined, parodically, an industry devoted to handling and commenting on the books of owners of enormous libraries who were, however, basically illiterate: O'Brien, "Buchhandlung," 17–22.

14. "Ab gai so cuindet e leri / fas motz e capus e doli, / que seran vrai e sert, / quan n'aurai passat la lima." (With music joyful and sweet / I also write words that are well polished / they will become truthful and trustworthy / once I have filed them well [my translation].) Daniel, *Poesías*, 142. There are many variants of this poem, which was widely circulated. Riquer, who edited this version, chooses "Ab gai so," although many manuscripts show some variant of "En cest sonet cond e leri"; the variants do not affect the next two verses, which use the verb *doli* (polish) and the noun *lima* (file), the ones that refer to the act of polishing the poem.

Strategies of Order

Part of a well-designed plan is the ability to separate spaces for reading. An example is one of the manuscripts of *Epitoma rei militaris* by Vegetius, in its Castilian translation by Fray Alonso de San Cristóbal: *Libro de Vegecio de la caballería y del arte de las batallas*. Fray Alonso was both the translator and the commentator:

> With the help of Our Lord God, I have planned to divide this work into three parts. The first will relate what Vegetius said in his books, translating them as clearly as I can. The second part will be placed in the book's margin in the manner of a gloss, and [will consist of] sayings of experts who agree with what Vegetius says & express their own opinions at certain points. And the third part will be placed below, and will speak spiritually, relating Vegetius's words to the virtues & sins & customs of this world we live in.[15]

This reordering of the material lends Vegetius's work a new meaning: it offers the central text as a support for something else, what is in the margin. Like Boethius's *Consolatio philosophiae*, Vegetius's *Epitoma* was one of the Latin treatises most read, translated, and quoted in the Middle Ages. The occasion of a new translation is related to the need to adapt its language to "the modern usage of today" (el moderno uso de agora), as the translator of the *Imago Mundi* put it. There is also the chance to construct, based on a well-known text, a body of knowledge that renews conceptually the uses to which Vegetius's work had always been put: military training and strategy.

Alonso de San Cristóbal, a master of theology and member of the Order of Preachers, worked within a discipline that was constantly exploring its affinities with other disciplines or fields of knowledge. Think of the intellectual labor of Thomas Aquinas, another Dominican, in his *Summa Theologiae*, which articulates how to appropriate other sciences, from logic to ethics, as parts of the discipline of theology. The affinity between chivalric knowledge, which in the Middle Ages

---

15. "Ayudandome el señor dios pense de partir esta obra en tres partes. La primera parte fablara & dira lo que dixo Vegeçio en sus libros, romançandolos lo mas claramente que yo podiere. La segunda parte sera bien como glosa puesta en la margen del libro, que es de dichos de los sabidores que concuerdan con lo que dize Vegeçio & declaran sus dichos en algunos logares. E la terçera parte sera puesta ayuso, que fablara spiritualmente trayendo los dichos de Vegeçio a las vezes a las virtudes & a los pecados & a las costumbres desta vida en que bevimos." M-94, fol. 1v, Biblioteca de Menéndez Pelayo, Santander.

included the study of Vegetius, and ecclesiastical law, religion, and theology, was not a new one in the late fourteenth and early fifteenth centuries. Royal coronations, knightly investitures, and narrative genres in poetry and prose were manifestations of a political theology that affected chivalry in particular, as an artifact for transforming society and its structures of power—for instance, the nobility.[16]

Alonso de San Cristóbal participates in this theological-political exploration, aware of the central role of chivalry in creating models of behavior, codes, moralities, beliefs, and statements of political theory conceived of as social engineering. In his political and social world, a prominent voice was that of Bartolo da Sassoferrato, who declares that chivalry, dominated by rulers, is the instrument that makes it possible to create a noble person out of a plebeian one. This is the creative power of chivalry in the fourteenth and fifteenth centuries, the power that is confronted by a text that theologizes chivalric knowledge, like that of Alonso de San Cristóbal.

The theologian's proposed separation of types of knowledge into blocks establishes a cognitive hierarchy that can be seen as the opposite of what Alonso de San Cristóbal expresses. The text's center consists of the column containing the translation of Vegetius's text by the Dominican. But this translation may yield its doctrinal importance to the two groups of marginal elements that share the page. Alonso de San Cristóbal begins the description of his plan with the gloss that is clearly on the side margin, which contains "allegations" and "concordances"; these function in accordance with the systems of glossing and "ordering" of biblical and legal texts. Alonso de San Cristóbal wants all of that to culminate in what is "below," placed immediately after or under the first gloss. It is hard to determine if he means that the spiritual gloss simply comes after the concordances and allegations, or if he means to place it deliberately on the lower margin of the page, as the doctrinal ballast of the text and the formal conclusion to the reading of Vegetius and related authorities. Elements that the client for the *Imago Mundi* translation called the "fundaments," the hermeneutic rules of the text with all its concordances and allegations, are located in that zone in

---

16. I have written on these topics. See, for example, Rodríguez Velasco, *Plebeyos márgenes* and *Order and Chivalry*.

which one "speaks spiritually" (*fabla spiritualmente*). Please read my mea culpa in this footnote.[17]

Just as in manuscripts of Boethius, in this version of Vegetius by Alonso de San Cristóbal the lexical hierarchy, and how it relates to the rest of the page, allows us to draw a conceptual map and a dictionary that, with its perceptiveness and inclusiveness, allows the reader to interpret texts that have not been marked graphically in any other way.[18]

The structuring of these spaces of perception, their hierarchies, and their relationships or imaginary connecting lines, reflect a need to control the space on the page, and copyists and even the patrons who requested the copies may have pushed back against that control. Authors and translators, as well as patrons, try to direct ways of reading that affect both the presence of the text and the construction of meanings and rules for the reception of ancient-language texts now, in the present, in Castilian. Perhaps we see most clearly this attempt to appropriate the space and rules of the page in the practice of autoglossing: works in which the author not only creates the master text but also fills the page's empty spaces with glosses. We will be studying some aspects of autoglossing below.

The Ruler and the Rhetorician

I am going to borrow for a moment, purely as an analogy, the concept of the satellite as it is used in cognitive semantics. Cognitive semantics claims that the gravitational center of a word (for instance, its lexical root) is what carries its recognized meaning; but the satellite that

---

17. Mea culpa: while writing my doctoral dissertation in 1993 I was able to see very briefly manuscript M-94 of the Biblioteca Menéndez Pelayo in Santander, which contains Alonso de San Cristóbal's *Vegetius* translation. In my haste I *thought* that its form was that designed by Alonso de San Cristóbal, with one column of translation and another column with two types of glosses. I relied on my perception and have not been able to see the manuscript since. Fortunately José Manuel Fradejas Rueda noticed and corrected my error in his recent edition: Alfonso de San Cristóbal, *La versión castellana medieval*, 76–77. I repeated my mistake in several publications, and I am happy to be able to address it now.

18. Alfonso de San Cristóbal's translation is preserved in seven copies, some with glosses, but none of them displays the order designed by its author. In addition to M-94 at the Biblioteca Menéndez Pelayo, II/569 at the Biblioteca Real, Madrid, copies the glosses but does not preserve the page layout that San Cristóbal intended. Ms Fonds Espagnol 211 and Ms Fonds Espagnol 295 of the Bibliothèque Nationale contain only Vegetius's text translated by San Cristóbal but omit the glosses entirely. For a detailed study of all the manuscripts, see Alfonso de San Cristóbal, *La versión castellana medieval*, 35–61.

orbits around that known meaning exerts an attraction that alters its meaning, forcing a semasiological or onomasiological interpretation. In order to do so the satellite becomes the main focus of the meaning.[19] In other (and perhaps simpler) words, if the page's center holds a meaning based on the aspects that confer authority on a body of knowledge and the intellectual networks that have sustained it over time, then glosses exert a special attraction, an unexpected focusing of the attention that transforms that body of knowledge.

One could argue that the gloss's role as a satellite is part of the order of a discipline, that is, the need to construct a science on the basis of a given corpus. Attraction is not merely assigning a different meaning to a known quantity; rather, it is a chance to project into the future a given whose political value should be subject to criticism in the present. Here actualization is combined with action. It is an "act-of-glossing" (a marginal speech act with which things are *done*), a way of constructing the contemporary.

Some of the individuals who wrote glosses, or wrote about them, at this period were also in the process of discovering the practice of literacy and its effects in their milieu—I mean literacy in the sense of literature. They were discovering it not only in themselves, through what this literacy allowed them to do, but also in those who employed them, either regularly or occasionally. Discovering the power of literacy could prove essential for constructing one's public image and one's political subjectivity and identity, that is, what Stephen Greenblatt called "self-fashioning."[20] Some of these persons strove to become intellectuals, individuals whose discursive expressions could have an impact on their contemporary world: in pacifying civil conflicts, in building new forms of civic association for the increasingly powerful cities, and above all in introducing new political ideas that could prove useful for

---

19. Talmy, *Toward a Cognitive Semantics*, 220–22. I could have used similar analogies like theme/rheme, or Roland Barthes's very attractive analogy in his study of photography based on the *studium* (things that seem to be part of a tradition) and *punctum* (something that rubs up against tradition and creates a wrinkle in the process of reception) in the construction of an image. But the satellite analogy has the virtue of evoking a mental picture in which one thing orbits around another, as glosses orbit around the central text. Barthes, *Camera lucida*.

20. Greenblatt, *Renaissance Self-Fashioning*. This way of constructing one's self follows specific models of imitation, but more important than the models and the imitation is the individual's consciousness of changing, and the resulting creation of a subjectivity that is both a response and a resistance to modes of cultural and political control at certain moments and in certain networks of power.

transforming the social circumstances in which they lived.[21] Becoming an intellectual meant, for them, appropriating the margins, the satellites, the points of focus needed for constructing a new field of knowledge.

These glossers, taking inspiration from legal or biblical glosses, as well as from early moralizings and commentaries on literature in the vernacular, did not merely inject the vernacular into an established genealogy of academic glosses—much less into the bibliographic industries of the *glossa ordinaria* in general. Through their work they redefined the very act of glossing, transforming it into a contemporary challenge. How are we to understand the intellectual efforts that underlie the different definitions they proposed for the meaning of the gloss? For these individuals a gloss neither completes nor complements (or supplements) the central text but constitutes something different and differentiated from the central text. It is this difference that calls for deeper exploration, because the production of the margin is, ultimately, the production of this kind of difference.

Bishop Alonso de Cartagena of Burgos, part of an intellectual dynasty whose members were fully aware of the public power of intellectual labor, offered a definition of the gloss or the act of glossing that, I believe, explains the burden of subjectivity and political identity that underlies this marginal endeavor and its expansion into new spheres for exerting authority. In one of his texts about the theory and practice of translation, among his exchanges about rendering Greek works into Latin and as part of his friendly debate with Leonardo Bruni about translating Aristotle's *Ethics*, he says: "In effect, just as one type of discourse is proper for a ruler and another for an orator, and one should speak in one way to a judge and in another to a lawyer, in the same manner the style [*locutio*] of texts and glosses should not be the same: the text teaches us with concision, while the glosses usually explain what the text means to say."[22]

The central idea of this argument is the special relationship between the forms of central power and the type of discourse (*locutio*) emitted, which is in turn a way that power circulates. What authority does this

---

21. See Rodríguez Velasco, "Diego de Valera," 81–102.
22. "Nam sicut alia principem, alia oratorem decet oratio et aliter iudicem, aliter aduocatum congruit loqui, sic textuum ac glossarum non debet similis esse locutio: nam breuiter textus nos docet, glossule uero quid textus senserit aperire solent." González Rolán et al., *Humanismo y teoría*, 208.

discourse have? What things can be done with this discourse? The judge and the ruler emit discourses, and these, which are acts, do certain things out of the sovereign space that the king and the prince inhabit; the lawyer and the rhetorician speak, and perform, other things. It is the same with the text, which speaks, as the ruler and the judge do, from the center; while the discourse of the gloss, on the margin, possesses the persuasive or differential capacity proper to the lawyer or orator. The authority of the decision still resides in the central text, in the ruler or the judge, but the responsibility for acting on or activating political action falls on the gloss—on the person who, by deploying the margin, seeks to persuade rhetorically or to advocate for an alternative. From this perspective, glosses imply the possibility of a change with respect to the traditional authority of a central text. Opening up the meaning, as Cartagena suggests in reference to the gloss, means not only infusing life into the letter of the law but exploring the spiritual possibilities of that letter to give life to the central text.

We can say, then, that glosses constitute deliberative and argumentative spaces that orbit around master narratives and discourses. While master discourses are distant in space and time and are invariable, glosses force these narratives and epistemologies down to earth, bringing them closer to contemporary thought and making them more open to transformation. The unchangeable nature of the central text is also expressed through marginal glosses: the best way to do things with that invariable text is to subject it to theoretical and literary pressures that might free it from its contextual chains. The male or female glosser (whoever that might be) responsible for the rhetorical or legal discourse has a particular responsibility: to construct forms of persuasion, based on the jurisprudence and jurisdiction of the master text, that open the door to meaning, and establish channels through which something from the past can be applied as if it were present.

The Manuscript as a Space of Civic Life

A manuscript book is one of the spaces of civic life. Many manuscripts were created to occupy a particular space, and often they are so large that the ritual of reading them is confined to the space where the book is located. Some manuscript books result from a commission that has meaning only within a certain space—like a king's chamber—that is also imbued with a high degree of hieratism; many of these manuscripts were created for a community of readers or a community of interpreters. It is

FIGURE 2.1. Pedro de Toledo's translation of Maimonides's *Moré Nevuchim/Mostrador de los Turbados*, MSS/10289, fol. 1r. Image from the collections of the Biblioteca Nacional de España, licensed under a Creative Commons CC-BY license.

true that the community of readers who occupy a given space is not the same as a community of interpreters, and it is precisely in that displacement that the book's margin proves especially significant.

Consider MSS/10289 of Spain's Biblioteca Nacional, titled in Philo-Biblon *El More en castellano traducido por el maestro Pedro de Toledo*, which contains Pedro de Toledo's translation of Maimonides's *Guide for the Perplexed*. It was made for Gómez Suárez de Figueroa, lord of Zafra (Badajoz) and butler to Catherine of Lancaster; the manuscript is dated September 25, 1419. That is the date of the first part of the book; the second part is undated but was produced later. The title that Pedro de Toledo gave it includes the glossed title or subtitle used by many translators: *Mostrador o Enseñador de los Turbados*. Both folio 1, which contains Pedro de Toledo's prologue, and folio 2, with that of Maimonides, are decorated with ornamental motifs in the margin colored with gold leaf and blue and red pigments.

Two different hands have made notations between the lines and on the margins. One of them is Pedro de Toledo's own, sometimes with instructions for the scribe. Through these notes we perceive a high level of anxiety about the process of translation. It is not enough for Pedro de Toledo to make excuses in his prologue, nor is he satisfied with the common practice of translating a single concept with two or even three terms so as to cover the whole conceptual range of the original.[23] At certain points he realizes that what he is translating, even though it can be expressed in Castilian, cannot be understood—that there is no way to reason with it other than with the reasoning of its original culture and language. Where Maimonides refers to rabbinical techniques of exegesis, Pedro de Toledo translates them, but complains, "This has no expression that can be put into Romance."[24]

Some of his renderings are interpretations, and his own literal translation (*de verbo ad verbum*) can put him in a hermeneutic quandary; in those cases he attempts an explanation with marginal notation, because he cannot be faithful to the original text. Pedro de Toledo claims that the words of Maimonides, with their glosses, would have to read as follows in Castilian:

> ¶ The Wise man said, golden apples in Nets | of silver through your heart in order to hear me. gloss of this Statement. that said that the nets are that the apples are netted because they have very small delicate piercings, which is the work of the goldsmiths & they are called nets because the eye sees through them & it is in their Chaldean language the meaning of "to look at" and "latticework". ¶ And the wise man says that just as the golden apple

---

23. Pedro de Toledo's wish to translate *de verbo ad verbum* (from word to word) is, in a way, incomprehensible from a theoretical perspective, if we consider Maimonides's letter to his Hebrew translator Samuel ben Jehudah ibn Tibbon (to which the second glosser refers at one point). In the letter Maimonides argues for a translation radically focused *ad sententiam* (on following the sense of the sentence), even if that means altering syntax, changing the order of the material, eliminating parts of the original altogether, or employing doublets or other tricks of translation so long as the resulting product has a character of its own. There is a full translation of this letter by Herman Adler in Löwy, *Miscellany of Hebrew Literature*, 219-28. I have now read Fernández López's splendid article, "An Intertextual Argument," where he also updates the bibliography and philology related to Pedro de Toledo's translation. He has also edited the text: Fernández López, *Mostrador e enseñador*. See other references and editions in my article, Rodríguez Velasco, "La producción," 249-72.

24. "Esto non ha rrazón que se pueda Romançar." *El More en Castellano traducido por el Maestro Pedro de Toledo*, MSS/10289, fol. 32va, Biblioteca Nacional de España, Madrid.

FIGURE 2.2. Pedro de Toledo's translation of Maimonides's *Moré Nevuchim/Mostrador de los Turbados*, MSS/10289, fol. 4r. Image from the collections of the Biblioteca Nacional de España, licensed under a Creative Commons CC-BY license.

in silver Netting has very small openings, so is the thing that is stated in two ways.[25]

In the margin, Pedro de Toledo tries to untangle this complicated passage: "note that he means two intentions [*entençiones*], one better although the other is good [also]." But this explanation leaves the problem almost unsolved. As Stern has shown, the interpretation is not incorrect in itself, since it suggests that both the outside of the apple (its silver netting) and the inside (the apple itself) should receive the same hermeneutic attention.[26] But the second glosser, who has the

---

25. "¶Dixo el Sabio mançanas de oro en Redes | de plata por tu coraçon para me oyr. glosa desta Razon. que dixo que las rredes son que las mançanas enrredadas por que han logares sotiles foracados mucho menudos segunt que es la obra de los orebzes & son llamadas rredes por que el ojo cata por ellas & su caldeo de catar es & en Redo. ¶Et el sabio dize que como la semejança de las mançana de oro en Redadura de plata que las sus aberturas son muy delgadas, asy es la cosa que es dicha en dos maneras." MSS/10289, fol. 4rb.

26. Stern, "The Maimonidean Parable," 209–47.

right to access the page and express his own opinion, does not seem equally satisfied.

This second glosser makes what look like innumerable interlinear corrections to Pedro de Toledo's translation. For example, in the transcribed text where Pedro de Toledo had written *dos* (two), the second glosser writes *sus* (their). The second glosser rebels not only against the translation but against every personal manifestation of Pedro de Toledo as translator, whose work he cannot abide. At the same level on which Pedro de Toledo wrote his note on the two *entençiones*, the other adds a comment that criticizes both the translation and the marginal note: "he should not say *dos* [*maneras*] here, but rather *sus maneras*, for that is what the text says further on in the author's words, where he says that every saying has two forms, etc. That is where this note should have been."[27]

Nothing the translator does satisfies this second reader, perhaps a scholar, who knows both the original text in Judeo-Arabic and the Hebrew translation by Samuel ben Judah ibn Tibbon (and perhaps also the one by Yehuda al-Harizi). His specific criticism of the placement of notes is a criticism of the translator's failure to organize the space of interpretation properly, his inability to grasp the process of reading with the support of the marginal comments a scholar needs when faced with a philosophical text like that of Maimonides.

At certain points the second glosser ridicules Pedro de Toledo's comments; drawing a box with two cells, he places the translator's note in one and his own scornful remark in the other:

| Note: what tanbil means in Hebrew. | I don't know what he means when he says this about Hebrew tanbil.[28] |

The page has become a battlefield, at least up to folio 20v, where the polemical voice of this reader, student, scholar, or annotator vanishes; he either will not, or cannot, go any further. Or perhaps the work he had undertaken and performed up to that point proved so intense that

---

27. "non ha de dezir aqui dos saluo sus maneras que ansi lo dize el texto mas adelante en las palabras del actor onde dize que todo dezir segun dos maneras etc. Ally convenia este notable." MSS/10289, fol. 4rb.

28. "nota que quier dezir tanbil en abrayco / non se que quiere dezir en esto que dize del ebrayco tanbil." MSS/10289, fol. 5r.

he decided not to continue, but to turn to another project. We do not know if he belonged to the *studium* (library) or the *schola* (that is, the court) of Gómez Suárez de Figueroa, but he clearly knew Hebrew and Arabic well; perhaps he was a Jewish intellectual charged with revising Pedro de Toledo's text and then became his rival, possibly without ever meeting him.

In any event his glosses are really non-glosses, if we mean glosses in the strictest sense of the term, having to do with strange or rare things. This seeming paradox allows us to make an important conceptual distinction. They are non-glosses because they refuse to establish criteria for explaining the text as the center of gravity of the content. They reject utterly the idea that the central text has authority, because it is lacking in meaning. But they are, in fact, glosses. They are glosses in how they are distributed on the surface of the page and work the space of the text, scanning it in every direction from the interlinear spaces to the margins, in a movement of tie mark and development, correction and commentary. They are glosses by virtue of how they establish the limits and boundaries of the territory, the system of signs vis-à-vis the text, through dots, lines, cells—in short, forms of restructuring the direction and order of reading, and of understanding the text both at the center and on the margins. The glosser reads, and in reading calls for reorganizing the space for reading. Since the central text is of no use to the glosser, he needs to exploit the manuscript's remaining space to the maximum.

Marking up the text is crucial to the process of appropriating the space of the page and redirecting the reader's attention to the points where debate is unfolding. A dagger marks a correction that is usually placed beside the column, written perpendicularly to the text. A dagger topped with a circle draws the eye to the margin, where the same sign is reproduced but now upside down. A bracket (perhaps a paragraph sign) marks the end of the passage to be commented on, where a half-bracket (maybe another paragraph sign) marked its beginning. The glosser also distinguishes every word of the commented portion by placing above it a trigon, three dots that form a triangle (∴). Underlining sends the reader to the reference in the margin, the usual practice in glossed manuscripts. Insertion and deletion are also indicated conventionally, with an arrow for insertion or a row of dots below a word to be deleted.

The second scholar's intervention cannot be called the experience of a reader; above all it is a theory of the production and emission of the text, and of the responsibility of the translator as philologist and philosopher. This intervention questions the basic principles of translating and interpreting, and therefore questions the principle that an untranslatable concept can be repaired through an explanation. It questions the practice of solving the problems of one translation through recourse to a second one; finally, it questions whether errors of interpretation in the practice of translation can have ecdotic motives, since these may be conditioned by the translator's linguistic, literary, and philosophical culture. Altogether, of course, it creates a pragmatics of reading that destroys the translator's authority and makes perfectly clear that the reader should approach the book with caution. This second glosser, through his action of glossing (or non-glossing), transforms the book into a totally different object.

Every reader of this manuscript will realize that it is like a labyrinth. That is why spatial marking is an essential instrument, being also an instrument of cognition, a vehicle for restoring a hierarchy of the many and diverse components of the page. The markup is Ariadne's thread, or maybe Tom Thumb's pitiful breadcrumbs.

The glosser treats Pedro de Toledo with irony and scorn. Sometimes he merely notes, "I do not know what he means by this"; he downplays the translator's good points and reproaches him for his mistakes. On occasion he goes on at great length, as if carrying on half of a conversation in the civil space of the page. Pedro de Toledo, when speaking about translation in his prologue, writes:

> I will do as I should & follow the Rule & custom of the learned [letrados] translators who came before me ⁋ And because translations vary & [are made] by different scholars, good & middling & poor [ningunos]:. ⁋ And all scribes likewise, [if] they were not learned, made obvious errors. If I should err let me not be blamed & and for what I express well, may thanks be given to God.[29]

This excuse gives the glosser an opening to place a trigon after the word *ningunos*: there he begins a comment that runs up the right side of the column, perpendicular to the text: "I do not know what ningunos means here [or] if it is a scribal error." The ironic remark turns into an

---

29. "yo fare lo que deuo & seguire la Regla & costunbre delos trasladadores letrados que amj son antiçipados ⁋Et por quanto los traslados son diuersos & de diuersos letrados buenos & comunales & ningunos:. ⁋ Et los escriuanos otro sy todos por ser non letrados erraron yerros manifiestos yo lo que fare sy errare non sea en culpa & delo que bien dixiere a dios las graçias sean dadas." MSS/10289, fol. 1ra.

irritable criticism of Pedro de Toledo's attitude: the glosser continues, now writing between the lines of the translator's prologue: "Not all scribes are deficient in learning [*non letrados*], and not all made mistakes; much less the translators, as he says (which will become clear further on). For the author himself saw Ibn Tabbon's translation and considered it good, although this translator may say that they all erred, as he says later about both translators. And he reasoned badly if he thought to excuse himself and accuse them."[30]

Perhaps this reader is a copyist and translator himself, because he seems to be nursing hurt feelings. It is so important to him to critique Pedro de Toledo's work as a translator as well as his text that, not content with writing between the lines, he asks the reader to look at "what it says in the lower margin" for the rest of the argument: "As for whether both translators erred: the author Rabbi Moses himself, bless him, saw Ibn Tabbon's translation & authorized it. It is true that al-Harizi's contains errors, and the Castilian translator's even more. It is good to trust in God, but that does not make his translation free of error & not a little. But as Solomon the wise said, many words do not remove the wrong."[31]

He continues his argument in the lower margin: "Perhaps this translation is as it is because the translator does not understand the author's intention. Even though he understands the meanings of the words he could not be free of error and it is not enough that he chooses the best translation (as he claims to have done) if he does not understand."[32]

In contrast to most glossers, this one does not want to agree, or allege, or point out, or establish doctrine, or craft an exegesis, or interpret; and probably he does not want either (something extraordinary in a glosser, who always hopes to be known for an ordinary gloss) to have

---

30. "Non son todos los escriuanos non letrados nin todos erraron, nin mucho menos los trasladadores, como dize segunt parecera luego adelante, que el autor mismo vio la trasladacion de abin tabbon e la ouo por buena, aun que este trasladador diga que todos erraron como lo dize luego de aqui adelante que amos trasladadores e rrazono mal sy penso descargar de si e cargar sobrellos." MSS/10289, fol. 1ra.

31. "quanto mas que amos trasladadores erraron. salua su graçia que el mismo conponedor Raby moysen vio la trasladaçion de abin tabbon & la auctorizo. verdad es que la del harizi es errada & la suya mas. Luego fiiar en dios buena cosa es mas non se quito por todo esto non es su trasladaçion errada & non de poco mas como dixo el sabio salemon por muchedunbre de palabras non se quita el yerro." MSS/10289, fol. 1r, upper outer margin.

32. "por ventura sera la tal trasladaçion como esta que quando el trasladador non entyende la yntençion del componedor puesto que entyenda las sygnificaçiones de los vocablos no pudo ser seguro de yerro & non satisfaze aun que tome la mejor trasladaçion como dize que la ha tomado se non entiende." MSS/10289, fol. 1r, lower margin.

his glosses reproduced in every new copy of the work. What he wants is for the text of this translation to disappear. In proposing the disappearance of the central text in its present form, he turns the act of studying it into a critical movement toward dominating the territory of the page and one's relationship to it.

A Margin for the Gloss

What, then, is the production of the margin? Above all, it is a task carried out in the vernacular sphere in order to change the dynamic that assigns intellectual value to marginal commentaries and the object book itself, which form part of the academic economy in non-vernacular languages. The gloss is not only a parallel text or mere added content. You could say that that is the least of its features. The gloss has a much more profound effect on perception, and that intuition was clearly present in theoretical texts, in treatises on reading, and in debates about memory.[33] Above all, the intuition existed in authors' individual products and in their attitudes and initiatives.

The cases I am studying in this chapter have often been placed in relation to the content they convey, considering them as forms of literal glossing. Scholars have also focused on the way in which traditional knowledge works, linking the act of glossing to the industry of gloss production. The glosses have also been interpreted as spaces for the emergence of the author. Sometimes they have been seen as ornamental elements whose endgame is showing off undigested knowledge on the part of authors who would like to present themselves as humanists but seem to do it in an acritical form.

The first argument I have presented is precisely about ordering the margin, needing to delineate what should go in the margin and how, and in what way that affects the reader. The second argument turns on certain authors' need to appropriate the entire space of the page so as to modify certain cultural tendencies, and, no doubt, to guard their own text and protect it from any hermeneutic interference, while imposing their own rules of interpretation. The third argument has to do with the production of the marginal space—and its marking off, or

---

33. Saenger, *Space Between Words*; Saenger, "Lire aux derniers siècles," 147–74; Illich, *In the Vineyard of the Text*; Carruthers, *The Book of Memory*; Carruthers, *The Craft of Thought*; Carruthers and Ziolkowski, *Medieval Craft of Memory*.

bornage—as a procedure for creating a movement of study based on networks and polemics.

I have confined my observations to questions of form, and of how these formal elements serve as a guide among the hierarchy of texts that occupy manuscript books in the vernacular produced in the fifteenth century. In this way I have tried to reveal how the production of presence is a crucial element in every process of constructing meaning. The creation of space, and its cognitive consequences, form the center of gravity for elaborating not just a particular interpretation but the ruling principles that make it possible. Analyzing the production of the textual space is obviously relevant for understanding how one forms, transforms, and experiments with codicological creativity, a central issue in the history of the book and the history of reading.

Chapter 3

Centripetal Glosses

So far, I have argued that the creative and historical order of a discipline is marked by the ways in which the commentary operates. Not just any commentary, but in particular the one that seeks to share the surface of the page with the text it comments on, adapting itself to the empty spaces, living within their narrow boundaries, sometimes creating by force a margin in which to express itself. This wish for material coexistence, for sharing the same home or the same real estate as another text—often a much older one—is surrounded by great signs of violence. This violence reveals the functioning of the discipline, its epistemological paradigm.

The multifocal, strabismic, and polyphonic page is a challenge to thought and to the senses. This is where the value of its fashioning, of its constitutive fiction, resides: in its industry. "Industry" here has the double meaning of something whose ingenuity is hugely productive, and something whose productive capacity belongs to a model of economic, social, and labor development. Neither form of this industry can escape taking a political or legal position; neither is neutral. Both tend to imagine, even in a fragmentary way, how a society—or a community, supposing that one exists—might function: what are its political or moral values, which of its actions should be considered legal and which not.

The ordinary gloss—its normal character, its inevitable presence beside a given text, its atemporal and permanent nature—abounds in the microliterary universe whether that universe is religious or juridical, whether it relates to forms of religious life or forms of civil life and experience. History promotes some glosses to the rank of *glossa ordinaria*, while others occupy that category as soon as they first appear. Still more wish they could enjoy that level of distinction, while a few seem to achieve it even without acquiring the name. In the following pages we shall explore one of this last kind.

The Shadow of an Industry

Occasionally a glosser, conniving with the industry that sustains, impels, and nourishes them sets a trap. With a hunter's cunning they make notes in the margins of a text. They may write very small, like Robert Walser, whose hand was difficult and almost microscopic but ultimately legible.[1] Others, like Thomas Aquinas, write in a *littera illegibilis* (unreadable script). Thomas writes and corrects until he achieves a logic that functions like clockwork. Since his works were not meant to be publicly known until their author had sanctioned them, his writing acted as a defensive shield until such time as the text assumed its final form.[2] Saint Bernard of Clairvaux knew the complications that could ensue if his works were launched into the world before their time, hence his many complaints and *retractationes*, or corrections and retellings.[3] Both Thomas and Bernard became an industry unto themselves: their names came to represent the works and ideas that they, their collaborators, the people in their workshops, and even their scribes and commentators produced; to denote the intellectual and bibliographical industry that transmitted their thought and the

---

1. Susan Bernofsky explains in her introduction to Walser's *Microscripts* how he used this traditional German form of writing. The code is recognizable, or, as Bernofsky says, it is not secret but it is magical. Some of Walser's microscripts were published in his lifetime, but others have only recently come to light.
2. See Carruthers, *The Book of Memory*, 4–5; Dondaine, *Secrétaires de Saint Thomas*, 10–25.
3. See, for example, the *retractatio* he includes in one of the versions of his *Liber de gradibus humilitatis et superbiae*. In the time it took him to verify a detail in his book, it had already gone to the scriptorium and been copied several times over: "Sed quia talem errorem meum multo post, quam a me idem libellus editus et a pluribus iam transcriptus fuit, deprehendi, cum non potui per tot iam libellos sparsum persequi mendacium, necessarium credidi confugere ad confessionis remedium" (I realized that mistake after it was already copied and transmitted through many transcriptions, so instead of trying to find out each faulty copy of the text, I decided to write this correction). Bernardo de Claraval, *Liber de gradibus humilitatis*, 170.

thought of those who subscribed to their way of writing and thinking—professors, writers, preachers—and their cultural weight was projected onto the public life of Christendom.[4] Or even onto overseas warfare: without Thomas there is no invasion and conquest of the Americas, and Bernard is largely responsible for what Marisa Galvez has called "the crusade idiom."[5]

The margins most exploited by glossers are those of the *Corpus Iuris Civilis*, the Justinian law code, and those of canon law: for instance, Gregory IX's *Decretales* or *Liber Extra*, edited and glossed by Raymond of Penyafort. These glossers also took as their model the glosses and commentaries on the Bible that several medieval scholars had anthologized, compiled, and ordered until, by the twelfth and thirteenth centuries, they had become *glossa ordinaria*. In other words, these models of marginal writing were directly related to law, whether civil, canonical, or divine. On these margins the glosses coagulate, living alongside the text throughout the centuries. They draw their lifeblood from the central text—what I sometimes call the tutor text—but the glosses aspire to be equally indispensable.[6] Some of the glossers' marginal comments come to be considered part of the tutor text itself, with the status of *glossa ordinaria*. Those compiled by John the Teutonic for the Bible or Francesco Accursio for the *Corpus Iuris Civilis* are the most prominent among the ordinary glosses and aspire to become the official science related to doctrine.

A gloss might spring from one person's desire to explain to themselves, or to their pupils, texts that are difficult to understand either orally or in writing. It might seek lexical clarity or point out allegations (parallel cases) and concordances (parallel passages) that would help to navigate a codex formally, contextually, and doctrinally. But some glosses became part of a lucrative bibliographic industry. Francesco Accursio, the power behind the *Glossa ordinaria* of the *Corpus Iuris Civilis*, organized the act of commenting not only as an intellectual movement but above all as an entrepreneurial and industrial activity. In Bologna he opened his own *statio*, a workshop in which scribes were given wide-margined quires with the *Corpus Iuris Civilis* written in the center; at

---

4. Boureau, "Peut-on parler?," 267–79; Foucault, "Qu'est-ce qu'un auteur?," 73–104.
5. Francisco de Vitoria is perhaps the best example for showing to what extent Thomas Aquinas and other Aristotelian scholastics are fundamental to the Spanish conquest and expansion in the Americas. See, for example, his *relectiones*: Vitoria, *Relecciones jurídicas y teológicas*. For the "crusade idiom," see Galvez, *The Subject of Crusade*.
6. I borrow the concept of tutor text (French *texte tuteur*) from Compagnon, *La Seconde main*.

the same time they received other quires containing the glosses that different commentators had produced in the previous two centuries, starting with Azo of Bologna, perhaps the most prominent (though there were glosses earlier than his); each gloss was marked with the initials of the scholar who wrote or dictated it. The *statio* worked with *peciae*, quires meant to be copied independently and later compiled into a single volume, so that the workshop's scribes could turn out complete copies of the text, plus glosses.[7] Their professional systems of references and abbreviations caused headaches even to Don Ximio, mayor of Bugía.[8]

The gloss forms part of the universe of knowledge, the universe of pedagogy, and the industries associated with both of those. In these industries it is hard to separate the intellectual from the economic—perhaps not just hard, but useless. Pedagogy is an enterprise in which certain persons are imbued with a social magic that authorizes them to understand, explain, and transmit the contents of certain hieratic texts that our cultures have endowed (through that same industry) with various kinds of authority. When we who belong to that industry reach out to something that falls outside the established canon, it is done to expand the canon, to bring new voices into the discussion that keeps the enterprise and the industry alive. This social magic, a concept developed by Pierre Bourdieu, forms part of a sociologically crucial class that he calls (in the rarefied French education system) the nobility of state. Bourdieu makes a sociological analysis of the relationship between the *Grandes écoles* and the development of the French state, particularly during the Fifth Republic: there the elites that govern the state's politics and economics are those who studied in this specific type of "great school" of higher education.[9] More broadly, the issue can be situated within a genealogy of social strata and their role in creating the political models of the state, especially from the fourteenth century onward.

---

7. Soetermeer, *Utrumque ius in peciis*; Murano, *Copisti a Bologna*.

8. Conte, "L'istituzione del testo giuridico," 51-88. On the *pecia* and its role in the legal industry of the Romanist Renaissance, see also Dolezalek, "La *pecia* e la preparazione," 201-17. And if you feel up to confronting Don Ximio, see Arcipreste de Hita, *Libro de Buen Amor*, stanzas 321-71.

9. Pierre Bourdieu has written about the issue of the academic *noblesse d'État*, analyzing and submitting to criticism the forms of élite solidarity within university and academic media, and also about the *homo academicus* as a sociological tool for transforming the fabric of power; he has written as well about the problems of distinction that result from the practice of knowledge, the canon, and the matter of judgment. See his works *Homo academicus*, *La Noblesse d'État*, and *La Distinction*.

I have mentioned that we are speaking of hieratic texts; hieratism is both the cause and the consequence of the gloss. The gloss admits the authority of the text it comments on, while conferring on it a new authority, rooted in the present, that seeks to transform the future of that text and its possible applications. Without the gloss (a sustained commentary that preserves the vital principles of the tutor text) this economy of authority could not exist. Think of Irnerius, the mythical (but not the only) figure responsible for recovering and systematizing the *Corpus Iuris Civilis* at the urging of Matilda of Canossa.[10] Irnerius will always be associated with that heroic moment in which the text in all its imperial authority is reborn, now digested, ordered, legible, and commented upon for pedagogic use. Likewise Gratian, with his commentary on and organization of the *Decretum*, breathes life into a renewed *Corpus Iuris Canonici*.[11] One may even wonder what would have become of Virgil if he had not been transmitted with a body of glosses like that of Servius. When Virgil's works were printed in the early sixteenth century, they were often accompanied by not one set of glosses, not three sets, but ten, together with some *comentarios historiales* (commentaries in images) in xylographic form.[12] Moreover, what is the function of Pietro Alighieri's glosses on his father Dante's *Commedia*? Are they a way of building up the father's authority, or of establishing the son's intellectual legitimacy?[13] What happens when a secretary and royal chronicler like Juan de Mena glosses his own poem *La Coronación* so as to construct political and social majesty for Íñigo López de Mendoza, marquis of Santillana?[14] We could keep asking questions like these, but

---

10. See Conte, *Tres libri Codicis*. The bibliography on Matilda of Canossa ought to be immense, but in fact it is short, repetitive, and antiquated. Hay, however, in *The Military Leadership*, made an effort to reconstruct the life of this Tuscan feudal noble and her consolidation of power.

11. Winroth, *The Making of Gratian's "Decretum."* Of course, Gratian is not the founder of canon law, but the inheritor of a long series of compilations and discussions of canons like those of Anselm of Liège and Ivo of Chartres. Gratian's work was known in several versions that Winroth studies in detail.

12. I will mention only the Venice edition of 1514 (Virgil, *Omnia opera*), which contains ten marginal commentaries plus the woodcuts. The workshop of Aldo Manuzio and his descendants, and that of Simon Collines in Paris, produced similar editions between the late fifteenth and the mid-sixteenth centuries.

13. See Alighieri, *Commentum Super Poema*.

14. I do not devote more space here to the *Coronación* because it deserves a book of its own. Mena's commentary on his own text recognizes the theoretical value of the fictional and metabolic elements of poetry. Mena divides (*trunca*) in order to establish the system of tie marks to the margin; later he expands on how truth, fiction, and the moral and political

the fact is that not all can be answered from the same perspective; each one would need to be taken up individually.

One of these perspectives—perhaps not the most showy or the most conceptual—consists of trying to understand how these questions were asked and answered by those responsible for creating a pragmatics of reading: the creators first of manuscripts and later of printed books. To give a practical answer to these questions—putting theory into practice—we should try to understand what kind of research was undertaken by craftsmen and intellectuals. The previous chapter posed this question in part.

To continue our questioning in this regard, we will now analyze the *Siete Partidas* and its relationship to marginal glosses. We will explore first the editorial history of this legal code, then its distribution, and later will turn to one of the glosses produced during that history by Gregorio López, a jurist and member of the Council of the Indies. López worked for years on the edition, which was published in 1555. The history of the editorial features of the *Siete Partidas*, and of its system of glosses, challenges the traditional forms of historical periodization. In fact, the lengthy gloss about war that López included in his 1555 edition attempts a transhistorical reflection on just war, conquest, colonization, and even capitalism and its norms. This gloss, which derives its essence from a thirteenth-century text and discusses texts from the entirety of the Middle Ages, would be subject from that moment onward to the life of this law code. The *Siete Partidas* were published in 1555 into a sort of void: Charles V was abdicating in favor of his son Philip II, with a council of regency presided over by Princess Joanna of Austria. And, in fact, the editorial history of the *Partidas* is linked to vacuums of power and played an important political role in those vacuums.

As I have been saying from the outset, I do not pretend to study these glosses exhaustively. The aim of this chapter is to explore how certain problems of social justice, which are endemic and systemic in Western thought and political legal practice, fit into a specific system of glosses. I also want to make clear from the beginning to what extent those issues or problems turn out to be inseparable from the material nature of communication, and from the philological problems that surround their production, reading, and transmission. I can postulate at once, and can justify in the present chapter, that beyond, or together

---

applications of what he expresses function in the relationship between the tutor text and the gloss. See the edition of the text with its commentary in Mena, *La coronación*, ed. Kerkhof.

with, the legal, theological, and political concepts that make a line of questions or investigations intelligible, there is a universe of concepts that are material and visual; like the structure of a book or the production of a margin, they bear a direct affinity to those textual or verbal concepts.

Restraining a Monster: The *Siete Partidas*

We have a relatively high number of manuscripts of Alfonso X's *Siete Partidas*: more than one hundred in all.[15] The second and third *Partidas* are either the ones most copied or the ones best preserved. The reason has to do with their content: the *Segunda* is a treatise on administrative law that proved enormously useful in constructing Spain's absolute monarchy through the eighteenth century; and the *Tercera* has to do with trial law, and with techniques related to the production and administration of both public and private documents. There are more than twenty extant manuscripts of each of these, and almost as many of the seventh *Partida*, devoted to criminal law and the rules of law.

Strictly speaking, none of these manuscripts goes back to Alfonso X's time. It is as if the ones that emerged from his workshop had been expunged from our libraries—and maybe that is just what happened. What aspired to be a law code was soon reduced to a codex. The reasons for this may be the same ones that explain why Alfonso was dethroned by his second-born son, Sancho, in 1282.[16] The monarchical overreach of the *Partidas* limited the jurisdictional capacity of the nobility and the cities, who believed that their privileges and their autonomy were

---

15. For a complete listing, see Craddock, *The Legislative Works*. José Manuel Fradejas Rueda directs the project *7PartidasDigital*, which will include every witness, both in manuscript and in print, direct and indirect, in the original language and in translation: *7PartidasDigital*, accessed December 2, 2024, https://7partidas.hypotheses.org.

16. Details of the conflict between Alfonso and Sancho may be found in recent biographies of Alfonso by both González Jiménez (*Alfonso X El Sabio*) and Martínez (*Alfonso X, el Sabio*), and of Sancho IV by Nieto Soria (*Sancho IV*). Martin has explored how a science of politics was built in the liminal space of the relations between Alfonso and Sancho: see his "Alphonse X maudit son fils" and "Alphonse X ou la science politique." For the construction of Sancho's legitimacy, central to the creation of his legal and juridical knowledge, see Bautista, *La Estoria de España*. Technical questions about the history of law have been explored magisterially by Pérez-Prendes y Muñoz de Arracó in *Curso de historia*. Francisco J. Hernández has just published *Los hombres del rey*, on the line of succession from Alfonso X through Sancho IV; although the whole volume was not available before the preparation of this book, he generously gave me access to the final chapter, which will break new ground in Alfonsine studies and on the reign of Sancho IV.

in danger. In Sancho's jurisdictional and legislative actions, he followed the *Fuero Real* and the trial procedures contained in the *Leyes del Estilo*, a set of new procedural regulations to complement the *Fuero Real*.[17] The *Fuero Real* would continue as a legal and political instrument for centuries and be used as a legislative compendium and an artifact for negotiating the sovereign power's forms of jurisdiction and dissemination. While the *Fuero Real* was produced in Alfonso's legal workshop, the *Leyes del Estilo* were created by Sancho's lawyers, thus bypassing other legislative works created by his father.[18]

There are no significant marginal comments on any of these texts of legislation or jurisprudence. This is strange, up to a point. In universities all over Europe (Alfonso and Sancho had each chartered several of these), legal commentary was invented as a marginal form, a systematic commentary on the great legal texts in Latin: the corpora of civil and canon law.[19] Neither the *Partidas*, nor the *Fuero Real*, nor the *Leyes del Estilo*, nor any other legal code produced in Castile and written in Castilian was studied in the universities or other schools of the Iberian Peninsula between the reign of Alfonso X (1252–84) and the death of Ferdinand IV in 1302—and we could probably extend that date to at least 1348. In universities at this period, what was studied was Roman civil law and canon law, both in Latin—just as in Bologna, just as in Orléans.[20]

I said that there are no manuscripts of the *Partidas* datable to the reign of Alfonso X, but there is one exception, which is a monument by virtue of its exceptionality. It is a manuscript preserved today in the British Library that seems to be a version of the *Primera Partida*, devoted to legal theory and canon law.[21] The codex calls itself *Libro del Fuero de las Leyes*, and it is best if we keep that title, because a comparison with other manuscripts of the *Primera Partida* reveals at once that they are two texts at very different stages of composition.

---

17. The *Leyes del Estilo* remain to be edited. See the two transcriptions made according to the norms of the Hispanic Seminar of Medieval Studies in Madison, by Mannetter: *Text and Concordance*, 1989, 1990.
18. See Rodríguez Velasco, *Order and Chivalry*, 138–44.
19. See Simonds, *Philosophy and Legal Traditions*; Kantorowicz et al., *Studies in the Glossators*.
20. See Kabatek, *Die Bolognesische Renaissance*.
21. Add. 20787, *Alfonso X, rey de Castilla y León, Siete partidas (1)*, British Library, London. Arias Bonet undertook an edition in *Alfonso X, Primera Partida*, but the problems of this text are much greater than what is presented there, as Craddock has shown in *The Legislative Works*.

FIGURE 3.1. Alfonso X, *Libro del Fuero de las Leyes/Primera Partida*. Add. 20787, fol. 1r. From the British Library collection.

FIGURE 3.2. Alfonso X, *Libro del Fuero de las Leyes/Primera Partida*. Add. 20787, fol. 1v. From the British Library collection.

The *Libro del Fuero de las Leyes* is a volume that contains images. It has twenty-seven miniatures, each of which is an *estoria* or narrative image; they are also graphic commentaries that establish a complicated relationship with the legislation that surrounds them. Since the images narrate something, they do so in parallel to the text, and make their own argument in a different way. These arguments do not necessarily correspond to the theses contained in the text of the law; or, they may broach different ways of referring to these legislative theses. In some cases, the images offer a visual imagining of the space in which the law functions: they put it into action. In all of this, they behave exactly like a gloss: they comment, bring up to date, provide a mise-en-scène, exemplify, agree, and, above all, redirect and alter the reading. The most obvious example occurs in the section devoted to legal theory, in title 1 of the *Libro*. There Alfonso explains, in the text, the origin of laws: what they are for, how they should be used. This part is complemented by four miniatures. The first presents the hierarchy of the kingdom, a family portrait with the king in majesty, surrounded by his officials: lay jurists, and arrayed behind them bishops and abbots in their mitres.[22]

The second miniature is the letter *A*, the initial of the king's name, the *alpha* that represents every beginning; this might look like a mere coincidence, were it not that elsewhere Alfonso explains how his name begins with *alpha* and ends with *omega* and has seven letters, like the seven planets and other groups of seven—like the *Partidas* themselves, in

---

22. For images of Alfonso X as a monarch or as "Justinian," see Fernández Fernández, "Folios reutilizados y proyectos en curso," 73–114.

fact.²³ Inside the *A* we see Alfonso kneeling while God himself dictates the laws to him.

The third miniature shows the king in the act of transmitting those same laws to the officials who will make them into a book. The fourth, another *A*, has Alfonso presenting that book to God for his approval.

In interpreting this series, we must bear three things in mind. First, the notion that the king is the direct interpreter of the laws, in personal contact with God, perhaps could not be written out as a legislative artifact but apparently could be painted. Second, although the law speaks of the origin of the laws, it never mentions this direct communication between God and the king. Third, this section of the *Partidas* occurs before canon law is codified, and the one codifying it is not any ecclesiastical authority but the monarch himself. In this case the miniatures constitute their own interpretation of the legal text, placing it in a realm of power that the text does not even hint at. In other words, the theory of power and its circulation is carefully constructed in four images that establish not only an internal narrative for each one but also a narrative that encompasses all four.

These images are "jurisgraphisms": imaginative expressions that offer their own thesis about the theory of power and its manifestation through the creation and diffusion of the legal code.²⁴ They make clear that, as Sonja Drimmer has argued for images in English literary manuscripts of the late Middle Ages, we must pay attention to the "act of allusion," that is, how "illuminators gave visual form to ideas and preoccupations arising from vernacular literary culture at large rather from exclusively the text at hand."²⁵ Drimmer asserts that the images of certain texts for which there is no sufficiently valid prior tradition are not mere illustrative reactions, but are actually constitutive: they create a visual concept.²⁶

---

23. All this is stated, for instance, in the *Setenario*, as well as in the prologue "Setenario," the second redaction of the prologue to the *Partidas*. See, for example, Gregorio López's 1555 edition (Alfonso X, *Las Siete Partidas*). It is well known also that each of the *Siete Partidas* begins with a letter of Alfonso's name: the initial of the *Primera Partida* is A, that of the *Segunda* is L, and so on.

24. I borrow the concept of jurisgraphism from Teissier-Ensminger, "La loi au figuré," 277–91. She considers jurisgraphism to be a visual accompaniment to the legal text. For me it meets that definition (and is not a mere image of a legal text) when the visual object itself constructs a legal concept that the text is not able, or not authorized, to construct. In other words, the important segment of the term is not *-graphism* but *juris-*.

25. Drimmer, *The Art of Allusion*, 12–13.

26. Drimmer, *The Art of Allusion*, 14.

Even these jurisgraphisms are strange. As I have said, they seem to be glosses with visual concepts, but at the same time they are not; in any event they proceed from the royal workshop, they are the king's voice. The theory of Alfonsine law as contained in title 1 of the *Primera Partida*, with its extensions in other laws of the *Tercera Partida* and the *Séptima Partida*, speak clearly of the laws' integrity as they are presented in the code: they must not be commented on, emended, or glossed. Only the king has that power, and in any case the margins of the *Partidas* are closed.[27] According to the law, the king alone can explain (*espaladinar*) the text.

After having examined the manuscripts that contain the *Partidas* I can affirm that, in fact, none of them is provided with glosses. Some contain marginal texts that consist of corrections, or occasionally contaminations: a reader who is able to consult two manuscripts may complete what they consider lacunae in one of them from the text of the other. A few manuscripts, of widely varying date but most from the late fifteenth century, contain notes of a professional nature as aids to producing legal arguments based on the text of the law. Many bear abstract reading marks such as keys, underlinings, or daggers.[28] And a small minority also contain images, like one preserved at Spain's Biblioteca Nacional in its *vitrina* collection, which belonged to the Catholic monarchs (although its history predates them). Many are astonishingly clean. The earliest marginal comments that resemble glosses begin with the pedagogical edition by Alonso Díaz de Montalvo in 1500, and the one prepared in 1555 by Gregorio López, the member of the Council of the Indies.

In 1348 Alfonso XI tried to reverse the fortunes of the *Partidas* in two articles of the *Ordenamiento de Alcalá*. In the first he determined the priority of the legal sources, incorporating the *Partidas* for all the cases in which the laws contained in the *Ordenamiento de Alcalá* itself and the *Fuero Real* did not apply. In this position, the scope of action of the *Partidas* is that of a suppletive law that, because of its broadly constitutional nature, can support a great deal of legal activity.

At the same point in that *Ordenamiento*, the monarch explains how he has arranged the *Partidas* and created two copies for the royal chamber, one bearing a gold seal and the other a lead one, to have them serve as a legal foundation. He does not consider sending copies to the

---

27. See Rodríguez Velasco, "Theorizing the Language of Law," 64–86.
28. See Velasco, *Dead Voice*, chap. 4.

various local administrations, as he did with the *Ordenamiento*.²⁹ He does something more important instead: he establishes by law that the *Partidas* shall become a text in the curriculum of the Faculty of Laws. Therefore, the *Partidas*, which had not been accepted as law nor studied in the schools, came to occupy the center of the canon.³⁰

Alfonso XI thoroughly understood the double burden that the *Partidas* placed on him. On the one hand he could not comment on them in the margins, but on the other, as king he had the power to change them. In the court minutes (*cuaderno de cortes*) that accompany the *Ordenamiento de Alcalá* of 1348 he responds to some complaints by representatives of the cities who feel unable to apply the laws of the *Partidas*: he will emend those laws so as to make them applicable.³¹ Did he make those changes? And if so, did they greatly affect the text? We actually cannot answer either of these questions with certainty, but everything points to his having introduced changes. We cannot assess their quantity or quality, however.³²

Apart from their specific use, the *Partidas* were studied in universities and schools of law, and they proved to be a first-class source of argumentation both in the political sphere and, more generally, in legal rhetoric and culture.³³ The *Partidas* consolidated a dialectical and rhetorical style of Castilian law, and perhaps not only of written law. The laws had to be freed from the blind alley they had entered in the fourteenth and fifteenth centuries. If we possess more than a hundred manuscripts today, it may be that a much larger number was produced at that time. The problem of the *Partidas* is comparable only to that of the other great source of law, the archive of the *ordenamientos reales* (royal ordinances) and the *cuadernos de cortes*, transmitted in massive volumes since at least the end of the reign of John I (r. 1379-90).

Every new monarch takes charge of the sources of law in some fashion. In some cases the very legitimacy of monarchs hangs on that thirst for appropriation. That is why the Catholic monarchs gave two orders

---

29. I discuss these issues of documentation and legal aesthetics in Rodríguez Velasco, *Ciudadanía*.

30. *Ordenamiento de Alcalá*, VITR/15/7, title 28, law 1, Biblioteca Nacional de España, Madrid.

31. *Cortes de los antiguos reinos de León y de Castilla*, 1:593–626, esp. point 3, p. 595.

32. García-Gallo's research and conclusions on these points in "El *Libro de las leyes*" and "Nuevas observaciones" have been cast into doubt on the basis of all the extant manuscripts by Craddock, "La Cronología," 365–418.

33. Craddock's critical bibliography, *The Legislative Works*, also includes many studies on the use of the *Partidas* on both sides of the Atlantic up to the nineteenth century.

to the jurist Alonso Díaz de Montalvo on leaving the Cortes of Toledo in 1481.[34] The first was to review and compile the *ordenamientos reales* and *cuadernos de cortes* that were still useful and had not been abrogated by others. The second was to prepare an edition of the *Partidas*. The new feature of the project was that both results would appear in print. The first was published in 1484 with the title *Copilación de las leyes del reyno*, and the second in 1491 as simply *Las Siete Partidas*. Montalvo had access to the royal codices, and probably to the manuscript of Queen Isabella's that had formerly belonged to the royal appellate judge Alonso de Zúñiga.[35] Montalvo took two further steps. First, he compared his sources with other manuscripts so as to choose the best readings, or those he considered the best. After having collated all the manuscripts in several sections of the *Segunda Partida*, we can affirm that in general Montalvo made plausible choices, although at times he preferred readings that are difficult to explain, or perhaps were altered later by typesetters and compositors whose errors were not detected in subsequent printings.[36]

The second step Montalvo took is even more interesting. For the first time in the textual tradition of the *Siete Partidas* he added some type of commentary, but he did so in a schematic way. In truth his comments are not glosses—nobody had dared to add them up to that time, and Montalvo did not think it right either to fill up the margins of his *Partidas*. It is reasonable to assume that in the manuscript he prepared for the press his *adiciones*, as he called them, were in the margin, but that is not the case in the printed book. His additions are placed at the end of the relevant law or title, in the same layout and typeface as the rest of the text, preceded by the word "adiçion."

The purpose of all these additions is to situate the *Partidas* within the tradition of Castilian law. They are a way of harmonizing the *Partidas* with the *Copilación de las leyes del reyno*, in an exercise that authorizes both legal sources in parallel. Here the printing press has become a fundamental instrument for creating something new: unified and consistent

---

34. *Cortes de los antiguos reinos de León y de Castilla*, vol. 4.
35. Biblioteca Nacional, Madrid, VITRINA/4/6.
36. See the collation in Craddock and Rodríguez Velasco, *Alfonso X, Siete Partidas 2.21*. It is available through the library of the University of California, Berkeley.

I will mention only two choices from title 9 of the *Segunda Partida*. One is the metaphor of the compass and the court, where Montalvo's edition reads *agua* (water) instead of *aguja* (compass); the other concerns the two elderly knights who are (plausibly) termed *pros caballeros* (excellent knights), when the original reading was probably *por caballeros* ([considered] as knights).

sources for the laws of Castile. The power of the press has a somewhat unreal feel to it: it assumes as ordinary legal tender what is really an upholding of authority. The additions indicate that the *Partidas* should be read in the light of the *ordenamientos* and the *cuadernos de cortes*, since these are the ones that actually impose legal restrictions on the longer code, which continues to have a suppletive character.

An Authentic Thing

I do not wish to slight the second edition of the *Partidas* that Alonso Díaz de Montalvo prepared for its first publication in 1492. This edition was reprinted a number of times in both Spain and other countries, including in Venice, one of the great centers for printing Iberian texts during the sixteenth century. In 1550 the last edition of this work appeared in print, with glosses, patronized by Alonso Gómez of Seville and Enrique Toti of Salamanca, at a press in Lyon (apud Iuntas). It is the other side of the coin with respect to the previous edition: the margins of every page are filled with extensive Latin glosses, and, if the prior edition was directed to professional jurists, this one is clearly meant for university students and also includes the *adiçiones* from 1491. It is another facet of the royal enterprise and its unbreakable tie to the university as an industrial artifact for constructing the kingdom—or the state, if you prefer; I don't mind being inexact in this case.[37] These glosses are a way to establish a direct connection between vernacular Castilian law and the traditions of Roman and canon law that make up the immense power of the *ius commune*, the exclusive common law on which the idea of Europe has rested for centuries.[38] Moreover, this edition would become the most important source for the one that

---

37. The central medallion in the old cloister of the University of Salamanca, from Charles V's time, is well known: it bears a relief of the Catholic monarchs surrounded by the Greek lemma "οἱ βασιλεῖς τῇ ἐγκυκλοπαιδείᾳ αὔτη τοίς βασιλεῦσι." Its chief innovation is the neologism ἐγκυκλοπαιδεία to mean the university. The approximate translation would be: "The monarchs for the university and she [the university] for the monarchs," although it is usually rendered as a mutual dedication (from the monarchs to the university and from it to the monarchs). I find the first translation better, since it also constitutes a palinode with respect to the support that many students and professors of Salamanca had offered to the *comunero* rebels against Charles V. See Hinojo Andrés, "Οἱ βασιλεῖς," 463–72.

38. Traditionally, *ius commune* is the combination of canon law, Roman civil law, and the so-called *iura propria* or local rules and norms. Perhaps the clearest exposition of *ius commune* as the law common to the European world is Bellomo's *L'Europa del diritto comune*.

changed radically the transmission and dominance of the textual monster that is the *Partidas*.

The edition of 1555, printed by Andrea de Portonariis in Salamanca and formally inspired by the 1550 edition with Montalvo's glosses, is the most universally recognized of all the editions of the *Partidas*, and we can assume that no future edition will attain the influence that this one has had (and still has).[39] Not even the one prepared by the Real Academia de la Historia in 1807 (the same year that the Treaty of Fontainebleau between Spain and France was signed) has kept most jurists and scholars from reading the *Partidas* in López's edition. When the dictator Francisco Franco designated Juan Carlos de Borbón as his successor, he marked the occasion with a facsimile reprinting of the *Partidas* of 1555 together with an accompanying law, all from the presses of the *Boletín Oficial del Estado*.

So, then, in 1555 a unique edition of the *Siete Partidas* of "King Alfonso Nono" emerges from the Salamanca press of Andrea de Portonariis.[40] Here the editor uses the Castilian numbering of the kings, although in fifteenth-century texts Alfonso the Wise was always assigned the ordinal of the Castilian-Leonese computation, that is, the tenth. This detail also seems to be inherited from Montalvo's 1550 edition, in which the editor wanted to maintain the Castilian royal succession. The editor in 1555 is Gregorio López of the Council of the Indies. The editorial contract for the *Partidas*, signed by López and Portonariis in July 1553, states that the lawyer from the Council of the Indies will supervise the whole edition, of which up to a thousand copies will be printed, all of which will be given to López so that he can sign them with his own hand.[41] Gregorio López was from Guadalupe and was married to a woman from Trujillo surnamed Pizarro (though despite the claims of López's descendants, she was not related to Francisco Pizarro). He had studied at Salamanca and been involved in the legal study and debate initiated by Francisco de Vitoria, a Dominican of the College of San Esteban. His work is not only that of a jurist; rather, it resembles that of a professional deeply aware of the public effects of his contribution. We must now examine the long editorial history of the *Partidas* "according

---

39. At least eleven different editions (without counting reprintings) of Gregorio López's edition appeared between 1555 and 1844.

40. For an editorial history of the *Partidas* in the sixteenth century, see López Nevot, "Las ediciones de las *Partidas*," 1–31.

41. Guilarte, "Capítulos de concierto," 670–75.

to López," because this is the official edition and the one with the most significant presence in Spain and her possessions from the time of its creation until the present day.[42]

Starting in 1555 and up to 1829, when the great modern legal apparatus begins to be built, the *Partidas* with their enormous legal weight on both sides of the Atlantic were normally read in the edition of Gregorio López. In 1969, when the *Boletín Oficial del Estado* publishes its facsimile of the *Partidas*, it notes: "Even today one must sometimes consult the Partidas to understand prevailing Law, but only the 1555 edition glossed by Gregorio López and reproduced here can be considered the authentic text."[43]

Later on, in comparing the differences between López's edition and that of the Real Academica de la Historia from 1807, the *Boletín Oficial del Estado* (speaking as an institution, without any particular author's name), states: "It is obvious, then, that the *Boletín Oficial del Estado*, concerned purely with the authenticity of the text, had to follow the edition of 1555."[44]

They key concept is that of the text's authenticity. The legal person called *Boletín Oficial del Estado* determines that this statute forever relates the central text of the *Partidas* to the history of Spanish law, and that this cannot occur without the authentication devised in the form of marginal glosses that support the text and its interpretation. In the prologue to title 18 of the *Tercera Partida*, devoted to trial law, Alfonso establishes the mechanism for communicating legal or notarial authority through a *persona auténtica*: an authentic person who can vouch for the authenticity of a text, while transferring or transmitting it to an archive in permanent form. This is what Gregorio López does; authorized by the regent of Castile, his text displays the authenticity of the legislative body of the *Partidas*, while at the same time his glosses make it contemporaneous. In other words, the text's authenticity consists of extracting it from history and restoring its present and future activity.

---

42. As an example: the "Real Decreto-ley 1/2015," dated February 27 of that year.

43. "Aún hoy es preciso acudir en algunos casos a Las Partidas para conocer el Derecho vigente, pero solo la edición de 1555 glosada por Gregorio López y aquí reproducida, puede considerarse como texto auténtico." "Nota del Editor," in Alfonso X, *Las Siete Partidas*. The note appears with no folio or page number at the end of the third volume of the work.

44. "Resulta obvio, pues, que el *Boletín Oficial del Estado*, preocupado exclusivamente por la autenticidad del texto, no podía por menos de atenerse a la edición de 1555." "Nota del Editor," in Alfonso X, *Las Siete Partidas*.

Gregorio López's edition was reprinted numerous times and received additions of indices and notes, to which his grandson, Gregorio López de Tovar, contributed beginning in 1576, sixteen years after his grandfather's death.[45] Use of Gregorio López's work became general as a source of knowledge of the *Partidas* even after the more scientific edition of the Real Academia de la Historia appeared. On March 27, 1860, when the Supreme Court had to rule on the use of editions of the *Partidas* (in relation to portions of the *Cuarta Partida*), it decided in favor of López's version, "which has in its favor the approval of many years of authority, and of established jurisprudence."[46]

The printing authorized by Alonso Díaz de Montalvo had a decisive effect on fixing the text of the *Partidas*. Comparing it with Gregorio López's edition leads to a first conclusion: the textual variations that López introduced are largely errors by the editor or the typesetters, but otherwise he is using the text established by Montalvo (until then, the canonical text of the *Partidas*). But López says that he is comparing it to other older codices ("antiquissimos Partitarum libros de manu conscriptos") in order to solve problems of reading ("in multis locis deficiebant integrae sententiae, et in multis legibus deficiebant plures lineae in ipsa contextura litterae multae mendositates") and determine the best form of the text ("quantum potui, veritatem litterae detegi"), but we have no idea what those other manuscripts were.[47] Printing, therefore, halted the entropic process of the earlier manuscripts and created an illusion: the notion that a text of the *Siete Partidas* exists. López appropriated that illusion in order to authenticate it and infuse it with new life.

A Very Lengthy Gloss

López, like Montalvo in his edition for students, decided that mastering the monster of the *Partidas* required buttressing it with a system

---

45. See Pérez Martín, "El aparato," esp. 486-87 on López de Tovar. Gregorio López de Tovar left a memoir in which he alluded to doing tedious work on his grandfather's glosses, preserved in MSS/19344 of the Biblioteca Nacional, Madrid. López Nevot transcribes the relevant pages in his abovementioned article, as a documentary appendix. Before reading this article I was unaware that the *Vida y memorias del licenciado Gregorio de Tovar, caballero natural de Valladolid*, existed, and I must say that it is fascinating.

46. "que tiene a su favor la sanción del largo tiempo que rige y la jurisprudencia establecida." Tribunal Constitucional, "Sentencia del Tribunal," 2051.

47. *Siete Partidas*, I, fol. 9v.

of glosses. Thinking of the Alfonsine text as a classical source of law, the editor built around it the most overwhelming colonnade of commentary imaginable. Alfonso's text, in two columns, is framed and surrounded by Gregorio López's onion-like layers of Latin glosses, with all their abbreviations.

Again like Montalvo, López sought his models in the Romanistic traditions of glossers and commentators that emerged from the schools where civil law, the *Corpus Iuris Civilis*, was studied, in the period extending from Irnerius (tenth century?) to Azo of Bologna (twelfth), from Francesco Accursio (thirteenth century) to Bartolo da Sassoferrato (fourteenth) and from Baldo de Ubaldis to Giovanni Andrea (both from the fourteenth century). These are the authors who occupied the margins of legal texts from the twelfth to the fourteenth centuries, becoming the essential sources of argumentation for all of Europe. Printed editions of the *Corpus Iuris Civilis* from the sixteenth and seventeenth centuries carefully reproduce their glosses and commentaries. They are not the only ones, but they do stand at the center of the canon, and Gregorio López wanted to resemble them; that means that his glossed text had to resemble theirs. López's gloss is an act of discourse that imposes a new, vitally important practice of reading: it situates the Alfonsine text within the study of Roman law, not inside the schools but in the public sphere of a global empire whose language is Castilian as well as Latin.

But López introduces a greater variant with respect to Montalvo. While the latter stops at Giovanni Andrea (perhaps following a decree issued by John II of Castile in 1427) and the fourteenth-century Italian style, Gregorio López continues the legal conversation in several more directions.[48] On the one hand he includes new, more modern, legal commentators in the work he is composing, all coming from the study of Roman law: Bartolomeo da Saliceto (d. 1412), Giovanni da Imola (d. 1436), and Filippo Decio (1454–ca. 1535), who wrote a commentary on Justinian's *Digest* that was published several times beginning in 1523. López also establishes direct lines of debate about the law with the schools of theology, from Thomas Aquinas to Francisco de Vitoria, and with Spanish jurisconsults like Rodrigo Suárez, active in the early sixteenth century.[49]

---

48. For the decree of February 8, 1427, see Pérez de la Canal, "La pragmática de Juan II," 659–68.
49. Pérez Martín, "El aparato," 492–93; Gibert y Sánchez de la Vega, "La Glosa," 448.

Montalvo's audience had been confined within the buildings where future professionals of the law studied, or within the law courts. But López has a political perspective on his activity. For one thing, his work is published in the midst of a unique and unprecedented historical situation: the regency of Princess Joanna of Austria (who in fact had authorized publication of the *Partidas*), with a regency council convened to manage the long, laborious process of Charles V's abdication from his kingdom and its territories, and the resulting investiture of all those fragments of imperial power in his son Felipe. Besides, Gregorio López is directly involved in the political administration of the kingdom beyond the borders of the Iberian Peninsula. He is conversant with the political and legal debates taking place both inside and outside the peninsula. From his study and library in Castile or in Extremadura, he exerts his influence as a "remote worker" in service to the empire, and keeps up his investigations of legal history and the challenges of the present moment.

This Is War

A key moment in López's involvement is the series of glosses on title 23 of the *Segunda Partida*, on the subject of war. The series takes up ten whole pages of glosses in double columns. It is not the only treatise in the form of a gloss in this edition (there is another on the royal succession), but it is among the ones that have proved most influential over the centuries. The glosser analyzes Alfonso's laws concerning war, relating them to theories of just war and to Saint Augustine's thought in *De Civitate Dei*. Gregorio López had studied law in Salamanca and had come into direct contact with the public academic debates surrounding the teaching of Francisco de Vitoria and other members of the so-called Salamanca school, both in the College of San Esteban and in other academic spaces. By the time López wrote his gloss on title 23 of the *Segunda Partida*, much of the work of Fray Bartolomé de las Casas had already been published, including the *Brevísima relación de la destrucción de las Indias* (*A Short Account of the Destruction of the Indies*) and his dispute with Juan Ginés de Sepúlveda. All this was essential material for López's political role, in which he administered relevant legal and political decisions and opinions (as if they were *responsa* or *consilia*), especially as they concerned the Dominicans and the development of the *Ius Gentium* (Law of nations). In the process he summarized and commented on the canonical texts of this debate, including Francisco de Vitoria's *Relectiones*—a kind of academic exercise that consisted of reevaluating a given subject.

All this may seem like an academic discussion, and in some ways it is. When we call something an "academic discussion" it is usually in a somewhat scornful tone: these discussions take place away from the world, in the proverbial ivory tower; they have little impact, and they belong to a universe of sociocultural and political elites who don't understand the genuine problems of real people.[50] This is not the place for calling this view into question: educational and academic pursuits— those of Western capitalism, or other forms of education—occupy many years of most people's calendars. The academy is both a multiform universe and in a constant state of crisis. So from that point of view, an "academic discussion" does not fall outside the world or the way of life of real people. However, academic discussions can be of very different lengths; they may last a long time, continuously or intermittently, as the focus of debate or criticism, or they may vanish in a fraction of a second, though with the possibility of reviving. Perhaps the most important feature of the particular academic discussion that Gregorio López continues in the margins of this point of the *Segunda Partida* is that it has remained alive for centuries, and may, unfortunately, continue for a long time yet.

In a profound piece of research, Rolena Adorno has explored the literary, rhetorical, and historical function of the polemic about possession. Her work emphasizes the tropes of conquest and possession among colonial historiography, and the persistence of the colonial in modern and contemporary narrative.[51] She locates the center of gravity of this persistence in the debate between Bartolomé de las Casas and Ginés de Sepúlveda. Adorno follows the polemic of possession into contemporary literature, an institution that manifests itself clearly in the public sphere. What I will now discuss is a supplement to her research, a proof of how this polemic about possession and its colonial arguments shows up atemporally and unseasonably in the underpinnings of the law—in the gloss.

One of the key points of the polemic about possession questions the legal, political, and anthropological status of Native Americans while they are being invaded by the Spanish conquistadors. The historical consequences of this discussion are not alien to the systemic

---

50. Asad, *Genealogies of Religion*, 6–11.
51. Adorno, *The Polemics of Possession*.

racism of capitalist societies, but form part of the sociopolitical and cultural paradigms of contemporaneity. The discussion that Gregorio López intended to continue turns on how forms of racialization, and the supremacy of the white Christian body, are superimposed on the other manifestations of civilization and justify founding and preserving Spanish rights through a new form of violence.[52] The mere fact that the possibility of involuntary servitude and slavery, and questions of race and social difference, can be placed on the potter's wheel of legal, scholastic, theological, and political logic, is sufficient to show how an academic discussion can flow into people's everyday life—the life that is felt empirically as well as the life that is not felt.[53]

López's lengthy glosses have not passed unnoticed by research in the least. In 1992, as part of the celebrations of the fifth centenary of the beginning of the Spanish invasion and conquest of America, Antonio Agúndez Fernández, a judge of the Supreme Court, published his book *La doctrina jurídica de Gregorio López en la defensa de los derechos humanos de los indios* (Gregorio López's legal doctrine in defense of the Indians' human rights).[54] I won't describe the style of this book, except to say that I couldn't quote a single passage from it without blushing. It begins by narrating Gregorio López's life, based on established research and on new documentation, most of it from the Archivo General de Simancas. It establishes the key moment that awakened Gregorio López's consciousness of Native Americans as legal subjects, during the visit of the Dominican Bernardino de Minaya to Valladolid in 1536; he was the envoy of his fellow Dominican Julián Garcés (1452-1542), bishop of Tlaxcala. The missive Minaya brought with him is thought to have provoked Pope Paul III's bull *Sublimis Deus* (and its satellite documents), dated May 29, 1537—the same day as the *Pastorale officium*, which forbids the enslavement of native peoples—and proclaimed on June 2 of that year. In 2005 Ana María Barrero García published her *La "glosa magna" de Gregorio López: Sobre la doctrina de la guerra justa en el siglo XVI* (Gregorio López's "Glossa Magna": On the doctrine of just war in the sixteenth century). There she edits and translates into Spanish the Latin text of López's gloss (of which Agúndez Fernández had also made a translation, full of errors and typographic problems); establishes the dates of its composition, with its interruptions and possible

---

52. Benjamin, *Toward the Critique of Violence*; Rabasa, *Writing Violence on the Northern Frontier*.
53. Mbembe, *Critique of Black Reason*.
54. Agúndez Fernández, *La doctrina jurídica*.

moments of inspiration (between February and July 1544, when the glosser encounters Vitoria's text; 1550, after [Barrero believes] he heard Bartolomé de las Casas in San Gregorio, Valladolid; and so on); and lays out Gregorio López's sources and conclusions.

Law 2 of title 23 of the *Segunda Partida* legislates "for what reasons men are moved to wage war" (porque razones se mueuen los omes a fazer guerra). A first gloss, with no apparent tie mark and preceded by an asterisk, marks the words *bello iusto*: it reads "concerning just war" (acerca de la guerra justa), even though it is the previous law that speaks of the war "that they call in Latin just, which means in Romance the same as rightful" (llaman en latín justa, que quiere decir tanto en romance como derechurera). That one receives its own gloss *e*, on the inside margin of folio 78v. Therefore, this gloss with an asterisk is a kind of catchword since it centers the theme of the previous law while connecting it to the present one. Two more brief glosses indicate legal allegations about the benefits of just war, citing Baldo de Ubaldis (1327–1400) and Lucas de Penna (ca. 1325–ca. 1390), to establish that the three benefits mentioned by Alfonso include other possible types (Lucas de Penna, for instance, maintains that there are thirteen benefits). The law first lays out three reasons for war, the first being "for the people to increase their faith, and to destroy those who may wish to confound it" (por acresçentar el pueblo su fe, e para destruyr los que la quisiesen contrallar).[55] Here López places a tie mark, the gloss *g*, on the inside margin of folio 79r. That gloss, called "for the people to increase their faith" (¶*Acresçentar el pueblo su fe*), is then extended from the lower part of that left-hand column as far as folio 83v. In the process it concentrates on the first clause in the sentence and leaves aside the second, "and to destroy those who may wish to confound it."

Although the gloss is hard to read (with a script size that challenges the strongest eyeglasses, thousands of abbreviations both standard and non-standard, and furthermore written in Latin), its text is actually transparent. It is perfectly marked for study, with paragraph signs to signal the different conclusions to each of the theses presented for discussion. Gregorio López acts here as a scholastic jurist, and his references leave no doubt about the fact. His arguments draw in particular on dialectic and concepts from theology. His most important interlocutor, though not the only theologian, is Thomas Aquinas. Most of

---

55. *Siete Partidas* 2.23.2, fol. 79r, col. b.

the others are canonists (specialists in ecclesiastical law), headed by Henry of Segusio or Susa (ca. 1200–1271)—also known as Hostiensis, *el Hostiense* as López always calls him—who discuss the power of the pope, his universal jurisdiction, the *plenitudo potestatis*. López is opposed to *el Hostiense*'s justification of violence, and indicates at the end of his gloss that he prefers violence as a reaction, not an action: that is, it should serve to preserve the law rather than be its foundation.[56] The next arguments proceed from Francisco de Vitoria and his *Relectiones de Indis*: "Et postea quam haec scripseram venit ad manus, quod in materia ipsa scriptis tradiderat Franciscus a victoria, Frater ordinis predicatorum" (And after I wrote all this, what Francisco de Vitoria, a Dominican, wrote on this very subject came into my hands). Therefore Francisco de Vitoria's "rereadings" reach López's hands after he had written all the foregoing; on the one hand he had explained all the theological theory and canon law surrounding papal power, and on the other he had compared non-Christian natives of the Americas with non-Christians in the Iberian Peninsula and the Mediterranean. All this in the context of the various holy wars, proclamations of crusades, massive forced baptisms, pogroms, and expulsions that had occurred in the medieval history of Europe. Within this careful exposition López also criticizes the theses of Francisco de Vitoria.

At the end of his gloss, in the middle of his sixth conclusion, Gregorio López expresses his *angustia decidendi*, the pain of having to make decisions or pass legal sentences. His nine conclusions summarize his posture and his decisions. First: it is the kings of Spain who have the right to conquer America. Second: that conquest should be accomplished by preaching, not by force of arms. Third: clear distinctions should be made and enforced between the converted and the not yet converted. Fourth: if war is declared, it should be in reaction to acts of violence by the natives. Fifth: one cannot declare war on those who do not accept conversion, which should come about voluntarily and not by force. Sixth: one should not use violence against idolaters, even though that may have been recommended in the past. Seventh: it is licit to declare war on those who perform human sacrifice. Eighth: war is caused by the violence of others; once that violence ceases, war should end. The ninth, and the only one that does not make a positive proposal, is a total rejection of the doctrines of *el Hostiense*.

---

56. Benjamin, in his *Toward the Critique of Violence*, distinguishes between violence that establishes law and violence that preserves it.

These conclusions in themselves cannot erase the arguments contained in the gloss, or the critical process that animates it. It is true that, as the gloss marked with an asterisk proposes about just war, López's gloss-treatise as a whole can be seen as an exposition and debate about the subject from the theological and canonical doctrines of the scholastics to the moment in about 1544 when López first saw Vitoria's *relectiones*. López may feel more comfortable explaining and critiquing than deciding—at least once, he was pained by having to decide. He is in general agreement with Innocent IV's conclusions about exerting violence, and Paul III's decisions about the character of the natives and rejection of any enslavement or exploitation of them. But López is still forced to criticize some of the topics that make up the systemic universe that, in different ways, excludes or discriminates against natives and their descendants, including offspring born from relations between natives and conquistadors, in light of the abuses and rapes that the latter perpetrated.

None of this can be seen as a defense of the human rights of Native Americans. This gloss cloaks itself in a series of discourses about the natives' humanity and full intelligence, while maintaining that the violence of seizing territory and promoting the faith and capitalism of the Spanish enterprise are not really forms of violence because, if this legal counsel is followed, there will be no war. López proposes a war without wars. That is why, where this law is concerned, the gloss with the asterisk repeats the very concept of just war.

Centripetal Force

A gloss has the specific ability to draw into itself whole texts of varying origins. Not constrained by time or by the temporalities of the tutor text, the gloss exerts a centripetal force that sometimes overcomes the value of the tutor text. Gibert, in his study of the *Partidas*, noted that on occasion lawyers, representatives, judges, and other legal professionals drew for their arguments on Gregorio López's glosses more than on the text of the *Partidas*, until in 1887 "the Supreme Court ruled that the *Glosa* did not form part of the legal text and a failure to follow it did not justify requesting a reversal."[57] The gloss's invasion of the legal universe is not exclusive to the *Partidas*. Beginning with the medieval

---

57. "el Tribunal Supremo declaró que la Glosa no formaba parte del texto legal y su no seguimiento no era motivo para pedir la casación." Gibert y Sánchez de la Vega, "La Glosa," 446.

origins of Roman law, the time lapse between the tutor text and the gloss make the latter into an essential resource.

This centripetal force has historical potential. Gregorio López deploys the gloss as a legal artifact, while its value as an authority is supported by the text of the legal document that it comments on. From this position of privilege López administers the basic texts that have served through the centuries to build the arguments about just war: whether interrupted commerce and economic benefit can justify a war, or not; when a war should cease; what it means to be a non-Christian, and if there are different ways of not being one; whether, in a process of conquest, one can view native peoples through a racialized lens, or not; what it means to possess reason, to be humanized or animalized; and many other things. All these matters, with arguments pro and con, are now contained in this gloss, which through the years and centuries, through printings, reprintings, and translations, is available for professionals and non-professionals of the law. But it always speaks in the voice of one who has legal authority and the power of decision (even when it is painful to decide). And his pain is not unjustified: it makes possible the foundation and preservation of law through acts of violence that, if they are less visible than open warfare, still create a system of oppression that follows the logic of imperial colonization.

The theory of the gloss is also its practice. It is flexible; it may be a single line, or ten pages of two columns each. It can refer to a tie mark, or it can construct a tie mark that did not exist before but that the gloss makes necessary. Inside it, information and argument accumulate; it works out dialogues in a time frame broader than the earthly lives of the actors who took part in the debate. And in doing so the gloss organizes a contemporary debate.

Chapter 4

Activism

Gregorio López, like the workshops that established the *glossa ordinaria*, acted from a position of official privilege. All were supported by the disciplines they practiced within the structures of power, from which they sent forth doctrinal materials or legal decisions. But some people who glossed manuscripts in the fourteenth and fifteenth centuries, mostly in the vernacular, did so from positions that, although not totally lacking in privilege, did not include duties or titles of authority. These were voluntary glossators and, as we will explain below, activists who did their work through these glosses.

From the Margin

The ability to combine activism with the structuring of a body of knowledge defines intellectual commitment. Those who consider themselves public intellectuals deploy a knowledge that they may have struggled to extract from the spaces and institutions in which knowledge is created and cultivated, in accordance with methods, practices, and theories of a scientific nature. In the spaces where knowledge is constructed, in the institutions created for that purpose—fortresses, "ivory towers," spaces isolated from other social and political currents (kinds of utopian islands or phalansteries, within urban and pedagogical territories where the paramount illusion is one of free thought and action)—trying and failing is not only permitted but sacralized: it is a basic feature of the method. Public intellectual labor puts knowledge into practice "out there," where the protocols of reception and discussion function through languages that are emphatically nonacademic or even antiacademic. To emerge from the fortress or the ivory tower is to strip oneself of the various forms of protection offered by the institution, and to take refuge solely in one's ability to create a social magic that often resembles illusionism or prestidigitation.[1]

How does a public intellectual figure emerge at those historical times when the formal knowledge of university culture differs in its public presence from that of a society with media of mass communication? Under these circumstances we should wonder how to propose the existence of a public intellectual—preferably lay or secular—and how to define the "poetics of the public" that this intellectual might attempt. In other words, how can public intellectuals create their own field of expression and action within a society to which they feel especially committed?

Is it of interest to identify a public intellectual in more or less remote historical periods that now seem to be inactive, or perhaps deactivated? Not at all, in fact, if all we want is to locate and single them out in order to compare them to others, establishing a genealogy based on repetitions and differences. But it can be of interest if we establish a different genealogy: the one that explores how the public intellectual allows us to understand a poetics of critical thinking, that is, a way of modifying, or rethinking, the relations among the humanities, their public and academic nature, and social and political action.

In order to pose, and perhaps begin to answer, this series of questions I will now analyze part of the work of Diego de Valera (b. Cuenca, 1412-d. Puerto de Santa María, 1488). He is a figure whom I consider, together with some of his contemporaries—particularly with women writers such as Christine de Pizan and Teresa de Cartagena, whom we will see again in the last chapter—a public intellectual of the period that, in an insidious way, has often been called "premodern" or "nonmodern." In this I adopt Kathleen Davis's discussion of "the politics of time," where she analyzes the hegemony of modernity and the consequences

---

1. See Behm et al., "The Case for Academics." The whole issue is devoted to academic freedom and to the academic as a public intellectual. I borrow the concept of "social magic" from Pierre Bourdieu, as he employs it in *La Noblesse d'État*.

of creating a binary opposition between nonmodernity and premodernity on the one hand and modernity on the other.[2] What interests me here is that, independently of what communication systems were available and when particular individuals (Valera, for example) joined them, we must extract a historical analysis of their works, actions, and feelings from a "politics of time," that is, from historiography's assignment of certain homogeneous traits to a given period.[3]

The public intellectual who appears in these pages is a microliterary artist. The microliterary artist I refer to is a male or female writer of the fourteenth and fifteenth centuries. In technical and formal terms, this artist puts at his or her disposal, and employs, the totality of the page, both its center and its margin, and thereby tests the potential polyphony of their thought, whether in the role of the "ruler" or in that of the "orator," as we indicated in the previous chapter. The microliterary artist creates a central discourse, then goes on to broaden the meanings of their own discourse in the margins. The gloss is a self-gloss, the result of an act of writing that explores at one and the same time the formal limits of the text being composed (a treatise or an epistle), the political limits of the society being addressed, and the material flexibility of the written manuscript that bears the message.

These contributions, then, are a form of research into the public sphere. The debate takes place on the surface of the manuscript itself, often at different times of writing and in different grammatical tenses, shaping a periodization that is appropriate for public writing as a slow and self-reflective process. This internal periodization is not merely the writer's return to a certain textual journey, but the fruit of a series of

---

2. For the discussion about premodernity, nonmodernity, and other periodizations that presuppose a hegemonic view and practice of modernity, see Davis, *Periodization and Sovereignty*.

3. In the second volume of *La Fable Mystique*, published twenty-seven years after its author's death, Michel de Certeau defines the *effet d'inscription*: how the history of the past is etched into our historicity. It is a far-reaching effect in which we as contemporary historians cannot avoid a double inscription of our object of study: there is one that seems distant, wholly separate from us, and another that, in contrast, is almost in the genetic code of our own history, whose mode of action we are ignorant of and yet must discover, in not just one but multiple ways—as many ways as there are histories that could be written. This inscription effect is in fact twofold: on the one hand, studying the past transforms our experience of contemporary history; on the other, contemporary experience struggles to retell the past with methods and theories that allow us not only to study the past but also to *think with the past* (De Certeau, *La Fable Mystique*). For Denise Baker, this means knowing how a historical source speaks *of* an event while also speaking *to* that event (Baker, *Inscribing the Hundred Years' War*). The *effet d'inscription* suggests a slightly different path, placing at the center of gravity not the event but the constellation of ideas that are under discussion.

acts of violence in which the topic under discussion, or the text itself, have been stigmatized and excised from the economy of the reception to which they were originally sent. Microliterary artists, rather than furling their sails and returning to port, spread and fill them once again with exegetical energy in the form of marginal glosses or iterations of the original expression. This, in large measure, is what marks the production of marginal glosses that accompany many texts by Diego de Valera and Christine de Pizan, among others; the same can be said of the second letter or treatise by Teresa de Cartagena (*Admiraçion operum dei*) as a response to the act of intellectual violence with which her first letter (*Arboleda de los enfermos*) was received.

We also find microliterature transformed into a politics and ethics that are manifested in the need to introduce into the vernacular tongue, and into its history, certain concepts (often through neologisms that did not survive), certain institutions (peace, about which we will say more later), or certain subjects (individual women with specific histories) that the microliterary artist thinks have been subjected to a politics of invisibility.[4]

A Certain Infelicity

I would like to think of the microliterary artist as a contemporary, as I stated in the introduction to this book. The adjective *contemporáneo* is relatively recent in Spanish, and Diego de Valera was one of the first writers to use it. Other users of his time were Alfonso de Palencia and Rodrigo de Santaella, each in their own dictionary, indicating a certain unease with a word that, being so new, had to figure in a list of untranslatables.[5] Valera uses this word to show himself especially fascinated

---

4. This concept is Robert J. C. Young's in "Postcolonial Remains," 19–42. For Young the "politics of invisibility," that is, the capacity of institutions to conceal the alternatives to hegemony, should be the object of postcolonial thinking as an active form of thought, not as a tendency or a school. The issue has been carried further—and in an intellectually more active way—by Walter Mignolo and his project of discolonial thought (Mignolo, *The Darker Side*).

5. In his dictionary for interpreting biblical texts, Rodrigo de Santaella translates the Greek *synchronon* as "contemporaneous or of the same time" (contemporaneo o de un tiempo): Santaella, *Vocabulario Eclesiástico*; Alfonso de Palencia, *Universal Vocabulario*, under "Ogiges." CORDE (Corpus diacrónico del español) offers other examples, in all of which *contemporáneo* means strictly "contemporary." In Valera's case, his way of referring to the contemporary as purely modern, and related to a particular technological advance that transforms a way of writing and a way of participating in public life, suggests a "politics of the neologism" similar to the politics of translation that Apter studies in *Against World Literature*. The question of "untranslatability" is crucial to the concept of the politics of the untranslatable because it

by the technological innovations that he is taking part in—for, as it happened, his *Crónica Abreviada de España*, better known as the *Valeriana*, would be the first vernacular work of historiography to be printed in the Iberian Peninsula. Valera expresses his hope that the *Valeriana* will have a strong impact just when the techniques of writing are being transformed, and that his radically contemporary history will circulate widely, "being renewed through multiple copies in knowledge of the past, present, and future, to the greatest extent that human inventiveness can achieve."[6] From his position in the contemporary, then, Valera can start a conversation with historical times and grammatical tenses, with the past, present, and future of present things, according to an Augustinian conception of time.[7]

This contemporaneity is what makes Diego de Valera an activist. So far, I have not defined what an active life might mean, or what an activism is that transforms the academic into an intellectual. To do so I will use a definition that may be strange, but that forms part of a culture in which secular occupations and their metaphysical interpretation are called into question. In this definition Saint Augustine refers to the worldview of the Neoplatonists and the three ways of life that one can live in the earthly city, through which one acts as a public citizen:

> Likewise with regard to those three kinds of life,—namely, the first life, which though not slothful yet is a life of leisure spent in considering or enquiring into truth, the second life, which is actively engaged in administration of human affairs, and the third, which is a combination of the two others,—when the question is asked

---

calls for not only constructing a series of equivalents but recognizing that to understand the concept one must study it both linguistically and culturally. Apter also bases her work on Cassin, *Vocabulaire Européen des Philosophies*. For translation/untranslatability, see also Meschonnic, *Poétique du traduire*, where the author focuses on something that is also important for the concept of Valera as a contemporary: translation is not a question of "source" or "target" (of translators who are *sourciers* or *ciblistes*), but rather of finding a rhythm that is somehow the rhythm of the contemporary, that has an effect in the language and culture that is translating.

6. "restituyéndose por multiplicados códices en conoscimiento de los pasado, presente y futuro, tanto quanto ingenio humano conseguir puede." Valera, *Crónica Valeriana*, 338. For Valera, brevity and influence in the contemporary (and in his contemporaries) is associated with a new "art of writing" (arte de escrevir) that puts an end to the "paucity of originals and copies" (penuria de originales y trasuntos) (*Crónica Valeriana*, 338). The interesting fact about this technology is perhaps just that: this art of writing transforms the pacts that govern the production of history and historiography.

7. Valera seems to have in mind a periodization that is related to Augustine's ideas about the past, present, and future "de praesentis" (about the present). Augustine, *Confessions*, 11:25–29. That is also what characterizes this contemporary thought.

which of them should be chosen, there is no dispute about the supreme good; the subject of the dispute is which of these three hampers or facilitates the attainment or preservation of the supreme good. When any one achieves the supreme good, it forthwith makes him happy, whereas a life spent in lettered leisure or in public business or in both by turns does not immediately make him happy. No doubt there are many people who may be leading any one of these three lives, yet who go astray in their quest for the ultimate good that determines human happiness.[8]

A little further on, Augustine articulates the concept more concisely when he summarizes the three ways of life in a single expression: "the inactive, the active, and that which has some proportion of both."[9] He finds all three to be different responses to a single question that we might call here the neurosis of existence, the impossibility of finding happiness *in this world*. The three ways of life are a way of accepting this neurosis in the earthly Jerusalem, the world here below.

The principal feature of critical engagement is the impossibility of finding the ultimate good, and therefore happiness, in any of these three ways of life. A person cannot always place his life on the line in the name of truth or of a just cause. He may run certain political risks, place his relationships or social networks in danger. The public intellectual knows that the critical act that carries those risks will negate the simple possibility of defining happiness, even of feeling it. Activism may mean accepting that happiness does not enter into the sphere of action of political criticism.

For the activist what matters is not the "negotium publicum" (public affairs) but the way of life that Augustine calls "ex utroque modificato" or, a little earlier, "ex utroque genere temperato," a moderate mixture of the active and the contemplative lives. That would be the life of a person who is in a continual process of change, through a combination

---

8. "In tribus quoque illis vitae generibus, uno scilicet non segniter sed in contemplatione vel inquisitione veritas otioso, altero in gerendis rebus humanis negotioso, tertio ex utroque genere temperato, cum quaeritur quid horum sit potius eligendum, non finis boni habet controversiam; sed quid horum trium difficultatem vel facilitatem afferat ad consequendum vel retinendum finem boni, id in ista quaestione versatur. Finis enim boni, cum ad eum quisque pervenerit, protinus beatum facit. In otio autem litterato, vel in negotio publico, vel quando utruquem vicibus agitur, non continuo quisque beatus est. Multi quippe in quolibet horum trium possunt vivere, et in appetendo boni fine quo fit homo beatus, errare." Agustín, *La ciudad de Dios*, 2:19.2.

9. "otioso, actuoso, et ex utroque modificato." Agustín, *La ciudad de Dios*, 2:19.2.

of "otium litteratum" (leisure with the study of letters) and "negotium publicum" (public affairs); or, to erase the false dichotomy between leisure and work, combining knowledge derived from study with the need to enter the political and ethical universe where public problems are managed. Augustine does not seem to care that academics prefer the third way of life (the mixture of the public and the literary), because he, in effect, does not accept that the neurosis of existence may constitute the goal of existence.[10] But in my opinion that is, in fact, existence's fundamental trait. And it is also what I want to set as an interpretative horizon for understanding the life and work of Diego de Valera.

There are many ways to evaluate this feeling, which is literary and public at the same time. For an individual like Diego de Valera, it was very difficult to join a political universe in which a public presence, and participation in the inner circle of power, were obtained through a mixture of lineage and cultural and academic achievements. Valera's biography is marked by a series of sociopolitical wounds that were hard to cure. His father, Alonso, was a converso physician; his mother, María Fernández de Valera (whose surname he always preferred to his father's, Chirino) came from a bourgeois family that had reached a certain hidalgo status within the knightly rank in Cuenca. Valera felt uncomfortable at the level of the nobility, to which he never managed to rise. Knighthood, for Valera and the followers of Bartolo da Sassoferrato (1313–57), the jurisconsult from Perugia, was an open door through which plebeians could attain noble rank through the king's grace. But Valera's experience as a knight was marked by his investiture by a non-royal hand.[11] At the same time, the mixture of lineage and formal education that could distinguish an individual in courtly circles was not predictable: no one could say just what dosage of each thing was necessary, making Valera's social experience at the Castilian royal court more difficult, and ruled by anxiety.

To confront these problems Valera deploys two different personalities, one in the interior of his treatises and the other on their periphery. In the center he establishes the rules of belonging to the lineage and genealogy of power, expounding on legally complex topics like peace, knighthood, and political theory. In all these media he proposes theses about what it means to belong to a noble lineage, including social

---

10. Agustín, *La ciudad de Dios*, 2:19.3.
11. The best modern biography of Valera is that of Cristina Moya in her edition of Valera's *Crónica Valeriana*.

groups whose individual access to power was limited, such as women and Jews, as well as other sectors of urban or even rural origin who make up the plebeian world.[12] At the same time, on the periphery, he plays a second essential game, sometimes beyond the margins of his texts: he reestablishes the rules for interpreting his ideas about political and social theory, forcing his readers (ourselves included) to read him in the key of the *bibliotheca*, the thesaurus, or, if you will, the cultural encyclopedia whose validity is always in dispute. There is no doubt, for instance, that Valera not only contributes to discussions or arguments with authors who belong to the contemporary cultural economy, whether through complete works or through miscellanies, indices, and anthologies; he also manages to introduce a few writers from his own experience as a researcher, like the elusive John the Teutonic, whom he shares with Francesc Eiximenis, or Bartolo da Sassoferrato who, though much sought-after among the lettered elites of Castile and Aragon, remained difficult for his contemporaries to locate and comprehend.[13]

Diego de Valera's microliterature acts within a logic of the whole that encompasses both the center and the gloss. It is, above all, an attitude, rather than a textual manifestation that can be formally identified on the manuscript pages that transmit his works. This attitude not only expands toward the margins in a centrifugal way; it defines his modus operandi as a writer of treatises. Valera's microliterature is everywhere at once, a kind of urgent participation in topics of burning current interest, which is what reveals his engagement in the public sphere.

We never have too many moral and political models. Crises have an insidious way of shaking the solidity of some of those models. What I propose is by no means a moral model, nor a style, not even an example. I only want to do what any historian should do: to seek out theoretical concepts and problems that help us understand what responses

---

12. We should recall here that Valera was born and raised in an urban milieu that, as in Cuenca, contained a lower-class or plebeian rank of knights with aspirations to rise to hidalgo status. See Cabañas González, *La caballería popular en Cuenca*; Jara Fuente, *Concejo, poder y élites*.

13. Later on, I will again discuss how Valera introduced Bartolo into his political debates. In fact, he is not the only one; also involved are Alonso de Cartagena with his conciliar address, Juan Rodríguez del Padrón, and Ferrán Mejía. On all this, see Rodríguez Velasco, *El debate*; and González-Vázquez, "Représentation et théorisation." Francisco Bautista has argued that "Bartolo" is a name that conveys a certain debate about politics and society, and that was transmitted through a small selection of texts that includes *De dignitatibus* and *De insigniis*; this version of the Bartolo debate can be considered a Castilian invention: Bautista, "La idea de nobleza." It is a risky thesis that I nonetheless find convincing, because it explains not only the preeminence of certain texts (and the absence of others), but also the circularity of discourse concerning them as applied to certain specific cases in the Castilian milieu.

have arisen at critical moments, in my case in the humanities; and what value resides in this. In other words, we need to imagine a society in which the answers to social, political, public, and other problems do not come only from systematic and autopoetic discourses (the concept is Niklas Luhman's) like economics and law, but also from humanistic analyses that choose to be interdisciplinary and transversal.

Diego de Valera elects to participate in public life by writing. We may not need to stress that this was a singular choice: writing in the fifteenth century did not mean what it means now, when written culture overwhelms everything. In the fifteenth century writing was a marginal activity, and Valera devotes himself to it in all directions. His writing is a constant exploration of different ways to write. He doesn't so much cultivate as plow different textual forms; he breaks them open for the first time, gets certain results and, like a nomadic thinker, moves on to another field so as to plow it as well.[14]

This is what he does, for example, with one of his discourses written most clearly at a crosscurrent, on the subject of peace. There he wanders through missives, a letter sent to an imaginary friend, and a brief treatise with its glosses that is sometimes called an exhortation and sometimes a compilation.

Concerning Peace

The philologist bent on exploring Diego de Valera's sources will realize two things. First, that Valera seems to be an avid reader in several languages who can refer with equal ease to philosophical and theological

---

14. Here I borrow freely (but not faithfully to their moment) from certain ideas and concepts of Gilles Deleuze and Félix Guattari in their little book on Kafka and minor literature: *Kafka*. (But I am not acting *against Deleuze*, so to speak, as I believe Deleuze himself explains in speaking both of philosophy as a discipline and of his reading of Friedrich Nietzsche: Deleuze and Guattari, *Qu'est-ce que la philosophie?*; Deleuze, *Nietzsche et la philosophie* and *Nietzsche*.) The notion of nomadic thought, like that of linguistic stammering, which I discuss later on, serves me here in a specific way, as a metaphor of a metaphor, we might say. I know that Deleuze and Guattari are speaking of problems of a modernity that is not applicable to figures like Valera in any way, but that do serve as an analogy for speaking of this microliterary Valera. Valera's nomadism relates to his constant activity in exploring certain styles and forms of writing, which at the same time lead him to assume certain masks, or certain causes, as his own: he can become an imaginary friend, or a Jew who wants to retain noble rank, or an individual woman with a story to tell, or an agent of peace. In this sense his thought exploits different forms and foci of expression, with a certain taste for contradiction, a certain way of opposing common opinion or common sense of a specific form of governability, like that of eras that Marx called "of Don Juans and Henrys." Karl Marx, "Revolutionary Spain: Fourth Article," originally published in the *New York Daily Tribune*, October 27, 1854.

treatises, historiography, law, and poetry, or any other text in the library, whether that is a real room with shelves or a virtual space of oral debate and authorial ideas that are in the air. Second, digging a little deeper, that Diego de Valera is very fond of name-dropping: he draws not so much on a detailed reading of all the works and authors he cites but on glossaries, indices, anthologies, and other artifacts prepared for the purpose in the libraries he frequents, and he likes to show that he knows the names in the literary pantheon. Neither of these two tendencies can detract from the intensity of Valera's writings about peace. In that intellectual project, although we can recognize the jigsaw puzzle of microliteratures that makes up his argumental process, we also see the ethical and political commitment that overrides any criticism of his sources.

His first two letters about peace and processes of pacification are addressed to King John II.[15] In both, the superficial thesis is the same diptych of ideas: pacification is preferable to civil strife, and in the pacification process clemency is preferable to vengeance. This dual thesis has a recognizable political and ethical genealogy that Valera has no desire to conceal. He draws on a plethora of quotations and examples from a sort of vulgate that includes Valerius Maximus, Seneca, Saint Isidore, and other authors whom he names. The fact that he cites them explicitly does not mean that he has read them all in detail; often it is relatively easy to establish how far he depends on secondary sources, indices, or compilations. The more or less predictable nature of these sources, their lack of originality, should not interfere with our reading of Valera's letters, for which the sources serve as a kind of virtual library; it exerts on his theses a symbolic power of attraction rather than a concrete form of argumentation. In other words, these sources are like the quicksilver that allows extraction of the precious metal, and not necessarily the point of arrival for the theses that Valera wishes to propose and defend.

The thesis of pacification and clemency can be considered a major premise with two stages for a logic of peace. In a first stage it serves to organize a vocabulary, a series of major concepts that make up

---

15. I read both the letters and the *Exhortación* in the original manuscripts but cite the edition by Mario Penna: *Prosistas españoles del siglo XV*. The most recent edition of the *Exhortación* is Baldissera's ("La *Exhortación de la Paz*"), but it is thoroughly traditional and adds little to earlier studies and editions.

the frontier of intelligibility of the problem of peace.[16] These major concepts state that the peace of the kingdom resides in the tension between maintaining royal power and establishing a sociopolitical contract based on clemency. In a second stage it serves to place the whole system of argumentation within a discourse of the history of political doctrines, in which the authors cited, and the examples quoted, also make up a horizon of intelligibility as examples or as ethical and political models.

All this is simply the greater premise in Valera's logic, in which he devotes great effort to producing lesser premises and concepts. It is here, in fact, where Valera departs from the universal nature of major concepts and abstract political theory in order to focus on concrete political action.

The first of these minor concepts has to do with public participation, or activism. Valera defends it from the beginning of the letter, when he states that "each subject [is] obliged, according to divine and human law, to tell his opinion to his king or lord in the matters that much concern him."[17] He observes closely the political conflicts that divide the kingdom, tracing them back to the confrontation with the princes of Aragon, the Castilian factions, the opposition to Álvaro de Luna, the confrontation between John II and his son Henry, who was supported by some of the nobility, and other factors. In view of all this Valera decides to participate in the least predictable way for a knight like himself. He distances himself, rejects military solutions and the sovereign's supposed right to mete out punishment, and offers a series of strategic solutions that could preserve the unity of the kingdom, based on a concept of permanent peace that would later be glimpsed by political theorists from Hugo Grotius to Immanuel Kant.

Valera has no interest in finding the formula for victory in this civil conflict; he cares more about constructing a new solidarity within the kingdom. With this motivation he draws up a brief list of minor concepts, all of which run counter to the experience of civil war. In the second letter he expresses them as follows: "To achieve tranquility and calm and perpetual peace in your kingdoms, in my opinion, four things are needed; without which, or lacking any one of them, I see no way or

---

16. I use "major concepts" and "minor concepts" following Rorty, "The Contingency of Language," 3–22.

17. "cada uno de los naturales [es] tenido, según derecho divino e humano, dezir su parecer a su rey o señor en las cosas que mucho le va." Valera, *Tratado de las epístolas*, 3a.

path by which we can expect it [peace], to wit: total concord between you and the Prince, restoration of the absent knights, and freeing of prisoners; and for the guilty, a general pardon."[18]

Valera's vision includes a series of Augustinian concepts such as tranquility and calm, but also that of perpetual peace, which is not strictly Augustinian (Augustine situates the possibility of perpetual peace only in the heavenly Jerusalem). Authors of Valera's time such as Alonso de Madrigal "el Tostado" insist that perpetual peace is impossible; or, as in a charter oath issued by John II in 1436, they define perpetual peace as a type of contract, that is, a pact agreed upon by two parties whose duration is limited by the fulfilment of the contract.[19] Perpetual peace also enters into historical forms of pacification, but is usually centered on this type of contract that is frequent in fifteenth-century chronicles and documents.[20] Valera's perpetual peace, in contrast, is intransitive and does not depend on any contractual intent: it is an operation that presumes unilateral moves on the ruler's part. These moves are surprising because they require not only concord between the parties but also a general amnesty for the knights involved. They call for political and legal structures of forgetting, a voluntary amnesia about the uprisings and protests led by those knights.

Valera writes sternly to the king, in the parrhesiastic tone of which Foucault spoke in the course he left unfinished at his death. He tries to frighten him by referring to the prophecies of Benahatín from the chronicle of the chancellor of Castile, Pero López de Ayala, under the pre-Trastámaran archtyrant Peter I (r. 1367–69), murdered by his half-brother Henry II (r. 1366–79). Valera's severity earns him the opposition

---

18. "Pues para dar tranquilidad e sossiego e paz perpetua en vuestros reinos, según mi opinión, quatro cosas son necessarias, sin las quales o falleciendo alguna dellas, yo no veo vía ni camino por dónde nin cómo esperarla devamos, conviene a saber: entera concordia de vos e del Príncipe, restitución de los cavalleros ausentes, e deliberación de los presos; de los culpados general perdón." Valera, *Tratado de las epístolas*, 6b.

19. Madrigal, "El Tostado," 102. Obviously, El Tostado takes his cue from Aristotle, *Nicomachean Ethics* 8.1.1155a: "καὶ φίλων μὲν ὄντων οὐδὲν δεῖ δικαιοσύνης" (And if men are friends, there is no need of justice between them). Translation from H. Rackham's edition (Cambridge, MA: Harvard University Press, 1926), 452–53. For John's charter, see Sánchez-Prieto Borja, *Carta de juramento de 1436*.

20. In other texts such as *El Victorial*, the legal institution of "perpetual peace" is a contract that is perpetual not in the sense of "permanent," but rather of "indefinite" and "unconditional," or without obstacles: Díaz de Games, *El Victorial*. The same assumption is made in Pulgar, *Crónica de los Reyes Católicos*. See Real Academia Española, Database CORDE: "Corpus diacrónico del español," under "paz perpetua." For the issue of pactism, see the fundamental work directed by Foronda, *Avant le contrat social*.

of many of his contemporaries, to whom he replies in a third letter that is, without doubt, the most fascinating. Written on the subject of peace, it is addressed to an imaginary friend. This is not the first example of writing to such a "friend" (Cicero and Petrarch come immediately to mind, as well as my oldest son), but it is the first time for Valera. It will not be the last: the imaginary friend (the same one or another, who knows?) will also serve him for speaking about certain women in his preamble to another glossed text that we will discuss further on.

Valera's political subjectivity appears and is constructed in this letter. The letter does not, in fact, claim to change the theory about peace, but rather to affirm it while focusing on the subject who is stating the theories about peace. For his critics the issue is not whether the theory is adequate or inadequate, but whether the political subject who expresses it is a proper one or not. Valera opposes that judgment consistently, because he knows that the question simply reproduces the ways in which the traditional structures of power perpetuate themselves.

This declaration of subjectivity is crucial to understanding how Valera places himself in relation to his contemporaries. It also endorses the activist stance he wishes to take. He means to transform how objective power is organized: how (as he recalls in his letter) the role of counselor seems limited to ecclesiastics and nobles and excludes persons of his own social class and political opinions. In this sense his activism is based on a view of society with roots in the Gospels, without any "difference between persons and States."[21] Breaking through this barrier and introducing persons and states into the economy of power means extending the scope of sovereignty, in which every subject is endowed with personal political feeling—a sort of phenomenology of political events that, for Valera, is the key to political knowledge.

The *Exhortación a la Paz* (Exhortation to peace), perhaps composed after 1447, is in large measure a rewriting of these earlier epistolary microliteratures, and also a pioneering form of treatise on the subject of peace. Only Christine de Pizan's *Livre de Paix* (or *de la Paix*), written in 1414, can be remotely compared to it, with common references that suggest that Valera may plausibly have known Christine's text at an early date.[22] Christine is concerned with the breaking of pacts and

---

21. "diferencia entre personas y Estados." Valera, *Tratado de las epístolas*, 7a.

22. This link between Christine's work and those of several Iberian authors has yet to be demonstrated. But there are very intense resonances, both political and in techniques of writing, between works by Christine de Pizan and Valera and, above all, by Pedro of Portugal.

truces, and of how to restore the process of pacification in the face of the civil conflicts that were dividing France.

The *Exhortación*, like the first two letters, is dedicated to John II. In it, Valera gathers ideas from several authorities who define peace and relate it to political practice. He shows his concern for contemporary views: if most of his doctrinal and philosophical sources are ancient and medieval, his chief authority for defining political practice is a contemporary piece of great international renown, Alonso de Cartagena's *Libro de las Sesiones* (Book of sessions), which conveys Cartagena's address to the Council of Basel. Sixty-three marginal notations, with conventional Latin abbreviations, indicate the genealogy and bibliography of its ideas, protecting and preserving on its margins the thought of Diego de Valera.

A sense of political urgency releases the public intellectual within Valera, an intellectual who seems to emerge from within the inner ranks of the kingdom's establishment, an apparent "organic intellectual." Rapidly, however, Valera shows his need to depart from the immediate practices of power and, using similar intellectual resources, he assumes the uncomfortable position of a political subject whose very voice is called into question. From this uneasy perch Valera places on the political horizon a series of microliterary views on peace, not only as a major concept but also in terms of their concrete applicability to current circumstances.

Against All Generalization

Something similar happens with another matter that impels Valera to place himself on the margins of official thought: the importance of certain individual women in the history of political practice. Federica Accorsi devoted a book to Valera's *Tratado en defensa de virtuosas mujeres* (Treatise in defense of virtuous women), a text that is emblematic of a microliterary attitude.[23] With her characteristic philological tenacity Accorsi followed up every one of the references inherent in Valera's text, placing it within the cultural parameters of the fifteenth century. Accorsi's book is a model in every sense of the word.

To demonstrate these strictly contemporary connections, and how they relate to a politics of gender, one would have to open a line of research that differs from a criticism of sources—though I confess that I don't know what that alternative might be.

23. Valera, *Defensa de virtuosas mujeres*. I cite this edition by page number only.

CHAPTER 4

Good books always raise questions, and to some we have not yet found adequate answers. There is a full line of studies on fifteenth-century misogyny, fifteenth-century pro-feminism, and the so-called *querelle des femmes*. Its genealogy is very clear, and almost everyone can draw up a list that begins with two works by Boccaccio (*De mulieribus claris* and *Corbaccio*), continues with Christine de Pizan—who brings in retroactively Mathieu de Boulogne and Jean de Meun (*Querelle du Roman de la Rose*, as well as *La cité des dames*)—and then meets dueling opinions south of the Pyrenees with authors like Juan Rodríguez del Padrón (*Libro de las donas*), Álvaro de Luna (*Libro de las virtuosas e claras mugeres*), Juan de Mena (the triple prologue to Álvaro de Luna's book), Alfonso Martínez de Toledo (*Arcipreste de Talavera*), Pere Torroella (*Maldezir de las mugeres*), and others. Valera is among them. This genealogy of texts is matched by a genealogy of scholarly studies, notably those by Robert Archer, Julian Weiss, Federica Accorsi, Julio Vélez, Barbara Weissberger, and Lola Pons.[24]

Among all these studies I will distinguish Julian Weiss's article, "'¿Qué demandamos de las mujeres?,'" published in 2002. For Weiss, the literary debate about women during the fifteenth and early sixteenth centuries needs to be seen in a context of social and political change, not as a mere courtly fashion followed with greater or lesser consistency. These literary artifacts should be viewed not within the "transhistorical cycle" of misogyny but as part of the transformation of cultural contexts.[25] Valera is playing within the masculine hegemonic arena, while his interlocutor Queen Mary, as Weiss points out, is really a silent interlocutor; the treatise is actually addressed to the imaginary friend with whom he shares both habits and structures of symbolic violence: a way of speaking, cultural references, forms of ventriloquism. In my opinion Valera does not stand outside the economy of symbolic

---

24. Boccaccio, *Il corbaccio*; Boccaccio, *Famous Women*. For Christine de Pizan's *Livre de la cité des dames* one should consult the manuscripts now almost all available at gallica.bnf.fr, simply because most of Christine's concepts are expressed not only textually but also visually. David Hult has prepared a dossier on the *querelle des femmes* in Pizan, *Debate of the "Romance of the Rose."* See Rodríguez del Padrón, "Triumpho de las donas." There are two editions of Álvaro de Luna's text, respectively by Julio Vélez (Luna, *Libro de las virtuosas e claras mugeres*), and Lola Pons (Luna, *Virtuosas y claras mujeres*). These editions also contain many other pieces of an ideological and political puzzle about which much still remains to be said. Federica Accorsi also discusses it in her introduction to the abovementioned edition of Valera. The relevant bibliography is extensive, but I will mention only more recent works by Archer, *The Problem of Woman*; Weiss, "'¿Qué demandamos de las mujeres?,'" 237–81; Weissberger, *Isabel Rules* and "'Deceitful Sects,'" 207–35; and Vélez Sáinz, "*De amor, de honor e de donas.*"

25. Weiss, "'¿Qué demandamos de las mujeres?,'" 239.

masculine power, nor outside the anxiety felt by many fifteenth-century men over the political and economic emergence of several women of the time—the prime example being, perhaps, Isabella of Castile. I will show that when he refers to "women" and objects to generalizations about them, he is accepting that in the symbolic paradigm of masculine hegemony there is a series of identifiable individual women (therefore only a few) who are exceptions to the rule. But even if we follow the thread of this argument we can find, at a more microscopic level, other ideas that help to transform the context of feminist thinking—I use "feminist" deliberately—during the fifteenth century.

Valera's microliterary attitude shows a special sensitivity on this point, beginning with the purely grammatical and continuing throughout the center and the margins of his book *Defensa de virtuosas mujeres*. The grammar can pass unnoticed: he does not speak of "women" or "woman" in general but of particular women, individual subjects. This precision fits his stated purpose, to confront precisely those who "usually denigrate the female nation," showing to what extent a general criticism should be countered with particular examples.[26] This opposition between the general and the specific appears both in the epistle to Queen Mary, to whom the treatise is dedicated, and in the preamble, where he again conjures up his imaginary friend to show him "these founders of the new sect who are brazenly pleased to curse all women."[27] In this rhetorical exercise in which epistle, satire, and deliberation are mixed together, Valera lays out his arguments around three theses concerning this opinion, whose greatest offense is its generality, both subjective and objective.

Valera's text is conceived as a satire, that is, a fifteenth-century moral genre that Julian Weiss reassessed in a study of Juan de Mena's *Coronación*.[28] This satire in prose allows a pun on its popular etymology, *satura* (a fruit salad), saturated with fruit. And this is what Valera does, in some sense: he creates a supersaturated solution in which the marginal text added to the central one overwhelms it; is more than the central text can absorb. While the central text names, one by one, examples of women in the worlds of morals and politics, the marginal text spins out the history of each one, becoming a space or site of memory.

---

26. "de la femenil nasción generalmente detraen." Valera, *Defensa de virtuosas mujeres*, 229.
27. "el fundamento de aquestos començadores de nueva seta que rotamente les plaze en general de todas las mugeres maldezir." Valera, *Defensa de virtuosas mujeres*, 229.
28. Weiss, "Juan de Mena's *Coronación*," 113–38.

Designing a site of memory on the surface of the page does not mean merely recalling. Rather, it constructs an alternative to ways of remembering and to the very use of memories. This site of memory is by no means a shrine or a mausoleum, but rather a way of initiating a contemporary activity: redefining the public to make it include new female interlocutors who can have a specific effect on action in the present. Constructing a site of memory is, in this sense, a form of intellectual activism.

Scholars of the *Defensa* have focused on these marginal glosses as literal or historical. A literal gloss is nothing but a technique of commentary whose doctrinal genealogy lends it historical value. What seems to me the basic question has gone unasked: Why are these stories told in full? My theory is simple: narrating them is the only way to reincorporate these minor, displaced, and untimely stories into the modern discourse of a growing historiography. In this historiography an ethical and political reading is ever more essential, and Valera understands that a renovation of history requires including, or reincorporating, these women into it.

Valera, unlike his contemporaries, decides to move these individual histories to the margins, refusing to mix the space for theory and apology with the space for biographical essays. These essays, placed at the periphery of most of the manuscripts (some gather the glosses at the end of the treatise, or even at the end of each chapter or section), show Valera as author of microliterature: each story can be read independently and each contains an urgent lesson, just as happens with the innumerable legal-political glosses that surround the legal texts that Valera admires so much.[29] Valera's microhistories, individualized and displaced from the center, resemble him a little: they are put there "to mean something" (puestas a significar), and their presence requires thinking about the meaning of these stories and about why they have traditionally been silenced by history.[30] With the margin and the center linked by invisible lines, this satellite of stories is composed of narratives that have lives of their own and display their brilliant uniqueness.

Julian Weiss, in his splendid article, maintains that male writings about the cultural value of certain women in history should be

---

29. For the various manuscripts of Valera's *Defensa de virtuosas mujeres*, see Accorsi's edition (202-97).

30. "Puestas a significar" is an expression used by Luis de Lucena to explain his own annotations: *Repeticion de amores y arte de ajedrez*, fol. ciiij^r.

understood as part of the sociology of masculinity.³¹ There is no need to seek in Valera's writing what does not appear there. He is neither a feminist nor a misogynist. Both notions prevent us from speaking of Valera's project, because they do not belong to the intellectual economy of his time. But sometimes Valera, like us, is incapable of creating new conceptual systems and must seize on moral concepts that were inherited or common in his age. So it is with the role assigned to chastity, which seems like a particularly perverse way of breaking with "misogynist" discourse, not to speak of being "feminist." But as Michael Baxandall has shown, behind many fifteenth-century concepts lies a system of interpretation that, while it may be opaque to us, should not deceive us with its apparent triviality.³² Theories about this concept lead us into political complexities: Stephanie Jed, in *Chaste Thinking*, proposed that the idea of chastity had been politicized in narratives about the rape of Lucrece to the point that it became a civic virtue that allowed popular and democratic action by the republican system; both chastity and Lucrece's suicide were presented as expressions of female virtue.³³

Another way of interpreting these stories is to see them as historical forms that consolidate the patriarchal and political colonization of the uterus. Paul B. Preciado offers us the vocabulary for interpreting this type of colonization:

> Among all the body's organs, the uterus is without doubt the one that historically has been the object of the fiercest political and economic exploitation. A cavity with the potential for gestation, the uterus is not a private organ, but a public space fought over by religious and political leaders, and by the medical, pharmaceutical, and food and agriculture industries. Every woman carries within her a laboratory for the nation-state, and the purity of the nation's race depends on how she manages it.³⁴

---

31. Weiss, "'¿Qué demandamos de las mujeres?,'" 237–81.
32. Baxandall, *Giotto and the Orators*.
33. Jed, *Chaste Thinking*.
34. Stephanie Jed's thesis is problematic from the viewpoint of a "colonization of the uterus" like the one Paul B. Preciado proposes in "Déclarer la grève des utérus." ("Parmi tous les organes du corps, l'utérus est sans doute celui qui, historiquement, a fait l'objet de l'expropriation politique et économique la plus acharnée. Cavité potentiellement gestatrice, l'utérus n'est pas un organe privé, mais un espace public que se disputent pouvoirs religieux et politiques, industries médicales, pharmaceutiques et agroalimentaires. Chaque femme porte en elle un laboratoire de l'État-nation, et c'est de sa gestion que dépend la pureté de l'ethnie nationale"). In fact, the politicization of chastity (to which fifteenth-century treatises

We cannot be unaware that, even without this vocabulary, the public nature of the female organ is what is under discussion by both men and women who write about chastity, or even about legislation on marriage and reproduction, in legal texts such as Raymond of Penyafort's *Summa de Penitentia et Matrimonio* and Alfonso X's *Cuarta Partida*. Introducing classical texts and commentaries on female chastity as a political ideal of national purity, using humanistic concepts, merely establishes a broader genealogy for this colonization of the female body. In effect, it offers one more argument in support of Julian Weiss's thesis that ultimately, texts about women, even those that seem to contain the greatest doses of feminism in the fifteenth century, only help to perpetuate concepts of masculinity as the system's norm.

Orality in Writing

As I have already observed, Valera is often concerned with establishing or even reestablishing the rules for participating in public affairs. This is a political thesis, and he sets out to construct it in essays on political theory. By "essay" I mean two different things. On the one hand I wish to identify the treatise (*tratado*) as a category of the essay genre and, as such, a form of research whose rules are established within the text itself, not depending necessarily on any external theories or expectations.[35] The best example may be, once again, the *Defensa de virtuosas mujeres*, in which the rules for the text's composition appear at different points but above all in a gloss in which rhetorical and poetic theory, as well as the theory of the art of letter-writing (*ars dictaminis*), belong to the type of project Valera wishes to carry out.[36] Several of Valera's treatises tend, explicitly or implicitly, toward this self-definition.

The noun "essay" (*ensayo*) has a second, more tentative, meaning. The term *tratado*, relatively new in Castilian in reference to a written genre, comes from an argumentative form of particular interest to Valera, the legal treatise developed by the post-glossators or commentators of the *mos italicum* (the "Italian style" of legal commentary) from the fourteenth century onward. This type of treatise also establishes its

---

on women are not immune) forms one of the central problems of gender studies. See also Preciado, *Countersexual Manifesto*.

35. The notion of considering the treatise as an essay was proposed by Marichal, *La voluntad de estilo*.

36. Rodríguez Velasco, "Autoglosa," 10–33.

own functional rules, by setting out general topics and converting them into legal-political arguments. Valera shows particular skill in converting these relatively banal ideas and questions into reflections on the functioning of objective politics. We have seen the full extent of this talent in how he refers to the construction of peace, and in how his microliterary approach floods the affective space of the glossed page with individual biographies, synchronizing it with asynchronous lives.

Where Valera does this best is, without doubt, in his political treatises, especially the *Espejo de Verdadera Nobleza* (Mirror of true nobility), also edited and studied by Federica Accorsi. Like the *Defensa de virtuosas mujeres*, the *Espejo* is an argument for confronting specific, particular problems so as to deactivate the negative consequences of general or popular opinions. To this end Valera turns to Bartolo da Sassoferrato, his intellectual fetish and favorite author, declaring that if he is to follow in "his footsteps" it is because Bartolo "argues in a very lively manner against all these opinions," that is to say, the commonest ideas about the nobility.[37] Here it is Valera with Bartolo (and as Francisco de Quevedo would have said), against all.

In an unnumbered gloss in the *Defensa*, Valera declares that "I wish to put in writing what I had often maintained in [spoken] words, because in matters expressed in words there are many cavils and deceits; and not wishing to give occasion for those, I was moved to write."[38] The same feeling about oral debates motivates Valera as he is writing the *Espejo*: "I remembered having heard many times, not only in your splendid house and court but in others of very exalted kings, illustrious princes, and great men, discussions about nobility and high estate"; and he adds that they all sounded wrong to him.[39] Both reactions to orality do not only relate to scenes of courtly life; they bring up two additional problems. The first is that the specific interest aroused by these matters at court must be linked to the fact that they question concrete assumptions about the exercise of power: specifically, the primacy of the male and the primacy of hereditary nobility. The second is that writing can

---

37. Valera, *Espejo de verdadera nobleza*, 297.
38. "querer en escripto poner lo que muchas vezes por palabras avía sostenido, porque en las questiones que por palabras pasan ay muchas cavilaçiones o engaños, a los quales non queriendo dar lugar, yo fui movido escrivir." Valera, *Defensa de virtuosas mujeres*, 252; see also 251n1.
39. "acordávame yo muchas vezes aver oído no solamente en vuestra magnífica casa e corte, mas aun en otras de muy altos reyes e ilustres prínçipes e grandes varones, de la nobleza o fidalguía tractar." Valera, *Espejo de verdadera nobleza*, 291.

replace the fluid pragmatic elements of a conversation with a system of argument and authority that leads to a debate's conclusion. In other words, a written reaction to orality is not a mere transcription but rather a dialectical improvement, a thesis in itself. Here we are truly at the base camp of Jacques Derrida's *supplément*: writing is a supplement, and therefore a subproduct of orality that partakes of the anxieties of the permanent.

The microliterary attitude of the essay feeds on the structure of a treatise with glosses, in which both arguments and their narrative conditions are expressed in brief and definitive form. We see not only the Valera who is activated by a certain stimulus, but also the Valera who theorizes about the conditions of the stimulus that forces him to become a public activist by means of writing.

In a legal text, and especially in the *mos italicus* tradition, an *exemplum* is a jurisprudential note to a juridical rule. Normally these *exempla* are not long narratives, but they are illustrative since they tend to make an abstract regulation concrete. One of the *exempla* that form part of this microliterature is preserved by Valera in his interpretation of and commentary on Bartolo. Further, this *exemplum* helps to connect the *Espejo* to the *Defensa*, showing how a single intellectual endeavor can be constructed from two different viewpoints of political analysis.

Bartolo and Valera maintain that to verify the essential dynamism of the concept of nobility one must consider the role of women more than that of men, and in general those who receive nobility unawares, such as children. It is these marginal subjects who place the continuity of nobility in danger. Nobility must be examined in women because legally nobility is patrilineal, making women into variable subjects who are at the mercy of genealogical forces.[40] And nobility in children should be closely watched because, although they inherit it genetically, they are later obliged to renew it through their own practice of virtue lest they lose it for themselves and their descendants.[41]

Among these marginal subjects are also Jews and Muslims. Can they preserve the nobility they once had after their conversion to Christianity? Valera, employing Bartolo's terminology, distinguishes among theological nobility (of divine origin), ordinary nobility (which pertains mostly to objects and to a form of speaking), and civil or political

---

40. In Rodríguez Velasco, "Microbiographies," I analyze a specific case related to female nobility based on Boccaccio's narrative about Filippa da Catania.
41. Rodríguez Velasco, *Plebeyos márgenes*.

nobility, that is, the kind based on the selection by rulers and kings of the best plebeians to join the circle of power around the monarch's central jurisdiction. Diego de Valera does not deny the Jews' civil nobility before their conversion, but he does deny their theological nobility. It is true that upon converting, by recognizing the true faith, they recover theological nobility, but the question is whether they retain civil nobility or not. Valera invokes the principles of *equitas* (which he translates as equality) and of justice to claim that they should not only retain their civil nobility but increase it, to the extent that conversion is an act of heroism or virtue. Justice is an absolute legal value, but *equitas* is a relative one: as Kathy Eden has shown, it arises from the interrelation between ethics and law.[42] Does Valera speak for and about himself? Was he not the son of a converso doctor? Certainly, but speaking for oneself does not mean ceasing to speak for others. The *Espejo* was written at one of the historic peaks in the volume of conversions, while the Trastámara monarchs were painstakingly reorganizing the structures of the nobility and the jurisdictional agreements that connected them to those noble ranks.

It was not Valera who introduced Bartolo's theory of civil nobility into the Castilian tradition: that had been another illustrious converso, Alonso de Cartagena, in his address to the Council of Basel on September 14, 1434. But Cartagena's treatise was not translated into Castilian until many years later, and besides, his intent was not to uphold a different theory of nobility but to show that the king of Castile's civil nobility preceded, historically, that of the king of England; that detail ought to establish the hierarchy of interventions in the sessions of the Council.[43] Valera, in contrast, arrives at Bartolo independently of Cartagena: the latter is interested only in a few short passages from Bartolo's *De dignitatibus*, and he takes them out of context in order to build his defense. Valera reads Bartolo much more extensively, and his reading introduces into Castile something innovative that, in an earlier book, I called "the poetics of the plebeian." The poetics of the plebeian implies an important political contribution: if what matters is not whether or not nobility is inherited, but the deed(s) through which a plebeian becomes noble, then the political issue shifts to the nature

---

42. Eden, "Poetry and Equity," 17–43; Quaglioni, *La giustizia nel medioevo*.
43. See Olivetto, "Política y sermón," 222–31. Olivetto provides details about Cartagena's speeches to the Council, together with the necessary bibliography of old and modern editions.

of the virtuous acts through which a plebian ceases to be one. Therefore nobility is a problem not of the noble classes but of the plebeian experience.[44]

Valera's Name

One may wonder about the value of Valera's name. Or, perhaps, how to use Valera, how to put him into practice. Another way of asking something similar is this: what is the ethics and politics of studying Valera in a crisis as great as the one we now live in? The crisis does not assail us, it has no agency; it arises from actions by specific actors; or, if you prefer, the crisis is a setting of something in motion, an ethics and a politics. Valera is, to begin with, an ethical and political response to the ethics and politics contained in the practical concept of "crisis."

Perhaps this is not the most brilliant of all possible answers, but for that very reason it is also highly interesting. Valera is not Petrarch. Valera is not Lorenzo Valla. Valera is not even Íñigo López de Mendoza, nor Juan de Mena, nor Alfonso de Palencia. His writing style is not sublime in any consistent way, and it often stammers, in a manner of speaking. Part of its worth resides in that stammer: he uses it to break down the resistance that broad swaths of the society of his time, his contemporaries, offered against great changes occurring in narrow social spaces.

Valera skillfully unveils a "politics of invisibility," and reveals through his stammering obvious essential problems: that civil war requires unending pacification; that individual women must be reincorporated into historical and political discourse and everyday ethics; and that if power is to be transformed, the categories that give rise to it must first be transformed themselves, must be reinterpreted in the light of virtue. He is neither the first nor the last to point this out, but Valera does so like a true contemporary: fully committed to the essential issues of a time that exceeds his own lifespan, he acquires enough political subjectivity to distance himself and undertake a critical discourse with the materials that are actually and virtually at his disposal.

---

44. Rodríguez Velasco, *Plebeyos márgenes*. Federica Accorsi devoted part of her work to Bartolo's usages in the *Songe du Verdier*, and the problems of transmission of the text of *De dignitatibus*: Accorsi, "Estudio del *Espejo de verdadera nobleza*." See also Bautista's piece on the invention of Bartolo in Castile: "La idea de nobleza." Breaugh's *L'Expérience plébéienne* is a splendid theoretical point of departure for the critique of the plebeian; but it is, as he promises, a "discontinuous" history that should be questioned and enriched through other contemporary experiences such as Diego de Valera's.

In traditional terms, reading Diego de Valera is not a particularly elevated aesthetic experience. Rather, it is an ethical and political experience. But precisely for that reason, aesthetics should be redefined in ethical and political terms; for Diego de Valera truly operates out of aesthetic principles that seek to make a concrete impact on the consciences, affections, and emotions of the persons he addresses.

Poetry or Activism

The most sublime aesthetic experience is, by definition, poetry. But it is no less true that poetry is one of the avatars of activism and, in that sense, an equally sublime ethical and political experience. Here "sublime" means, as Longinus says, something unforgettable. The most effective of these experiences is the one that remains in memory so as to be sung if there is music or recited in the most intimate of spaces (while walking, while struggling to fall asleep). In the final pages of this chapter, we will speak of an activism that plays out on the fields of theodicy, political theology, and opposition to prevailing administrative structures.

For this purpose, we will examine a poem in short meter (*arte menor*) by the poet and politician Gómez Manrique, titled *Exclamación y Querella de la Governaçión* (Exclamation and lament for governance). We have no way of knowing whether walkers and insomniacs, or his sociopolitical networks in general (which included men and women prominent in public life, like his own wife and the nun-author Teresa de Cartagena) recited those verses to themselves in silence. The quickness of the short lines, the perfect rhymes, the musicality of the verses, plus the combination of keen critique and moralistic aphorisms, might have made them easy to memorize. Who knows. But the surviving manuscripts make clear that the work was generously distributed and received.[45]

---

45. The *Catálogo-índice* by Dutton and Fleming includes sixteen manuscript copies of the poem in fifteen songbooks (GB1-43; MN6a-25; MN23*-55; MN29-3; MP3-67; MP3-135; MP3-137; MR2-11; PN5-27; PN8-73; PN9-23; PN13-9; SA4-2; SA10a-9; SA10b-99); three more copies transmit the poem with glosses by Pero Díaz de Toledo (MN24-130; MP3-136; MN43-2). Sara Russo's MA thesis contains a more detailed count of all the manuscript and printed versions of Gómez Manrique's work: Russo, "Aproximación a la tradición textual." This count is far more complete and exact than the one found in the edition of Gómez Manrique's works by Francisco Vidal González: see Manrique, *Cancionero*. Here I always cite Vidal's edition, for several reasons, but above all because it edits the gloss by Pero Díaz de Toledo.

The poem entered the political and social debate perhaps in 1464, the date proposed by Nicholas Round.[46] The poem was directed to, or found a ready audience in, the circle of Cardinal Alonso Carrillo of Toledo; there it had to face its critics, who responded with their own poems in opposition. Among the responders were the fairly enigmatic Pedro Guillén de Segovia and Antón de Montoro, nicknamed *el Trapero de Córdoba* (the ragman from Cordova).[47] Both of them adopt a style similar to Gómez Manrique's: frankly allusive and without specific details. All of them possess something that we have to a limited degree only: while they could feel the effects of the poem combined with its political circumstances—since they were deeply involved in political life—we lack that sensibility in our own time. But one thing is very clear: if poetry is activism, individuals are, by definition, active life itself. And there is certainly a huge difference between political activism and political activity.

Neither Pedro Guillén de Segovia nor Antón de Montoro cared much more than Gómez Manrique did to offer facts about the political context. Neither of them seemed to be writing for posterity, but rather so as to start a discussion, a debate. What is most certain is that the central topic of that debate was the theological-political governance of Cardinal Alonso Carrillo. But posterity does not care if people wrote for it, for posterity; and it makes its decisions autonomously and sometimes arbitrarily. Therefore, the poems have passed, with greater or lesser brilliance, into the history of literature, which speculates (as philology does) about the circumstances of the texts that form a dynamic part of it.

In relation to this need to learn the possible conditions of texts, an abundance of studies has sought to determine as exactly as possible the dates and circumstances in which a poem was composed. The works by Nancy Marino, Nicholas Round, Eloy Recio Ferreras, and Sara Russo

---

46. Nicholas G. Round establishes a complete biography of Pero Díaz de Toledo, with the dates of his public interventions, in Díaz de Toledo, *Libro llamado Fedron*. For greater detail, see Round's article discussing the date and sociopolitical milieu of the composition of Gómez Manrique's poem: "Gómez Manrique's *Exclamación*," 149–74.

47. For more details, see the works by Russo ("Aproximación a la tradición textual") and Round ("Gómez Manrique's *Exclamación*"), as well as Vidal González's edition (Manrique, *Cancionero*); also the work of our late lamented friend Nancy Marino, "La Relación entre historia y poesía," 211–25. Nancy Marino's intellectual project is based on her outstanding knowledge of *cancionero* poetry and its textual tradition, and on the need to study it in terms that combine historicism with sociology and political practice. See also Recio Ferreras, *Gómez Manrique*.

mentioned in footnotes reconstruct the historical and political context of Gómez Manrique's poem, while advancing different interpretations according to its presumed date.

The poem and its hermeneutics change when we read another response, one that would accompany Manrique's poem during much of its existence in both manuscript and printed form. Unlike the other reactions, this one is intimately joined to Gómez Manrique's poem, engulfing, surrounding, and embracing it so as to lend it meaning. The gloss is by Pero Díaz de Toledo, one of those whom I venture to call public intellectuals in Castile in the first half of the fifteenth century; he was of Gómez Manrique's own generation, scarcely two years older than he, and died at the age of fifty-six in 1466. We know that Pedro Guillén de Segovia, Antón de Montoro, and others who replied to Gómez Manrique in verse were not interested in the context. That is to be expected, perhaps, when poetic concision is a factor. But it is perhaps more striking that the glossator, Pero Díaz de Toledo, does not care about the context either, and never alludes to it in the explanations he sees fit to compose.[48] His gloss on Gómez Manrique's poem is also addressed to Alonso Carrillo, who, obviously, did not need to be put in the picture.[49] But that fact never seems to have discouraged any of the glossators in prose from the Iberian Peninsula, whether Catalan, Portuguese, Navarrese, or Castilian: in their glosses, including those related to contemporary events, they do not hesitate for a moment to mix spiritual readings—allegorical, moral, and transcendental—with readings that touch on current affairs.

Still—"the letter killeth, but the spirit giveth life" (2 Corinthians 3:6). What I want to know in this case is what spiritual reading animates a poem beyond its historical context. In other words, what is Pero Díaz de Toledo's theoretical project, based on his reading of a radically contemporary poem? What is the meaning behind the fact that he avoids commenting on circumstantial details? This seems crucial to me, in an intellectual sphere that not only includes Pero Díaz de Toledo but constitutes a great project for many fifteenth-century intellectuals. Díaz de Toledo himself, the amusing humanist Juan de Lucena, and Bishop Alonso de Cartagena all mention this project: how can philosophy, which lives in an unattainable realm, find a home (*morada*), a chamber

---

48. Manrique, *Cancionero*, 578.
49. See the dedication on p. 577 of Manrique, *Cancionero*.

(*aposento*), or a habitation (*habitación*) in civil life? (These authors deploy all those metaphors, referring to a comment on Plato by Cicero.)[50]

Active Leisure

Díaz de Toledo takes up his pen to write his gloss as a distraction from his work on a book that he calls *Enchiridion*. Contrary to what Francisco Vidal supposes, this *Enchiridion* is neither that of Epictetus nor that of Saint Augustine, but a sort of index and dictionary of legal concepts that is Díaz de Toledo's own; he was writing it between 1464 and 1466, and it is preserved today in a manuscript in the library of the Complutense University in Madrid.[51]

The *Enchiridion* is an important element of Díaz de Toledo's intellectual project. It sets forth in alphabetical order the most important concepts in juridical science, and it offers the references and *allegationes* (proofs of authority) needed for arguing with the concept in question during a legal trial. Like all legal indices it contains an abundance of definitions, together with specific reflections on the oath, the fiduciary questions, the condictio, and so on—all the terms that make up that mass of false friends that is the language of the law. These are terms that do not say what they seem to say to an ordinary speaker, but really mean something technical in a profession that, nonetheless, invades the whole of public and private experience. Besides these concepts there are others that are also sometimes found in indices but in a more limited way: philosophy, fable, fiction, poetry. Díaz de Toledo is interested in how such notions function within the complex relationship formed by culture, law, and social change. For instance, he does not care merely to define poetry but also to know whether one may argue a legal case with quotations from poets—and if so, what the political and social

---

50. See below in the chapter "A Vernacular Society." MSS/6728 of Spain's Biblioteca Nacional transmits some glosses on the *Diálogo de vita beata* by Juan de Lucena; both Jerónimo Miguel and Olga Perotti believe that they are anonymous and not penned by Lucena. Whoever the author might be, the glossator read the translation of, and glosses on, Plato's *Phaedrus* by Pero Díaz de Toledo (*Libro llamado Fedron*). Gloss number 5 on Lucena's text (folio 11) cites almost word for word gloss number 5 by Pero Díaz de Toledo on his translation of Plato, of course without attribution (and with a mistaken reference, since it actually appears in book 5): "Socrates, as Tullius [Cicero] says in the fourth *Tusculana* [*Tusculanae Disputationes*], called philosophy down from heaven and established it in the cities" (Sócrates, según dice Tulio en la cuarta *Tusculana* llamó desde el cielo la filosofía y asentóla en las ciudades): Lucena, *Diálogo sobre la vida feliz*, 166; Lucena, *De vita felici*, 141.

51. It was identified by Herrero Prado ("El *Enchiridión*"): Biblioteca Histórica, Universidad Complutense de Madrid, BH MSS 84.

consequences would be.⁵² In other words, the legal concepts, though they appear in alphabetical order, stand always in a reciprocal relationship to each other.

It therefore becomes necessary to define a "case." In an extensive passage, Díaz de Toledo gives it a series of definitions that gradually reveals how a case, necessarily "in the past" (*de preterito*)—something that has already happened—is nonetheless designed to achieve more stable and universal norms; those norms should create a present or future event that can be treated as a matter of law. A case is therefore an attempt to understand a legal future through knowledge and examination of jurisprudence; it is a future that is past.⁵³ Some of these terms show Díaz de Toledo's concern about how to insert philosophical discussion into the public sphere of the city to ensure that it has a concrete effect on society and politics.

In his *Glosa* on Gómez Manrique's poem, Pero Díaz de Toledo attempts some of these intellectual operations. As a jurist by profession, one interested in developing and understanding the language of the law, he does not fail to notice that Manrique called his poem *exclamación* and *querella*. The former is a rhetorical concept, once defined by Enrique de Villena as "one of the ornaments and colors that embellish rhetorical sayings" (una de las guarniçiones y colores que afermosiguan los retoricales dezires), a first-person discourse in direct style that "can be used where there is reason for sorrow or indignation or amazement" (puédese causar en donde ay razón de dolor ho indignaçión ho maravilla).⁵⁴ The second expression, *querella*, is clearly related to trial law, the equivalent of a suit; so it appears in almost every medieval source, including the *Enchiridion* itself. Díaz de Toledo will concentrate on just such a complaint about governance.

Political Theodicy

Díaz de Toledo does not approach his gloss while considering the context in which the poem was composed. Rather, he asks himself a different question: how a living contemporary poet can contribute, conceptually and ideologically, to a much more universal debate that,

---

52. As I have mentioned, the *Enchiridion* follows an alphabetical order and all the entries to which I refer will be found under the word in question.
53. Koselleck, *Vergangene Zukunft*.
54. Villena, *Traducción y glosas*, 41.

in Díaz de Toledo's opinion, poets and prophets throughout history have held before God. This is the theological and political problem that the seventeenth-century German philosopher Gottfried Wilhelm Leibniz baptized with the name "theodicy" in *De Théodicée: Sur la Bonté de Dieu, la liberté de l'homme et l'origine du mal*, published in French in 1710. The notion did not exist as such in the fifteenth century, but it is useful for understanding Díaz de Toledo's intellectual project—perhaps more so than another that Díaz de Toledo in fact employed but that has lost some of its luster from overuse: divine providence. What is perhaps most interesting about theodicy is its political and legal nature, bearing in mind that Pero Díaz de Toledo will deal with exactly that in his examination of Manrique's poem. According to Leibniz, theodicy as a philosophical discourse for theological-political debate originates in Saint Augustine and his legal arguments in *De Civitate Dei*—an essential work for Díaz de Toledo's argumentation, as we shall soon see. In speaking of "theological-political" I do not equate the terms in the manner of the Nazi political theorist Carl Schmitt, who asserted that political concepts arise from the secularization of theological ones. Rather, I mean the complex and multidirectional relationship that, throughout history, forms of political government have maintained with the emergence of theological notions.

First of all, Díaz de Toledo acknowledges an exception: Gómez Manrique is not only a living poet but an active one, who may produce more poetry in the future. Díaz de Toledo actually hopes to witness how that poetic activity will develop, and includes Manrique in a genealogy of prophets and poets who initiated the debates about theodicy—revealing a political asymmetry in relation to theological concepts of divine justice.[55] This is precisely Augustine's argument about theodicy (according to Leibniz): how is it possible that in civil and political life, on whose stability the lives of citizens depend, God permits tyrannical governments, or bad governance in general?

Díaz de Toledo defines this genealogy with a few strokes. The library to which Manrique refers begins with the legal poetic books of the Bible; it continues with the early Greeks up to Homer, includes a few Latin poets between Virgil and Persius, and then moves to "our Spain" with a list that includes a few deceased poets such as Fernán Pérez de

---

55. Manrique, *Cancionero*, 578.

Guzmán and Íñigo López de Mendoza, finally reaching Gómez Manrique, who both "begins and starts" (*pryncipia e comiença*) and who, "if time allows him to live on and he does so, will overtake those men and show his genius by publishing good and fruitful things."[56]

What can this new living poet contribute to the genealogy of dead poets? All of them were the object of glosses that describe their theological, political, and legal implications, so that they have come to form part of an economy of knowledge connected to transformations in the practices of power.[57] Although they all can be contextualized and interpreted within their immediate chronology, they are also essential for understanding a different temporality of knowledge that, in Augustinian terms, is a knowledge of the present as a machine for constituting events: the bishop of Hippo calls this "the present of present things, the present of past things, the present of future things" (praesens de praesentis, praesens de preteritis, praesens de futuris).[58] This is a temporality that always points toward the contemporary, what produces the presence of what happens in history. Like all the poets of this genealogy, Manrique must be excised from the specific context of the Castilian factions (the centers of action of the civil wars) so as to be connected to a universal project of "prosperity"—a notion of particular interest to Díaz de Toledo.

The story that must be told is the very hypothesis of the poem: there was a time when Rome prospered.[59] What conditions made that prosperity possible? Díaz de Toledo relates the history of Rome's prospering with a slight twist: although the information is found in Livy, Díaz de Toledo decides to tell it through Augustine's interpretation of Livy's

---

56. "nuestra Yspania" (Manrique, *Cancionero*, 581); "sy el tiempo le da logar a continuar e continua, yrá en alcançe a los caualleros nonbrados e publicará su ingenio de buenas e fructuosas cosas" (581–82).

57. See Weiss's catalogues of glossed texts ("Comentarios y glosas vernáculas" and "Vernacular Commentaries and Glosses"), as well as Dutton and Fleming's *Catálogo-índice*, whose volume 7 contains a section devoted to glosses in both poetry and prose.

58. Augustine, *Confessions*, book 10, 20: 230.

59. The first verse of the *Exclamación* reads in different manuscripts "Quando Roma conquistaua" (When Rome was conquering the world) or "Quando Roma prosperaua" (When Rome was at its peak). Most manuscripts show "conquistaua," and it is more likely that Gómez Manrique would have written that originally, even if he might have changed it later. But Pero Díaz de Toledo (writing, remember, in Gómez Manrique's lifetime, and in fact Manrique outlived Díaz de Toledo by many years) prefers, and comments on, the variant "prosperaua." For the distribution of these two readings among the manuscripts, see Russo ("Aproximación a la tradición textual"), and Dutton and Fleming's *Catálogo-índice*.

text. What he narrates is not simply the history of Rome but the history of Rome's conversion, told by one of its converted Christian citizens.[60] That history is a universal achievement, not only one of its own time. Contemporaneity and universality make the literary criticism relevant: it is a way of obtaining theoretical concepts for that triple, permanent Augustinian present, on which his political vision is based (Augustine calls this vision or theory *contuitu*, and also theorizes it in his *Confessions*).

Díaz de Toledo recalls that in this history of Rome's prosperity there is a crucial turning point: the dissolution of the monarchy and its replacement by the consulate and the republic. This is the center of gravity of the republic's master narrative, whose semantics form part of late medieval European political conversations, often beginning with the rape of Lucrece by the last king of Rome, Tarquin the Proud. One text that reinterprets that episode in translating it is by Coluccio Salutati, the chancellor of the Republic of Florence; it was translated into Castilian in the mid-fifteenth century, possibly for the Marquis of Santillana. It is preserved in one of the latter's manuscripts, together with, among other texts, Leonardo Bruni's *De militia* in Castilian.[61]

This master narrative of prosperity contains four elements in addition to the monarchy itself: Rome's local governments (*regimiento*) or transfer of power to the cities, its expansion into Africa, the style of its historians (Livy in particular), and the role of Roman women in the balance of war and peace.

These four elements are equally fundamental to fifteenth-century political theory, although some have not been studied in that context. Díaz de Toledo stresses two of them within a single thesis: that the city's government is not independent of how it is narrated. The pilgrim who visits the city, both physically and intellectually, does so not only to visit its holy sites nor the objects that have been imbued with meaning throughout its history—its relics, so to speak. The pilgrim also needs to encounter the public intellectual, the "man of science" who is

---

60. Díaz de Toledo was also a converso, who attained civil nobility in the course of a long political and legal career. As a nephew of the legal recorder (*relator*) Fernán Díaz de Toledo (né Moshe Hamon), he forms part of an intellectual and sociopolitical history in which conversion is a key to interpreting people's active lives and political positions in the fifteenth century—perhaps especially in the city of Toledo, and particularly after the great uprisings against the Toledan conversos at mid-century. See also Herrero Prado, "Pero Díaz de Toledo," 101–15. The gloss in question is found in Manrique, *Cancionero*, 582–88.

61. Aside from Stephanie Jed's book mentioned above (*Chaste Thinking*), see Morrás, "Coluccio Salutati en España," 209–48.

recording in permanent form the whole history of the city—either in works already published or in those that are still being published as a contemporary contribution to the poetics of the city's politics. Intellectuals are the agents of past times that reveal themselves in the present. It is they who narrate a political biography of the city, with its residents, its governments, and its tyrannies, that elucidates the history of law.

Providence and theodicy serve as conceptual heuristic systems that reveal both the faults of the governors' system of governance and the political life of the governed. In this sense, Díaz de Toledo's discourse about providence and theodicy, inspired by Manrique's poem, is a theoretical device that sees, simultaneously, that power resides everywhere (which is why the monarchy can be questioned) and that such power is asymmetrical: it cannot always be applied with equal force in every case.

But Díaz de Toledo connects his reading to the legal ethics of the biblical Book of Job, which he reads in the light of Saint Augustine and his theory of theodicy.[62] He asserts, with Augustine, that bad governance is part of the divine plan:

> God's providence is not disordered; in ruling and governance it is not fortuitous or casual that idiots should be lords over wise and informed men, and bad men over good ones. For as Saint Augustine says in the fifth book of *The City of God*, in Chapter XIX, the providence of our great God disposes that bad men should have powers and estates, when He judges and determines that the men whom they must conquer and rule deserve such masters.[63]

With this assertion he accepts that government is bad government and that rulers are both stupid and tyrannical; and, furthermore, that the whole populace deserves this kind of government. Divine providence is meted out proportionally: if power derives directly from divine law, and that law is both proportional and retributive, then the people themselves have *chosen* that wicked government through their own acts.

---

62. Manrique, *Cancionero*, 569.
63. "No es desordenada la prouidença de Dios, no es regimiento e gouernaçión fortuito e casual por que los neçios sean señores de los sabios e entendidos e los malos de los buenos, que según dize Sant Agustín en el quinto libro de *La çibdad de Dios*, en el XIX capítulo, estonçes la prouidençia del gran Dios dispone que los malos tengan potestades e señoríos quando juzga e determina que los onbres a quien han de sojuzgar e señorear son dignos de tales señores." Manrique, *Cancionero*, 569. Díaz de Toledo's reference to Augustine's text is exact and precise.

CHAPTER 4

Contemporary observations about this assertion would be so obvious as not to need recording here.[64]

After reaching this conclusion Díaz de Toledo paraphrases Augustine once more; perhaps more surprisingly, he cites through him a passage from the Psalms: "for about this, says Saint Augustine, the voice of God speaks, when He said: 'By me kings reign, and princes decree justice.'"[65] The true political issue is not so much that kings reign, which is what Proverbs 8:15 says and Augustine repeats, but also that it is divine justice that allows tyrants to rule the earth. This notion, which Díaz de Toledo offers as part of the citation of the psalm, is not in fact in the psalm, but is added by Augustine to that chapter of Proverbs.

The proposal in Manrique's poem is connected to his own position as *regidor* (city governor), which he held in Salamanca (1454–57), Burgos (1463), and Toledo (1477–90, the year of his death). As such he was one of the instruments of royal jurisdiction in the kingdom. Through this position he understood the asymmetry of the practices of power between the central and local jurisdictions. Díaz de Toledo is concerned with the universal nature of this problem; to that end, in his gloss, he analyzes the logic behind Manrique's position from the viewpoint of political philosophy.

The intellectual operates as a jurist, and therefore Díaz de Toledo analyzes the political problem as a *casus*, that is, from the standpoint of the possible conditions of a legal ruling. This legal case presents the close relationship between jurisdiction and sovereignty and explains how jurisdiction can be delegated without diminishing sovereignty. Sovereignty as a whole rests on the extensive legal knowledge of those to whom jurisdiction has been delegated:

> The presupposition: when there must be a governor in the communities and the kingdom for the health of the people, because he cannot be present everywhere, it is necessary, according to the laws, that in each place there should be persons who govern the people by his authority; and they should be like the eye of the people, for without them all things will be in confusion, as

---

64. But note that I write this in December 2020, in the United States, at a time of political and institutional crisis equaled only by the health-care crisis we have been living through since March.

65. Manrique, *Cancionero*, 596. The English is from the King James Version. The text of Proverbs 8:15 in the Vulgate reads: "Per me reges regnant, et legum conditores iusta decernunt; per me principes imperant, et potentes decernum iustitiam"; the speaker, referring to herself in the first person, is Sapientia (Wisdom). The Vulgate edition is that of Colunga Cueto and Turrado, *Biblia sacra iuxta Vulgatam*.

Cassiodorus says, and the flourishing and even the existence of the town or city would perish; and they should be expert and wise and learned in law and custom.[66]

The *casus* is part of a strategy for interpreting politics with the language and methods of legal science. In the *casus* the result is obtained by making a specific narrative universal; by eliminating, so to speak, its surrounding context so as to make it part of a philosophical-political analysis. Giles of Rome, in about 1280, had decided that jurists had become "political idiots" (his very words), because they had brought into fashion a technique of argumentation and analysis that was based on narrative rather than dialectic.[67] Of course his diagnosis (actually a complaint) arose from the fact that jurists were having much more public success than experts in political science, thereby gaining superior influence and privileges. Their true weapon was their ability to control the universe of narrative.

Díaz de Toledo is doubtless fighting for the preeminence of legal science and of jurists in political affairs, to the point of invoking, in two different places in his gloss, Aristotle's aporetic treatment in the *Politics* (1281b). Aristotle considers the ethical problems that arise from citizens' collective knowledge and the processes of public participation; he ends by recommending the formation of a senate as a consultative body. Díaz de Toledo does not refute the aporia itself nor its consequences for reorganizing the city, which would imply expanding the public sphere, now limited to the governing elites. Strategically, however, he condenses the discussion into an aphorism: it is better to have good law (that is, a collective regime) than a good king, since the former is more universal than the latter and outlives him. To argue this position, the glossator recalls that the *Partidas* had ended (at least in theory) with the principle "rex a legibus solutus," that is, the monarch is not subject to prevailing laws. This argument was well-known to, and debated by, jurists, but the gloss is not intended for them; rather, it is a public pronouncement within a general debate about politics.

---

66. "Presupuesto este: vn gouerandor que ha de auer en las comunidades e reyno para salud del pueblo, porque este non puede ser presente en todo lugar, fue cosa nesçesaria, según dizen las leyes, que ouiese en cada lugar perssonas que gouernasen los pueblos por actoridad de aqueste; los quales han de ser commo ojo del pueblo, ca syn ellos todas las cosas andarán confusas, segun dize Casyodoro e el trihunfo e avn estado de la villa o çibdad peresçería; los quales han de ser expertos e sabios e entendidos en la ley e costunbre." Manrique, *Cancionero*, 601.

67. Rodríguez Velasco, "Political Idiots," 86–112.

Díaz de Toledo's reading is not simply an interpretation of Manrique's poem. It also demonstrates that contemporary poetry is none other than theory: that is, a type of vision (Greek θεωρέω, or Augustine's *contuitu*), an epistemological device for giving shape to political science and social practice. Poetry is a heuristic system for finding the expressions and stylistic elements that, linked to particular events or problems, reach far beyond them, resulting in the genealogy of a certain profoundly political and theological complaint.

Paradigms of Activism

In the dyad of Diego de Valera and Pero Díaz de Toledo we see deeply the anxiety of individuals who belong wholly to the structures of power, where their voices are heard; but who, in some sense, place themselves in a series of marginal spaces that allow them to contrast their organic position with a critical voice. This position is not only that of their own urban, bourgeois, and converso lineage, but also their physical position in relation to the texts that occupy the center of the doctrinal and cultural canon of contemporary politics. These are the paradigms of intellectual activism in fifteenth-century Castile, and it is hard to view them from a radical perspective. But in the end, radicalism is not independent of its context.

Nicholas Round, in his study of Pero Díaz de Toledo's gloss on the *Exclamación*, maintains that the glossator takes a moderate position. I am wholly in agreement with this point of view. Menéndez Pelayo, who lived a long time ago in a different context of Spanish culture, said that Diego de Valera was a mixture of an arbitrator and an opposition journalist.[68] And I agree with this also. In all this activist movement there is a peculiar mixture of moderation, conciliation through a series of rhetorical processes, and opposition journalism, that is, a certain ability to document specific information about a political event so as to make it obvious and combat it. At a time when leaders lack empathy, try to divide the space of civil cooperation, and tend toward authoritarianism, it seems that the effort to organize responses that are moderate, conciliatory, and opposed to movements of power can be called by only one name: radical activism.

---

68. Menéndez Pelayo, *Antología de poetas líricos*, 220. Penna (*Prosistas españoles del siglo XV*, xcix) transmitted a similar viewpoint.

CHAPTER 5

Assemblage, Subject

An *impossibilium* was a logical demonstration of something impossible and the Brabantian philosopher Siger was a master of that genre. Once, he defended six impossible things in front of the students and professors of the University of Paris. In the third of these he proposed that the Trojan War is happening right now ("Proponebatur tertio quod bellum troianum esset in hoc instanti").[1] That is, of course impossible, in the time measured by my watch; even to propose it is a provocation. But it is possible in the very instant of saying it and when saying it is a repetition. We are never so close to history as at the moment when we repeat it, trying to narrate it anew. In fact, it doesn't matter if we recount the facts as they really happened, or if we choose the more philosophical path (according to Aristotle) and narrate everything as it might have happened.[2] This more philosophical approach makes "what could have been" present and allows us to

---

1. The manuscripts containing Siger of Brabant's *Impossibilia* start with the sophist (Siger) proposing to demonstrate and defend many impossible things in front of the most learned members of the Parisian university ("Convocatis sapientibus studii Parisiensis proposuit sophista quidam impossibilia multa probare et defendere"); Siger de Brabant, *Écrits de logique*, 67. The third *impossibilium* reads: "Quod bellum troianum esset in hoc instant" (that the Trojan War is happening right now), 77–79.
2. Aristotle, *Poetics*, 1451b.

examine it close up. That closeness is a very strange kind of time that we sometimes call history. The Trojan War is happening right now because we need it to be active, to be present, to be synchronized with the questions and problems that assail us. In her novel (at least, the phrase "a novel" appears on the cover just below the title) *How to Be Both*, Ali Smith narrates a conversation between George and his mother about the action of history. The mother asks, "Do things just go away?... Do things that happened not exist, or stop existing, just because we can't see them happening in front of us?"[3] Writing in the humanities is a way of seeing before our very eyes those things we cannot see.

In the following pages we will explore the experiences and risks of a particular medieval author, the Portuguese prince Pedro of Aviz, who wrote down the things we cannot see in order to make them visible. He thought that the best way of exploring those experiences and risks was the creative task of constructing a manuscript book. His work is not extensive, but three of his compositions, completed in his youth (in any case he died young, at thirty-six or thirty-seven) reveal different experiments in relating the master text to the gloss or marginal comment.[4] We will now examine two of his manuscripts with their glosses.

In studying these glossed manuscripts I am not much concerned with their sources and I will not try to relate them to the intellectual movements that contribute to a master narrative about Western culture, such as vernacular humanism.[5] Other scholars have already done this in masterly fashion.[6] I prefer to dwell on the experience of reading these glossed manuscripts, on the poetics of reading them. The experience and poetics in question consist of the montage and assemblage of the elements that make up the manuscript, as a complex texture. Beyond the achievement of the literary work, this experience crosses barriers of time, space, and language as well as disciplinary boundaries. My first thesis in this regard is that what we normally call the "material text," that is, the complicated confluence and collaboration between

---

3. Smith, *How to Be Both*, 104.

4. For a recent biography of Pedro of Aviz, see Pedro de Portugal, *Sátira de Infelice e Felice vida*.

5. Weiss, "Comentarios y glosas vernáculas," 199–245; "Vernacular Commentaries and Glosses," 237–71.

6. See, for example, the works by Jeremy Lawrance ("On Fifteenth-Century Spanish Vernacular Humanism"; "Humanism in the Iberian Peninsula"), Ottavio di Camillo (*El humanismo castellano*), María Morrás ("Coluccio Salutati en España"), and Guido Cappelli (*El humanismo italiano*).

the written text and the writing materials, should be thought of as artifact, something constructed in order to establish a certain vision, like an epistemological device—an eye, an I.

This chapter speaks about the assemblage of the subject, which is one form of the poetics of subjectivity. I believe that one of the most illuminating moments of activism and social justice occurs when we can observe the process of constructing a subject. This construction requires recognizing a knowledge and a thought, a time, a history, that supersede those forms of codified knowledge that cluster around the subject like a heavy encyclopedia. It is our responsibility to recognize the moment of illumination in which someone offers a narrative about him- or herself, and which emerges from this code of knowledge. It is our responsibility to embark on this transhistorical conversation and to accept as a valid interlocutor one who has taken on the heavy emotional and physical labor of displaying the poetics of his subjectivity before our eyes. This narrative surrounding the "I," in order to be heard, requires us to recognize the subject who is speaking, and to establish a close relationship with this subject.[7]

Pedro's manuscripts are epistemological artifacts that tend toward the construction of this subject, whose experiences and risks belong to him and constitute a philosophical way of interpreting or narrating events in the world. The best way to study this epistemological device is to try to activate it. Ultimately, my research not only tries to explain how things were in the past, but also questions how we can reactivate the past productively, so as to make it relevant to contemporary debates. Deactivating the past, eliminating the possibility of drawing near to historical activities, undermines the efforts of the humanities and critical thinking.

My aim, therefore, is not to read these glossed manuscripts as the chance result of a given tradition of known sources. It is important to recognize that tradition, but more essential to study these manuscripts as an experience, a process, sharing in the sense of innovation that their authors and artisans felt and expressed when they designed their material texts.

I would like to refocus the meaning that I give to the word "experience," as I use it when saying "experience of reading" or "experience of

---

7. Butler, *Giving an Account of Oneself*; Cavarero, *Tu che mi guardi*. These two works are central to reconfiguring politically what is involved in exercising subjectivity: it is not enough to illuminate the emergence of the subject; more important is ethical recognition, and projecting that recognition into the political arena.

writing." I would like to stress the notion of experience as a risk, a form of testing everything, in which writer and reader explore the limits of possibility in the activity they are engaged in. In this sense, though outside the theoretical purview of Georges Bataille, I will reuse some of his ideas, in particular his perception that an experience is a journey that one may make or not; but if one does, it must be done while calling into question the very concept of authority and the expectations for this journey in particular.[8] As I have noted, the experience I am interested in is the construction of the subject. This is an experience at the limits of authority, and a reconfiguration of the ways in which history can be narrated.

This private experience, that of Pedro of Avis or other glossers, has sometimes been considered a failure, simply because it did not result in any empirically verifiable changes in direction; we could also say that their epistemological project was not even understood. For Marina Brownlee the failure is even greater, to the degree that the different epistemological strategies displayed by someone like Pedro seem unable to solve the *psychology* of the figure called the author, whose life Pedro himself expresses through his narratives and lyrical descriptions.[9] I reject this idea of failure categorically. It may be unfortunate that the epistemological strategies were not understood; and perhaps we can acknowledge that a character cannot be cured of anything, since characters exist to demonstrate an ethics and a politics and submit them to interpretation, but not to provide a solution. Pedro and the other glossers, from the most radical to the most traditional, managed to create the terms with which to relate their experience, one of whose risks, which they pushed to the maximum, was not to be understood. And they were not; so much the worse for us. But that does not mean that they need to remain misunderstood forever, or that we should not try to understand them. The humanities and their activities are not simple, but they require a constant effort of critical thinking.

What Genealogy?

Do all glossers belong to the same genealogy? Does each glosser create his or her own genealogy in the art and practice of the gloss? To approach these questions, we must explore the problem of novelty in

---

8. Bataille, *L'Expérience intérieure*.
9. Brownlee, *The Severed Word*, 126.

the glossing experience: many of the authors who interest me here were convinced that they were doing something completely new and were not copying any tradition. Sometimes they thought that they were breaking the rules of traditional commentary.

In glossing his own literary work, Pedro built a complex piece of cultural engineering in which the central text and the marginal gloss combined into something that seemed radically new. We could deny, minimize, or simplify that notion, but that would mean rejecting the recognition being sought by someone who is speaking for himself. In the prologue to his *Sátira de Infelice e Felice vida*, Pedro argues that ancient authors were not in the habit of glossing their own works.[10] It is true that ancient authors did not gloss themselves, that we know of; but in Pedro's own generation the great Cordovan poet Juan de Mena had already published his autoexegetical *Coronación*, and Christine de Pizan had done the same in works such as the *Epistre Othéa*.[11] Pedro, who was of Burgundian ancestry, knew the French traditions; it is not likely that he was unaware of Christine de Pizan's oeuvre in particular, although the silence that surrounds her in the Iberian Peninsula is puzzling. Long before this, Dante had written an allegorical commentary on his own poetry in *Il convivio*, which was partially known at least in Castile, through the commentators and translators of the Perugian jurist Bartolo da Sassoferrato.[12] But the issue is not whether Pedro was

---

10. "Fize glosas al texto ahun que no sea acostumbrado por los antigos auctores glosar sus obras": fol. 4r, p. 76. I cite the manuscript of the Biblioteca Nacional, Madrid, MSS/4023. I have been unable to see the other manuscript, which is in a private collection in Catalonia. I also give the page numbers of the Guillermo Serés edition, although some of my own readings differ.

11. However, it would be hard to understand the *Sátira* without the *Coronación*, to which it owes huge doses of inspiration that include narrative resources, metaphors, and ways of interpreting. For recent critical editions, see Kerkhof's edition of Mena, *La coronación*, and Parussa's edition of Pizan, *Epistre Othéa*; both give no more than a faint impression of the respective works. Christine de Pizan's *Othéa*, in particular, is a highly sophisticated work in which the epistemological device has been explored and extended to its limits by including different levels of autogloss together with images for thought and meditation. It has been studied from the viewpoint of montage (one that I will use in this chapter also, though in a different sense) by Desmond and Sheingorn, *Myth, Montage, and Visuality*. This study also offers a rough idea of the complexity of the manuscript traditions. See also Mombello's classic essay, *La tradizione manoscritta*.

12. Dante, *Il convivio*. Bartolo da Sassoferrato, in his treatise *De dignitatibus*, commented at length on Dante's ideas about the nobility in the *convivio*. Bartolo was widely read and cited in Spain, thanks in part to his inclusion in Alfonso de Cartagena's addresses to the Council of Basel in 1431. See Cartagena, *Discurso sobre la precedencia*. Bartolo's treatise was discussed by other authors, including Diego de Valera in *Espejo de verdadera nobleza*, Juan Rodríguez del Padrón in *Cadira del honor*, and Ferrán Mexía in *Nobiliario vero*. See Rodríguez Velasco, *El debate*.

right or not. The issue is that his activity as a glosser and a creator of the manuscript artifact seemed new and innovative to *him*, and that he acted accordingly, suggesting to his readers that their experience of reading would also be novel.¹³

Argos Panoptos

Pedro's innovation surpasses that of all other authors of his generation because of the detailed planning that his works required. In this sense, his *Sátira de Infelice e Felice vida* is perhaps an astonishing achievement of radical literary art. The *Sátira* forms the central text, which "tells and relates" the "passionate life" of the first-person subject. The same manuscript contains both the *Sátira* and, at the same time, another work with a different title, *Argos*. The two are intimately intertwined, each with its own literary being. They coexist in a single space, assembled in a manuscript that shows all the complexity of its poetic and intellectual artifice. Argos is the name of the hundred-eyed giant whom Hermes hypnotizes and kills. Argos was once "a real man," to whom "the poets gave a hundred eyes . . . which they ordered that while some slept, the others must keep watch."¹⁴ His task, then, is to oversee the things that a given culture considers most valuable. It is precisely this unsleeping vigilance that, according to Pedro of Aviz (who cites his sources), makes him intolerable to the gods—especially to Jupiter, since Argos, under orders from Juno, is protecting the nymphs like Io whom the thunder god tries to seduce. After the rape of Io and her metamorphosis into a heifer, Jupiter realizes that he cannot conceal his deed because Argos has witnessed it. Argos's death, planned by Jupiter, falls to Mercury, and Juno, aware that she is now powerless, "desiring that so much beauty might not perish, placed the hundred eyes of Argos on the tail of the peacock, the bird sacred to her, as an ornament forever."¹⁵ Those watchful eyes now become the adornment of and witness to this story.

---

13. The perpetual anxiety about novelty is the object of Ingham's book *The Medieval New*. It offers an ethical perspective on discussions of novelty, in a cultural system in which, even though the idea of preservation dominated, it was manifested through innovation and investigation.

14. "cien ojos le dieron los poetas . . . a los cuales tal orden dieron que, unos dormiendo, otros velasen." All quotations are from the Guillermo Serés edition: Pedro de Portugal, *Sátira de Infelice e Felice vida*, 77–79.

15. "queriendo que tanta beldad non peresciese, los cien ojos de Argos en la cola del pavón, ave a ella consagrada, por perpetua apostura asentó." Pedro de Portugal, *Sátira de Infelice e Felice vida*, 79.

ASSEMBLAGE, SUBJECT

Pedro continues: "In each part of Ovid's tale [he means *Metamorphoses* I, vv. 624–746] there are different poetic integuments not worth pursuing here, but we can understand that Argos stands for prudence; Mercury, for the senses; and the sweet song of the syrinx [with which Mercury lulled Argos to sleep] for the pleasant blandishments that induce the sleep of everlasting death."[16]

The technique of commentary that Pedro attempts consists not of adding interpretations, but of rejecting possible exegeses if they do not fit a particular ethics, perhaps a politics. The "poetic integuments"— that is, the creative activity that surrounds and envelops the deeper meaning—appear to the reader as so many occasions for commentary; it is hard to resist their pull, so as to choose only what is necessary. In this case Pedro concentrates on those hundred eyes that watched over Io and tried to protect her:

> And because they assigned one hundred eyes to this Argos, as we have said, the author wished to call the resulting little work "Argos." For just as the man had a hundred eyes, the work contains a hundred glosses; and just as the physical eye enlightens and guides the body, so the gloss on the text does likewise, removing the readers' doubts. And just as the eye gives, brings, and causes joy and happiness, so does the gloss gladden, resolving what is obscure and revealing what is hidden. And if among the glosses one finds that some are lengthy and others brief, it was convenient to make it so, because in that earlier narrative pious Juno, moved by compassion, transformed the head of the dead Argos into the beauteous peacock's tail, which has many large and small eyes. From which we presume that that shepherd [Argos] had eyes not all alike, but diverse and different; and therefore the author, imitating that, set out on his path and continued his journey in a similar manner.[17]

---

16. "En cada parte de la ovidiana estoria son diversos integumentos poéticos non dignos aquí de proseguir, mas por Argos la prudencia entender se puede; por Mercurio, los sentidos; por el canto e dulzura del instrumento siringa, los falagueros delectes inducientes el sueño de la perpetua muerte." Pedro de Portugal, *Sátira de Infelice e Felice vida*, 79.

17. "E porque a este Argos cien ojos atribuyeron, como dicho es, quiso el autor llamar a la subsecuente obreta Argos. Ca así como aquel cien ojos tenía, así aquella cien glosas contiene; e así como el ojo corpóreo al cuerpo alumbra e guía, así la glosa al testo por semblante manera face, quitando dudas a los leyentes. E así como el ojo da, trae e causa gozo e alegría, así la glosa alegra, satisfaciendo a lo obscuro e declarando lo oculto. E si de las glosas algunas grandes e otras pequeñas se fallarán, así fue convenible de se facer, porque en la narración precedente dice la piadosa Juno, de compasión movida, la cabeça de Argos muerto transmutar

So ends the third gloss in the book. In it, obviously, Pedro explains the theory behind the practice he plans to employ. That practice is ruled by the desire to know, the pleasure and diversity of viewpoints and lengths that arise from each gloss as a function of its extent. The hundred eyes of Argos undergo a new metamorphosis, turned into a hundred glosses that oversee the whole of the text. Like Argos's hundred eyes, the hundred glosses carefully curated throughout the manuscript also impose different rhythms of reading and thought, different rhythms of theorizing. And of course, there are actually a hundred and five glosses.

Pleasure and Profit

In the first installment of his "Marginalia," published in the *Democratic Review*, Edgar Allan Poe wrote: "All this may be whim; it may be not only a very hackneyed, but a very idle practice;—yet I persist in it still; and it affords me pleasure; which is profit, in despite of Mr. Bentham with Mr. Mill on his back."[18]

Poe writes in the margins of his books because that brings him pleasure, the same pleasure that Pedro of Aviz expresses in his own gloss. Marginal writing is a tremendous source of pleasure. Poe does not elaborate on his feelings about the joys of marginal writing, even though they have been a component of that writing from Chaucer and Pedro of Aviz up to our own day. Pleasure is a positive good in Poe's eyes, something that he achieves and equates with an economic benefit, a profit, an interest payment, or perhaps a surplus (he doesn't explain which) that arises from writing these marginal notes; no one has requested them, they are merely a whim. Pleasure and profit are synonymous in spite of Jeremy Bentham, who leans on the economic guidance of John Stuart Mill. Those two men are not named simply to *épater le bourgeois*: through the pages of the *Democratic Review* Poe is citing the founders of modern liberal thought, the intellectual idols of the liberal philosophy in political economy. Poe adds something polemical to the liberal and anti-statist mindset of the readers of the *Democratic Review*: perhaps Bentham, and certainly John Stuart Mill,

---

en la fermosa cola de pavón, la cual muchos ojos grandes e pequeños posee. De lo cual es de presuponer el mencionado pastor no iguales ojos, mas diversos e dispares obtener; e por ende el auctor, imitando a aquello, por la semblante orden començó su camino e siguió su viaje." Pedro de Portugal, *Sátira de Infelice e Felice vida*, 79.

18. Poe, "Marginalia," 484.

are the chief examples of liberal thought and the individual's liberty vis-à-vis the state. But what they have not been able to scrub from the face of culture is that liberty, the individual, the liberal subject, seeks not only material gain but also another type of benefit, which is pleasure. In this sense, marginal notations are one of the bases of a political economy of pleasure. Poe invests in this marginal note because it earns him that profit or benefit.

Each one of the glosses is an investment in pleasure. It is the same with Pedro of Aviz, even though he doesn't translate that feeling with the vocabulary of political economy. In his case, the interest payment or surplus consists of knowledge and clarity, which are among the values of the humanities. Argos, with his hundred eyes that are a hundred glosses, administers that pleasure; every form of administration is also a kind of watchfulness. Argos, known in mythology as the Panoptos (the all-seer), is in charge of watching, but in Pedro's work he does it with a hundred glosses—a few more than a hundred. Bentham enters into our analysis once more, this time with his panopticon: a design for watching in which everything that happens is seen at once by the security forces, who are not seen themselves because they occupy the central "inspection house."

Pedro's Argos is also a panoptical system but, so to speak, in reverse. The population subject to oversight is Pedro himself with his passions, moods, and emotions, as they happen in the middle of the page. It is sorrow, unhappiness, sometimes happiness, depression, change of life, love, distance, a new language, the struggles and whims of a man barely out of adolescence (for Pedro wrote the *Sátira* before he turned twenty), all of it under scrutiny.[19] There is only one resident, in the center of the page. The highly visible inspection house consists of fragments of a cultural system that subjects to reason and narrative, and to understanding, the sufferings of the subject who is constructed as such and who speaks from inside the page.

The Silence of the Margins

The count of the glosses imposes a rhythm of reading. Every so often, 105 times, the reader's eye must leave the center in order to move to the margins of the page, and then return. This rhythm breaks deliberately

---

19. See an approach to Pedro's biography in the introduction to Guillermo Serés's edition: Pedro de Portugal, *Sátira de Infelice e Felice vida*.

with linear reading, with a genealogy of reading in which the landing lights that mark the locations of ideas are inside the text in the form of different signs, examples of punctuation art (periods, commas, paragraph signs) or of a way of organizing the book's interior (different colored inks for the initials or the paragraph marks). Along with these punctuation marks in the center, others (asterisks, daggers, letters) force the reader's eye toward the edges.

Among the markers of the rhythm of reading, the most visible is the horizon of expectations aroused by the construction of the manuscript. The people who prepare the quires for the volume know that they must lay out the page to accommodate the glosses. They know roughly how much space the text will occupy, and also where the glosses will be written on each page. They know the number of lines for each page. With these variables—among the skills of their craft—they score each page before the scribes begin to write.

Rhythms of reading do not apply only to texts, but also to the material nature of the manuscript itself: since the number of glosses is exact (one gloss per eye), even though the manuscript is prepared for more glosses, the only possibility available to the reader of the codex is to respect the silence of the margins.

This silence is relevant to the genealogy of the gloss I am studying here. Medievalists such as John Dagenais, Michael Agnew, and Sol Miguel-Prendes have argued that glossing is an activity that presupposes an *aliquid minus*, or something missing in the central text, implying a lack.[20] In the radical art of authors like Pedro and others, however, the count of glosses, like the length of the central text, has been established as part of the art of composition, and no one can really add anything without altering the complex equilibrium within the material text. Here, the silence of the margins presents a challenge: it offers potential readers a manuscript prepared to receive glosses, while it blocks those readers from completing or complementing it with new marginal comments.

Each of Argos's eyes represents a different way of seeing the passionate life of the self, which is expressed not only in the center of the *Sátira* but also encounters the characters and concepts that are invoked in each gloss. "Eye" and "I" are joined here as a theoretical device.[21]

---

20. Dagenais, *The Ethics of Reading*; Miguel-Prendes, *El espejo y el piélago*; Agnew, "The 'Comedieta,'" 298–317.

21. In ancient Greek, *theorein* meant "to observe" or "to spend time looking at something" (from θέα, "looking, sight" and ὁράω, "to look or see").

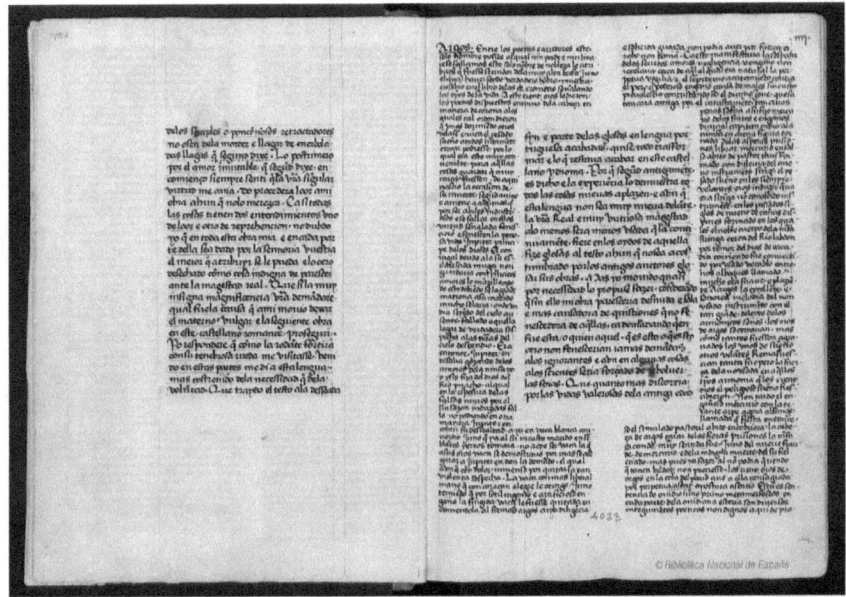

FIGURE 5.1. Pedro de Portugal, *Sátira de Infelice e Felice vida*, MSS/4023, fol. 3v–4r. Images from the collections of the Biblioteca Nacional de España, licensed under a Creative Commons CC-BY license.

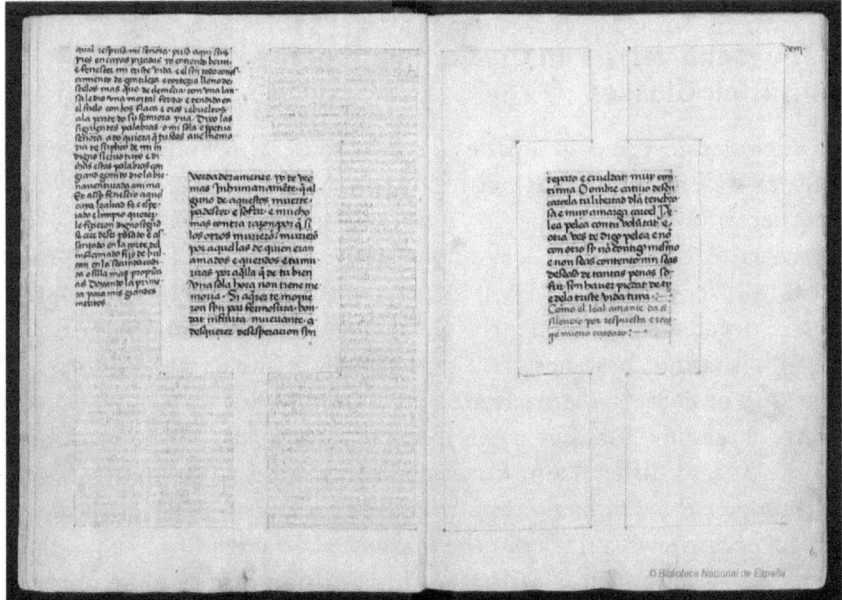

FIGURE 5.2. Pedro de Portugal, *Sátira de Infelice e Felice vida*, MSS/4023, fol. 10v–11r. Images from the collections of the Biblioteca Nacional de España, licensed under a Creative Commons CC-BY license.

148   CHAPTER 5

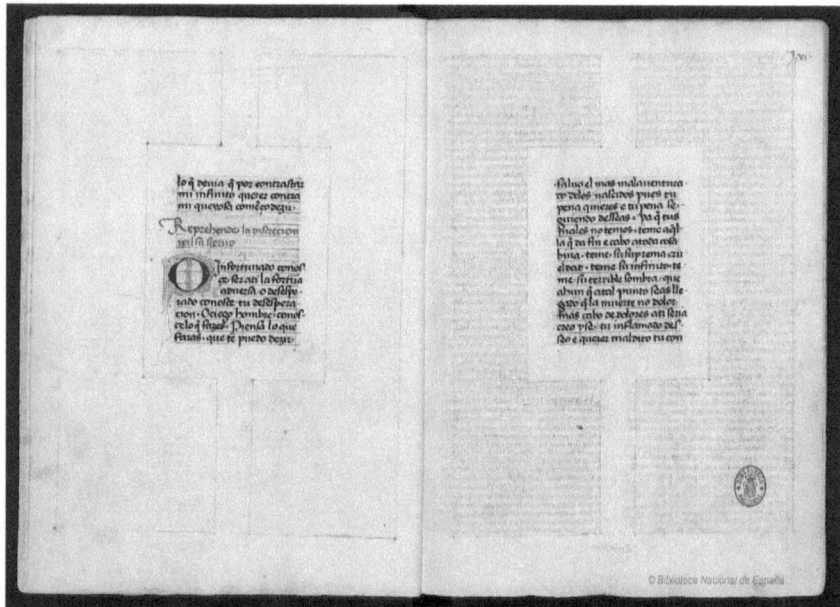

FIGURE 5.3. Pedro de Portugal, *Sátira de Infelice e Felice vida*, MSS/4023, fol. 12v–13r. Images from the collections of the Biblioteca Nacional de España, licensed under a Creative Commons CC-BY license.

A Thousand Verses on the Contempt of the World, with Their Glosses

To demonstrate the complexities faced by some who wrote on the margins, as well as the radical nature of their solutions, we can consider another work by Pedro, the *Coplas de contempto del mundo*. These *Coplas* allow us to develop a theory about new techniques of reading that I will call "serial reading." I will focus on just one narrative series in the *Coplas*, devoted to Alexander the Great. I will then explain the difficulties of situating these narrative series in the manuscript by analyzing one folio of Pedro's manuscript of the *Coplas*.

Serial reading does not mean reading at intervals, or one section at a time. It also differs from florilegia, a form of reading that seeks to anthologize the text being read: this technique is often visible because a reader has drawn a flower in the margin.[22] Serial reading is a possible response to an author's attitude. This attitude implies developing a

---

22. For an overview and analysis of this type of reading, see Dagenais, *The Ethics of Reading*. Marks made for an anthology or for extracting content include not only flowers (hence the

series of narratives and concepts in a fragmented way. Those fragments are later assembled in turn, and placed throughout the manuscript according to a narrative logic different from the internal logic that the original fragments might have had. This assemblage requires the reader to connect the fragments by traveling back and forth inside the labyrinth of the work and its structure—or to refuse to do so. While the epistemological device that I call "assemblage" is ever-present, serial readings are optional or possible but not required; they might even go unnoticed.

A single work, like any of the glossed works by Pedro of Aviz, Juan de Mena's *Coronación del Marqués de Santillana*, or Christine de Pizan's *Epistre Othéa*, can contain many narrative series. The multiplicity of series always includes the entire work and requires active reading in several dimensions at the same time, in which the reader exercises his memory and capacity to locate a given reading in its proper space. One's hands have their own memory, which has to be employed to the full in an active serial reading. Not every reader feels impelled by this need, but it exists within the structure of the work itself. From a cognitive standpoint it can prove extraordinarily complex, forming a challenge to the linearity of both reading and writing. Pedro's *Coplas de contemptu mundi*, our focus of attention here, displays the interaction of three series of intelligibility assembled within the codex: verses, rubrics, and glosses. This final series is divided into two parts since there are two different types of glosses.

The first series consists of a thousand verses of the poem. Unlike in the *Sátira* with its hundred glosses modeled on the hundred eyes of Argos, no explanation of the number is given here. In some sense, a series of a thousand verses is a complete series, probably linked to a millennial representation and calculation of history. A thousand, after all, is the largest number in the mathematics of the time: the concept of "million" does not yet exist in the early fifteenth century (although the word *millón* does), and the concept of "count" (*cuento*), sometimes applied to the *millón*, is unspecific. Here one thousand means the upper limit, the most. As in the *Thousand and One Nights*, it is the number that moves the narrative beyond, the one that breaks through the boundaries of history, the *plus ultra* (further beyond). The thousand verses of Pedro's poem condense the whole breadth of the concepts that express

---

Greek term ἀνθολογίᾱ) but other specific drawings (for example, a hand) or abstract marks (lines, dots, et cetera).

contempt for the world. A totality. Throughout these lines Pedro recounts the entire history of the world in terms that are historical as well as fictional or poetical. For this very reason it is a more philosophical system of narrative.

The second series is a counterpoint to the millennial calculation—the series that consists of the rubrics that order the text of the manuscript. These rubrics were inserted by Pedro and not by the scribes. They express the intellectual operations that govern the reading of the verses and announce whether there are other strophes that operate in the same way. Examples of these conventional rubrics are "aquí ejemplifica" (here is an example), "esto es una continuación" (this is a continuation), "aquí aplica (una comparación)" (here we apply a comparison), and so on. Other strophes seem independent of this pattern of repetition: the poem moves forward with announcements of how exactly to read certain strophes, for example, "concerning delights" (acerca de las delicias) and "concerning bad kings" (sobre los reyes malos). Traditional scholarship points out, very reasonably, that these rubrics help the reader to navigate the book and identify its basic themes: it is easy to see how a rubric like "on commendable generosity" (sobre la loable liberalidad) can achieve that. It may be harder to perceive that when different strophes throughout the book share a recurring rubric such as "aquí ejemplifica y procede," which is different from the ones that simply "exemplify" but do not "proceed," or the one in which the text "proceeds" but does not exemplify. Likewise, other recurring rubrics establish a typology of public interventions such as offering advice, invoking, adding something new, exhorting, applying, comparing, demonstrating, defining, et cetera. In such cases the phrase "navigating through the book" is an unsatisfactory way of explaining the effect of those rubrics on the whole literary process: once the reader accepts one of the conventional rubrics, a subsequent one will recall the first, creating a dynamic of comprehending the book that is more complex than the traditional concepts of *dispositio* (disposition) and *ordinatio* (ordering). Besides, these rubrics also point to the different operations that may be performed in the book, in the experience of writing as well as that of reading. In a certain sense, these possible operations are the terms of a contract about how to read the different layers of reasoning, comprehension, and emotion that have been placed on the page.

A third series is made up of two different types of glosses. Of the 119 glosses that the text contains, sixteen are Latin verses that appear in Castilian translation at the corresponding strophe. In this case the gloss precedes the center, so that the center is actually a translation of the margin. This arrangement imposes a type of serial reading that interrupts the linear reading, requiring a pause for thought. Since the verses are identified as biblical, they form part of a library that has its own rules for reading and thought, which do not exclude either prayer or singing.[23]

The second type of gloss in this third series is the one that interests me the most. It consists of 103 longer and more theoretical glosses. These constitute alternative ways of relating certain canonical historical narratives that were very familiar in the history of Western humanism. Each of them is especially relevant for the presence that occupies the whole epistemological space of these *Coplas*: the poetic "I," which is often confused deliberately with the author.[24]

Margins for Alexander

Aside from this superstructure of intelligibility, one can read serially within the series of longer glosses. I will comment only on the set of seven glosses in which Alexander the Great inspires the writing of the gloss, even if he is not always its chief protagonist. Alexander's presence generates an interaction with other series of glosses, requiring a participant who can read multidimensionally, in what I have called the strabismic order of the glossed page.

The prominence of the series on Alexander is hardly surprising, given the role played by Alexander narratives in medieval history and political theory, as well as in legal thought. It is also manifest in Pedro's prologue to his *Coplas*, perhaps in more precise terms. In the prologue Pedro dedicates the work to his sovereign and brother-in-law, Afonso V of Portugal, who had already named him a commander of the Order of Aviz. Pedro protests that the reader may be incapable of understanding the king's powerful personality, whose qualities are all equally praiseworthy and comparable to those of history's most famous men: "Afonso's counsel is as wise as Cato's, his greatness as notable as Alexander's." A cliché is a cliché, but some clichés can also generate movement, and this one sets in motion a series of glosses

---

23. See Boynton and Reilly, *The Practice of the Bible*; Nelson and Kempf, *Reading the Bible*.
24. The participation of the "I" can be read in the light of the notion of "autography" proposed by Spearing, *Medieval Autographies*.

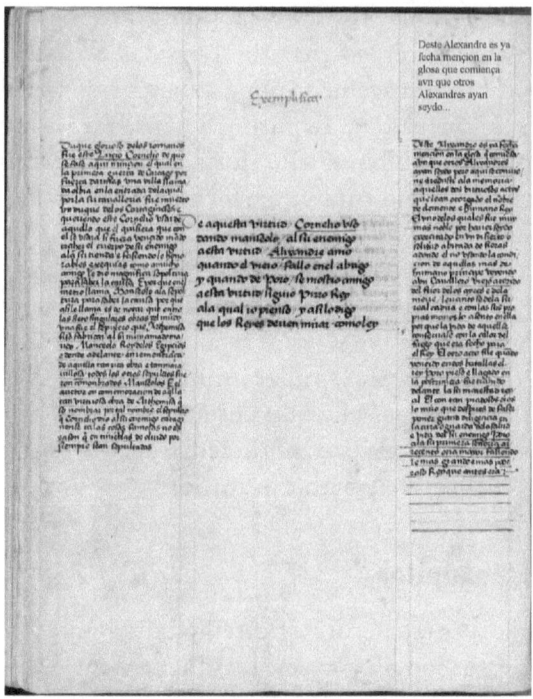

FIGURE 5.4. Pedro de Portugal, *Coplas de contemptu mundi*, MSS/3694, fol. 54v. Image from the collections of the Biblioteca Nacional de España, licensed under a Creative Commons CC-BY license.

about Alexander that make him relevant to the future relationship between Pedro and Afonso.[25]

This series of Alexandrine glosses is a reply to a basic question: why would it be better to tell a story in a linear way if, by fragmenting it and subjecting it to the unpredictable rhythms of a narrative series, we can achieve different effects, different hermeneutic outcomes, focusing on elements that could be lost or obscured in a linear narration? While linear narration allows for perspective (shaping a group of different voices), serial narration and assemblage allow perspectivism, that is, multiple and shifting perspectives that interact with each other in a polemical way.

---

25. All references to the *Coplas* are from the manuscript of the Biblioteca Nacional de España, MSS/3694, fols. 1r–4r. Note that all this makes sense only during the process of political reconciliation between Afonso of Portugal and Pedro, beginning in 1454.

The serial narrative of the neurotic emperor par excellence allows the subject himself to be fragmented. It literally permits him to be analyzed, separating his heroic life from his character, which is insecure (he is not even sure of his own identity within his lineage), sometimes choleric. It makes it possible to stress those aspects that call into question the creation of a subject beyond the master narrative transmitted by historians (in particular Plutarch's parallel life, and above all the work of Quintus Curtius Rufus).[26]

In most of the seven glosses distributed evenly throughout the volume, Alexander plays a secondary role; but this position makes his presence a convenient platform for theoretical observations. At one point the glosser tells the story of Darius.[27] This gloss does not come directly from the central text but is assembled on the basis of another gloss devoted to Polycrates, and both are offered as examples of the Wheel of Fortune. The rubric *ejemplo* (example) or *ejemplificación* (exemplification) is one of the intellectual operations encouraged by the order of discourse suggested in the manuscript, and here the universal "example" of the Wheel of Fortune is particularly well "exemplified" in these *casus*. In Latin, *casus* means not only a specific case with a legal or jurisprudential value (also called exemplum); it is also translated into Spanish as *caídas* (falls), the narrative constant in the Wheel of Fortune story: its protagonists are powerful people who "fall" from the wheel, who are ejected from the position of power they occupy.

The lexicon I use is deliberately legal because I believe that it helps to explain the theoretical procedure. Rolandino de' Passagieri, a thirteenth-century notary, explained that the exemplar is the model

---

26. The work of Quintus Curtius Rufus is amply represented in the libraries of fifteenth-century Iberia, often accompanied by glosses. His *Historia de Alejandro Magno*, the Castilian translation (Biblioteca Nacional de España, MSS/9220), was based on the Tuscan translation by the humanist and bookseller Pier Candido Decembrio. It is possible that the glosses in the Castilian manuscripts come from Decembrio as well. They go further than an *ordinatio*, yet fall far short of a desire to narrate. The characteristic of this manuscript's glosses is that they tend to create what we might call a poetics of admiration. A possible descriptor is "epiphonetic": when read after reading the text, they attract attention in a way that is directly related to perception itself. These epiphonetic glosses are introduced by one of three verbs: *nota* (note, which is very common, and gives rise to the name of a type of gloss, "notable"); *lee* (read); and above all, *mira*. This last verb is problematic because it not only indicates the need to cast one's eyes on something (*mirar*), but also contains the idea of admiration. Pier Candido Decembrio is a humanist, a Latinist, and profoundly Ciceronian, so this *mira* probably does not refer to the very popular verb *mirare* "to look"; more likely it reflects the passive form *mirari*, "to admire, wonder at."

27. MSS/9220, fol. 17r, Biblioteca Nacional de España.

and the exemplum is the case and its transcription; it was very common to call copies of letters and other documents "exempla," meaning simply "copies."[28] Another interpretation of the exemplum, like the one documented by Cornelia Vismann, is that of a "precedent" in a legal record, a meaning that is not far from the preceding one.[29] *Casus*, in turn, is the narration in the margin of legal manuscripts that gives particular details about a genuine legal and political issue that should (or at least can) be settled by discussing the legal statutes contained that are at the center of the *Corpus Iuris*, whether *Canonici* or *Civilis*.[30]

The Wheel of Fortune is part of a narrative whose political consequences fascinated many medieval intellectuals: they wondered how it was possible that something as unpredictable as fortune could exist, and form part of everyone's experience. Political phenomenology was, in fact, a phenomenology of fortune. We may no longer be able to understand the political and philosophical depth of this narrative because we observe it after the fact of its narration; that is, after the concept of fortune has been naturalized and therefore partly deactivated, turned into a banality. Nonetheless, fortune should be thought of as a heuristic concept that helps us to understand the multiple political viewpoints that enter into this master political narrative: good fortune confronts us with an ethical and political issue, insofar as it implies exploiting other individuals and groups and therefore creates bad fortune for another person. In this gloss, Darius could very well exemplify the theme of adverse fortune, but only through the actions of Alexander the Great. For the same reason, another question arises: will Alexander be capable, politically and ethically, of blocking his own adverse fortune in the future? Will he be able to control the agents of his own adverse fortune?

In other glosses, Alexander's secondary role is equally complex. He is the agent of vengeance or retribution in the gloss devoted to Pausanias, the celebrity hunter who assassinated Alexander's father—an incident that, in turn, brings up the issue of whether Afonso V had instigated

---

28. "Exemplar dicitur originalis scriptura, genus videlicet ex quo generatur uel sumitur exemplum; quod quidem exemplatur apellatur etiam originale et autenticum... unde uersus: Exemplar pater est, exemplum quod generatur." Passegieri, *Summa totius artis notariae*, bk. 3, chap. 10.

29. Vismann, *Files*, 48.

30. *Casus* appears as the rubric of initial marginal comments in many laws in the corpus. See, for example, the 1627 Lyon edition: Justinian, *Corpus Iuris Civilis*.

the murder of Pedro's father.[31] In the gloss devoted to Diogenes's wish to live close to nature, even if it meant rejecting his only possession (a ceramic jar), Alexander appears as an agent of culture as opposed to nature, whereas he appears elsewhere as an agent of culture against barbarism.[32] Other glosses devoted to Crito and Callisthenes deal with counselors of Alexander's who were dismissed for their verbal excesses.

The glosser, like the responsible historian he wants to be, feels surprised when he writes about cruel monarchs and claims that his own pen refuses to describe them. He calls up a picture of himself as a thoughtful, melancholy author who rests his elbow on the desk and leans his chin on his hand, contemplating his next literary step; at that point he sees a vision of Alexander standing before him. Alexander demands from Pedro his right to history, his right to the gloss. Pedro has spoken of Alexander so often, yet he has never devoted a gloss only to him—it's a scandal!

Seeking to be made into a gloss is also desiring to form part of the synchronic and contemporaneous dialogue with history. Alexander is actually demanding his right to be part of contemporary politics and ethics, together with all the other names that have been convoked around the author. Alexander's life has to take place right now.

The situation is frankly ironic. Alexander is not choosing the best moment for interfering in the creative process. The interaction among the three structural series (rubrics, strophes, glosses) tells reader that the *author* is now concerned about kings who do not seem to belong to the "responsible history" (a term advanced by the theorist of history Antoon de Baets) that the author is committed to criticizing.[33] Priam, Agamemnon, and Nero do not represent the values that Alexander wants to claim for himself; they are not proper ethical and political metonymies. Alexander demands, though with a large dose of vanity, the "greatness" and "magnanimity" that actually disappeared when he departed this earth at a young age. Alexander's history at this point could only be the story of his misfortune, not the story of his greatness. And the author, who genuinely admires Alexander, simply states that it is hard to determine if Alexander loved justice or not. This casts Alexander's generosity into doubt and will turn him into a counterexample: if there is any lesson here for the powerful, it is that greatness is fragile.

---

31. MSS/9220, fol. 13r.
32. MSS/9220, fol. 44r.
33. Baets, *Responsible History*.

The fictitious character of Alexander must have an impact on the glosser, who lays down his pen in his surprise at hearing how Alexander, now speaking directly, becomes the glosser of himself. The real glosser takes up his pen once more and travels from the right margin to the left without stopping at the strophe, so as to grant Alexander his right his own gloss.

An important gloss in this series coexists in the same folio, 54v, with the story of Lucius Cornelius and his role in the First Punic War. He is mentioned there on account of his magnanimity: after killing his enemy he wished to celebrate his funeral by raising a monumental mausoleum. Here is an occasion for the glosser to explain the history of the word "mausoleum," and its connection with the story. This is the folio's gloss *a*, which forms the left-hand column. On the other side of the central text, in the right-hand column, is the gloss about Alexander, labeled gloss *b*.

It seems that this was the moment for telling the story of Alexander as an example of compassion and piety, as a doer of good deeds who saved the lives of others, someone even better than Lucius Cornelius, who preserved the honor of his dead enemy. Here Alexander is not an agent of vengeance, nor of someone's else's adverse fortune, nor of culture as opposed to nature; he is the agent of culture against barbarism. But neither is he the monarch who does not love justice, as in the marginal note that Pedro addresses to the reader at the beginning of this gloss. And he is not, in fact, the lachrymose youth who complains to the young glosser, claiming at an improper time that his story must be told. Therefore, he is not the impatient, hybrid king who seems to appear in that other gloss, but rather a more human and more powerful one.

Up to now I have offered an example of a serial reading that connects the story of Alexander with histories of Alexander as an exemplary figure. One could certainly be even bolder and serialize certain secondary characters, exploring where and when they reappear in the needs created by a serialized reading. Although no one could dispute the importance of Alexander, others might raise their eyebrows on seeing how other characters occupy master narratives in the act of assembling and presenting the stories.

The series that coexist in the manuscript are varied in nature. One could make a series out of the story of Álvaro de Luna, or that of Pedro of Aviz himself. The history of individual women is also the object of a series, just as in the *Sátira de Infelice e Felice vida*. Each of these series winds through different glosses and strophes, but they all require a complete reading of the book and its cinematic montage, and very often they intersect with each other. They always require the person reading to become a radical reader.

Poetics of Reading

This is a good moment to draw even closer to the manuscript, and to do so I want to speak about montage, about the manuscript as a radical experience of montage. This is obviously a notion adopted from cinema, but it helps us to understand how Pedro of Aviz and others explore a poetics of reading. In this poetics, reading stands at the center of the work's ingenious construction.

This poetics of reading is eminently cinematic: it explores movement through multiple spaces that are also created as constituent elements of the work itself: the page, the book, the library (both virtual and physical). The codex is, in effect, an actual place to which one must arrive, since it is assigned to a library as a unique object; it is like a folding screen inside a building, and the reader not only reads it but uses it, moves through it, participates publicly in it, in the library's collaborative space. Reading becomes cinematic because it requires the reader's participation, the stitching together of space and time, the movement of the eye and the movement of the "I" over the surface of the page. To try to illustrate this type of movement I will now analyze folio 17v, as seen in figure 5.5.

This page summarizes three narrative series: Nero and the fall of Rome, Priam and the fall of Troy, and Alexander and his self-destruction, establishing a relationship among them. Fragments of these narrative series that were dispersed throughout the work meet on this page, where they interconnect not only as similar stories but also in a cinematic montage built around the writing and glossing of the "I," and around the reader's activity.

Reading this page can be difficult in several ways. The page displays a hierarchy based on the size or dimensions of the writing: the central text is larger than the marginal one and attracts more attention. There are also three letters, *a*, *b*, and *c*, that appear in the upper left part of the lower (*a*), right (*b*), and left (*c*) margins. This seems to suggest a recommended order for reading. But this order is not matched by any other recommendation: normally these letters would have a corresponding letter in the central text, indicating that there is a correlation between the center and the margin and a specific order to be followed. Of course,

158   CHAPTER 5

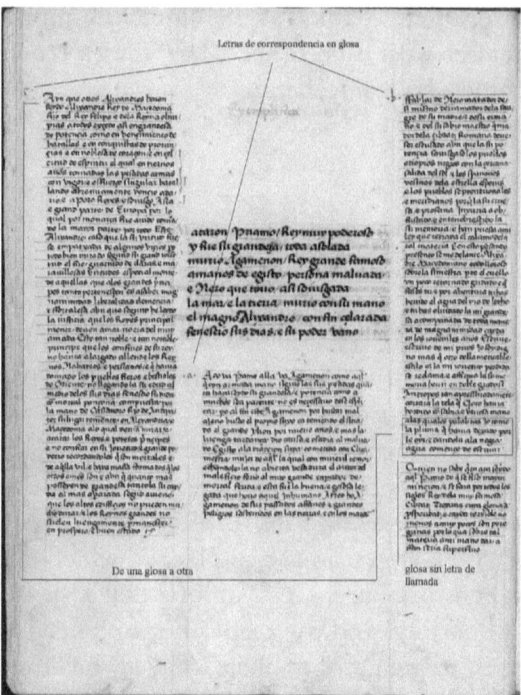

FIGURE 5.5. Pedro de Portugal, *Coplas de contemptu mundi*, MSS/3694, fol. 17v. Image from the collections of the Biblioteca Nacional de España, licensed under a Creative Commons CC-BY license.

the copy could be incomplete, lacking something that was meant to be added later. But the manuscript was produced in Pedro's lifetime and was probably copied for its intended recipient, Juana, Pedro's cousin and the queen of Portugal.

A letter also appears to be missing, since there are four glosses and only three letters. The fourth gloss, much shorter than the rest, has been relegated to the southeast corner of the page.[34] If we follow the rhythm of montage suggested by the central strophe, our surprise persists. Glosses *a*, *b*, and *c* are easily traced to the center, whether we begin our reading with the central text or not. Let's assume that we don't begin with the central strophe but first read the marginal glosses, proceeding from *a* to *b* and then to *c*. In that case we would have read first the story of Agamemnon, then that of Nero, and finally the gloss about

---

34. Pedro de Portugal, *Coplas de contempto del mundo* (1490). The book's printers didn't understand what had happened on this page and included the unlettered gloss as part of gloss *b*, because it was next to it.

Alexander. This is a deceptive story, of course, and I will explain why. If we then moved to the center, we would be surprised to see that the strophe also speaks of Priam, but that he is apparently disconnected from this economy of names. We would have to seek him out, only to find him hidden in a corner.

I have said that this is a deceptive narrative because the glosses are not simply one about Agamemnon, another about Nero, and a third about Alexander. Gloss *a* speaks of Agamemnon only after having explained that he always comes after Priam; gloss *b* begins with Nero, although the "I" who claims responsibility for this gloss bitterly rejects the need to explain all Nero's cruelty, and at this moment Alexander appears before him, claiming the right to have his own story written. Gloss *b*, generated by an unmarked gloss about Priam, then gives birth to gloss *c*, which acknowledges its dependence on, or at least relation to, gloss *b*. As a result, the gloss that lacks a tie mark in the form of a letter in the central text, the shortest one, is evoked in gloss *a*, and only in this way is the gloss integrated into the system of references.

In a way, gloss *a* is a flashback to the unlettered gloss about Priam, which additionally is disconnected. Because of that the whole system of alphabetic glosses makes the reader wonder why all the proper names in the strophe are glossed except Priam's—just before locating the sad hero of this Mediterranean tale in his remote corner of the page.

The cinematic aspect of all this is the movement needed for understanding the cartography or topography of the page. It forces the eye to shift in search of the connections between the different parts placed on the page's surface, and to learn how these interconnections create a flow that is very far from linear.

I have explained only one of the ways in which this montage is effected. The gloss about Priam connects not only with the one about Agamemnon but also with the final one, gloss *c* about Alexander the Great, to the extent that it also evokes other important Alexanders from history, such as Priam's son Alexander Paris, the true cause of the Trojan War.

Therefore the page becomes not a space for reading but a space for living, where one is forced to go back and forth among the glosses while forgetting the center, or to use the center as a center of gravity or reference point for establishing alternative orders for a variety of serial readings.

The radical montage of this folio 17v, and of all the *Coplas* in general, also has the power to condense different time periods of Mediterranean history and to make fictional and historical narratives simultaneous. Certain names evoke others, while some names are never developed, as if in a metonymy that cannot be actualized. Priam invokes Agamemnon, but Agamemnon does not open a separate space for the story of the traitor Aegisthus. Denied the right to a proper gloss, he is condemned to be no more than a name within the strophe, and only a passing mention in the gloss. Alexander the Great is shown shouting at the glosser and demanding that his life story be told, but perhaps at the wrong moment; then the glosser decides to divide the history of this great emperor (whose short stature his chroniclers never failed to mention) into two different glosses on this page and another on folio 53v, where the text also refers to folio 17v.

As the glosser explains at the end of gloss *b* (about Nero and Alexander), writing glosses is a continuous process, because after hearing Alexander out he decides to devote a gloss to him alone: "and then I took up the pen that I had just laid aside to listen to Alexander, and dipping it in the black liquid, I began to write" (y entonces, recuperé la pluma que acababa de poner a un lado para escuchar a Alejandro y, sumergiéndola en el agua negra, comencé a escribir). As a result we are sent from the right margin to the left one on a nonstop flight.

Nero, Agamemnon, Priam, Aegisthus, the writing of the "I," all become synchronic; they are no longer limited by the chronology of their stories, but are subject to a new synchrony that occurs in the dialogues that take place within the page, dialogues that do not merely coincide in space but are carefully conceived so as to occur at that precise moment. They draw closer through the art of manuscript writing.

Why would this kind of formal and narrative artifice be important? As I said before, materiality does not exist to be an object of study, but as a material concept with political-theoretical implications: it conceptualizes how fictitious and historical narratives come into contact when there is a need to activate them in the interest of sparking a political debate. This materiality dissolves temporal vacuums. It does not make them function in an ahistorical way, but facilitates the seriality and serialities of our communication with the past, making it possible to enter into dialogue with the past and reactivate it for contemporary ends.

Vulcan and the Phenomenal "I"

One radical way to read Pedro's work would be to look for the phenomenology of the "I." Not of just any "I," however, but of the one that is involved in the many layers and series that are being assembled and mounted in his works. It would be naïve to confuse the Pedro of

Aviz who lived a complicated life with the "I" whose voice we hear in all the *Coplas* and in the *Sátira*. But we are speaking of another kind of assemblage that is not only connected to a certain literary craft. This assemblage is the seed of the social, or rather, it is the social itself: it is a complex process in which the material text and lived experience establish a relationship. Here, the "I" is a collaboration between these two strange partners; it is a person who experiences both the material text and the lived experience.

Some people who have studied Pedro's *Sátira* have noted that the glosses are contingent: they are an effect added later to the central text and constitute a descriptive, literal, and non-allegorical way of confronting the task of interpretation.[35] They are contingent because they emerge from the questions inspired by reading the central text, and they ask those questions so that reading can provide answers, rather than leaving the questions open.[36] Furthermore, some of the glosses are composed directly in Castilian, while the text and other glosses were originally written in Portuguese; Pedro might have changed the plan of his work and decided to translate himself, but we do not know to what extent. This is a set of glosses that are descriptive and literal, because in fact their content is largely narrative; and when, on occasion, Pedro alludes to a story with a moral, he decides to ignore its "integuments" and the "profound meanings" (*luengos sesos*) that are hidden beneath them.[37] None of this is controversial, in my opinion.

Perhaps I dissent, however, about the reason for this attitude. The pleasure that Pedro gains from writing is purely therapeutic: "And the more I discoursed on worthy lives from ancient times, learning things at a closer range than before, the more my hand wrote with greater joy; and with greater intensity and interest—as much as I could seize amid my troublesome affairs—I continued my pursuit."[38]

Pedro finds pleasure in learning about these worthy lives because they offer him something he cannot find among the political and

---

35. Brownlee, *The Severed Word*; Lacarra, "Los discursos científico y amoroso," 109–28; Weiss, "Las fermosas e peregrinas ystorias," 103–12; Pedro de Portugal, *Sátira de Infelice e Felice vida*.
36. In the dedicatory epistle: Pedro de Portugal, *Sátira de Infelice e Felice vida*, 76.
37. Pedro de Portugal, *Sátira de Infelice e Felice vida*, 74.
38. "E cuanto más discorría por las vidas valerosas de la antigua edat, dándome a conoscimiento de las cosas con viso más propinco que de ante, tanto a mi mano con mayor gozo escrebía, e con mayor afección e estudio, aquel que arrebatar podía entre los enojosos aferes míos, yo proseguía lo procesado." Pedro de Portugal, *Sátira de Infelice e Felice vida*, 76–77.

familial affairs in which he is entangled. Every story illuminates one part of the "I" and grants it integrity, by extracting it from his own experience, which is fragmented among different languages, different political systems, different dynasties, different exiles. He finds knowledge of himself and of his capacities.

I think it is no coincidence that the first story he chooses to tell is Vulcan's. Vulcan is a god who has been sent into exile (*expelido*, Pedro calls it, from heaven) on account of his deformity from birth ("nasció . . . diforme"), to which is added another resulting from his fall: "having been expelled, he was left lame after falling" (siendo expelido, al caer quedo coxo). His own parents, Jupiter and Juno, found their son's deformity shameful: "not wishing to call him [their] son, they cast him onto the Aeolian Islands, and there he was raised by apes" (non lo queriendo llamar fijo, en las islas Ulcanias lo echaron, e, allí, de las ximias fue criado). The story of Vulcan is well-known, but that does not keep Pedro from retelling it in every detail, including his skill as a smith and goldsmith. Vulcan is not only an exiled and deformed god but also the only god concerned with crafts and artisanship. But he is also a god who is given a dubious reward by his father, whom he helped in the Gigantomachy; it finds him constantly enmeshed in strange romantic and sexual adventures, dominated by inconvenience and violence (first with Venus, then with Minerva), which ultimately end with his fathering Erichthonius by spilling his seed on the ground as he was pursuing Minerva.[39] Kings, say Sahlins and Graeber, base their sovereignty on imitating the gods.[40] But what is being imitated here? Where are the parallels? Obviously they are neither literary nor historical; the paradigm of Vulcan, as the first gloss on the "passionate" existence of the author's "I," is one in which the individual, the subject who seeks to rebuild himself, has been separated from his family, dispossessed of his physical integrity by entering a new language, and destined by his genealogy and lineage for ends that are unpredictable for the very young Pedro but that the story of Vulcan turns into a sordid premonition.

The phenomenology of this "I" is what matters in Pedro's glossed works. He is exploring the boundaries of the "I" that is himself and of the literary persona he is constructing. The former is experiencing exile, heteroglossia, migration, return, distancing, a whole complex universe

---

39. All the quotations are from the first gloss, dedicated to Vulcan: Pedro de Portugal, *Sátira de Infelice e Felice vida*, 72–74.

40. Sahlins and Graeber, *On Kings*.

of ethics and politics. The latter is synchronizing historical and fictitious experiences in a complex material text that, in turn, shapes a vision of ethics and politics that, in a process of serial reading, unites the cultural and the social into a single movement.

Mode d'emploi

Ferdinand de Saussure established, as one of the principles of the linguistic sign, that signifiers are linear.[41] They are like solid bodies that cannot occupy the same space at the same time. Signifiers are space, and to administer that space is to administer and control time. This is what happens in Georges Perec's novel *La vie, mode d'emploi* (*Life: A User's Manual*), first published in 1978: the narrator always moves in one direction, telling stories one after the other, only to reveal at the end that they all happened at the same time. Or, rather, that it was impossible to relate simultaneous events in any other way without dominating and managing the space that the signifiers are, so to speak, colonizing.

This is what all this serial reading and montage is about, and why it is important for a theory of history: in their montage and serialization, Pedro of Aviz's glossed manuscripts also manage to dominate space, to colonize it through their synchronic interpretation, their radical contemporaneity. Pedro of Aviz was a master of montage. Assemblage, for him, was really a uniting of materials from different sources and spaces so as to create a many-layered montage. Montage also meant, for him, establishing a profound relationship between the experience of reading and the experience of life, between the intellectual and the social, as an experience that is always beginning, inchoative.

But it is reasonable to ask, what is it that is being initiated? This is the question inspired by reading Pedro's experimental manuscript work. It is a subjectivity that is initiated: the possibility that the system of cultural codes created over the centuries can happen right now, right here, organized, synchronized, and controlled under Pedro's jurisdiction. It is he who emerges as a subject with a capacity for analysis and narrative more philosophical than a historian's, with a capacity to explore and judge precedents and cases, and thus to imagine a different future.

---

41. Saussure, Cours de linguistique générale, pt. 1, chap. 1, 116–17.

Chapter 6

A Vernacular Society

Pero Díaz de Toledo translated Plato's *Phaedo*. Since he knew no Greek, he took as his source Leonardo Bruni's Latin translation, made for Pope Innocent VII (1404-6, during the time of the antipope Benedict XIII, "el papa Luna"). He included a total of thirty-five glosses (if my count is accurate) in which, according to his editor Nicholas Round, the leading scholar of his work, Pero Díaz de Toledo, offers a counterpart to the image of Plato as a "good pagan," representing him instead as "the errant philosopher" (*el filósofo descarriado*).[1] In the fifth gloss Pero Díaz de Toledo recalls part of book 5 of Cicero's *Tusculanae Disputationes*, which reads as follows: "Socrates autem primus philosophiam devocavit e caelo et in urbibus conlocavit et in domus etiam introduxit et coegit de vita et moribus rebusque bonis et malis quaerere." He translates this as: "Sócrates . . . atrajo la philosophia del cielo e la aposentó en las cibdades, e fue el philosopho que se trabajó en dar ley e doctrina en el bien vivir de los honbres."[2]

---

1. Díaz de Toledo, *Libro llamado Fedron*, 129.
2. "Socrates . . . brought philosophy down from heaven and settled it in the cities, and was the philosopher who strove to give law and doctrine for mankind to live well." I cite Nicholas Round's edition, although the manuscript displayed in the Biblioteca Nacional de España is much more beautiful; Díaz de Toledo, *Libro llamado Fedron*, 229, in the Biblioteca Nacional de Madrid VITR/17/4, fol. 5r.

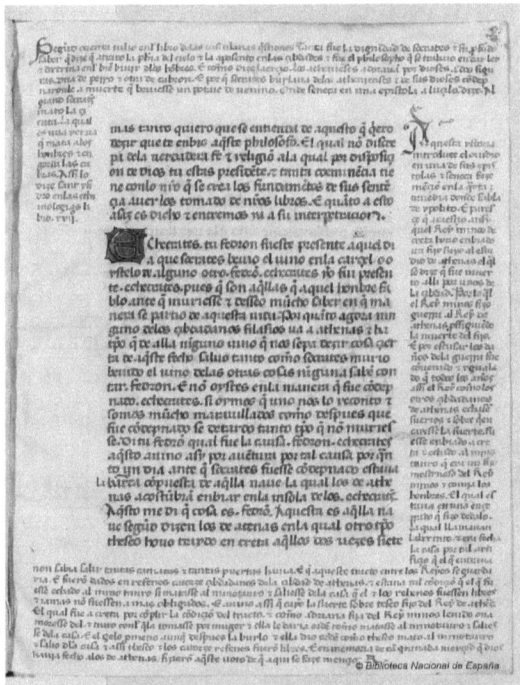

FIGURE 6.1. Pedro Díaz de Toledo's translation of Plato's *Libro llamado Fedrón*, VITR/17/4, fol. 5r. Image from the collections of the Biblioteca Nacional de España, licensed under a Creative Commons CC-BY license.

Pero Díaz de Toledo's translation is either concise or confusing, depending on your point of view, but it also plays well with the semantic field in Cicero's statement that Socrates called on philosophy, which resided in heaven, and installed it in the cities, later introducing it into the home. Pero Díaz de Toledo states that the movement from heaven to the city is a form of attraction, and that he *aposentó* (housed) philosophy in the cities; that verb contains not only the idea of location but also that of the home or house (*aposento*) where the issue is "liv[ing] well" (*el bien vivir*).

Anyone who has read these words and the works of John Dagenais and Mary Carruthers will wonder what the difference is between what I have just said and an ethical reading. Perhaps the central question is also the axis of my argument: the microliterary activity I am studying here is not specifically aimed at individual reflection, but at political action through the construction of networks and spaces of civil interchange. These networks are not new, and I believe they are related to the urban brotherhoods we find in the minutes of meetings of the Cortes, where representatives of the cities entered into discussion with the other three estates of the kingdom: the monarchy, the nobility, and the clergy. In these documents we often observe brotherhoods from the cities challenging the political and legal decisions, even the very jurisdiction, of the monarchy and its system of governing through the nobility and the clergy. Furthermore, urban brotherhoods join into networks that include several cities in a region, which in turn establish connections with other regions, weaving a fabric that gathers themes and concerns to be debated in the Cortes. These groups are acknowledged, and acknowledge each other, as interlocutors in the critique and theory of power. They are acknowledged as political and legal actors capable of speaking in the first person.[3]

I wish to spend a little more time with this movement of philosophical and political knowledge that Pero Díaz de Toledo saw in Plato, through Cicero's text. For many female and male intellectuals of the fourteenth and fifteenth centuries, both religious and lay, this philosophical transit from heaven to the city and the home is an immense discovery. And there is no doubt that we have Socrates to thank for it: putting philosophy within reach of civic life and even of the family, in the form of morally acceptable actions, makes a critical perspective available to anyone who wishes to stretch out a hand to touch and possess it. Philosophy, once it resides in the city and the home, is no longer an academic discipline but a body of knowledge with which to examine everything, including oneself. It is even more important insofar as this movement implies creating a space in which to philosophize, to think. As we studied in the first chapter of this book, those devoted to microliterature had to create the margin as a space for reflection and theorizing, endowed with certain cognitive advantages. Those same persons had to continue producing space so as to build a city in which to philosophize—that is, a system of interchange and circulation of ideas proposed by citizens.

As we read glossed manuscripts from the fourteenth and fifteenth centuries, we grow aware of the importance of this discovery. The

---

3. The use of the first person singular as an expression of the people's voice in the Cortes is an innovation owed to Fernán Díaz de Toledo, who served under King John II. He was an uncle of Pero Díaz de Toledo and a converso. He introduced this grammatical change into the minutes of the Cortes when he was protonotary of the kingdom, as I have suggested in Rodríguez Velasco, *Ciudadanía* and *Order and Chivalry*. In those books I also examine several aspects of the composition of urban brotherhoods, as well as how the legal dispositions resulting from the Cortes (*ordenamientos*) tried to exclude them.

margins of certain works like Pero Díaz de Toledo's translation of Plato's *Phaedo*, Pedro de Portugal's *Sátira de Infelice e Felice vida*, and Alfonso de Cartagena's glossed and expanded translation of Luca Mannelli's *Tabulatio et expositio Senecae* form an immense forest of philosophical interconnections that, like a constellation of ideas, bring philosophy down from the academic heavens to the cities and homes of the vernacular tongue, and to the civil and ethical issues that accompany persons who, whether nobles or burghers, make up the governing class. On those margins a history of philosophy is told that is synchronic, to the extent that it is also synoptic and has been called onto this dwelling space of the page through the glosser's voluntary act.

Alfonso de Cartagena, bishop of Burgos and Iberia's greatest intellectual, translated the text and glosses of the *Tabulatio et expositio Senecae* and made a few additions to it. One of these completes a gloss in which Luca Mannelli (barely) sketched a history of philosophy. Specifically in the *Título de la amistança*, the gloss numbered 38 in Georgina Olivetto's edition is devoted in principle to the issue of sexual reproduction.[4] Luca Mannelli's gloss contains a few lines that draw on the *Politics* of Aristotle (who considers sexual reproduction natural), and on Cicero's treatise *On Friendship*.[5] Cartagena is inspired by this gloss, first to explain who the Peripatetic philosophers were, and then to sketch out a history of philosophy. For him it is centered particularly on ideas about the soul: a philosophy that, although now supported by Seneca, is obviously based on the history of the science of the soul that Aristotle constructs in the first book of his treatise *On the Soul*. This discourse on the history of philosophy and the science of the soul leads to Cartagena's first thesis, that "we Catholics . . . cite the philosophers in the things that conform to our holy faith, but in others we reject and ignore them."[6] But Cartagena does not forget the statement that had brought him to this history of philosophy, the affirmation in Mannelli's gloss that, according to Aristotle, "man is naturally civil and political."[7] The whole history of philosophy is summed up in the fact that human existence occurs in the political sphere, in man's role as a "citizen" (*çibdadano*). If there is

---

4. Cartagena, *Título de la amistança*, 219-25.
5. It corresponds to Luca Mannelli's gloss number 40, in Cartagena, *Título de la amistança*, 218.
6. "los católicos . . . allegamos los philosophos en las cosas que son conformes a nuestra sancta fe, e las otras las desechamos e non curamos dellos." Cartagena, *Título de la amistança*, 223.
7. "el ome naturalmente es çivil e político." Cartagena, *Título de la amistança*, 223.

one thing that should be on the horizon of any philosophical inquiry, it is that it is inseparable from political life. Or, as Pero Díaz de Toledo observed for Cicero, that philosophy (thanks to Socrates) could reside in the city and in the home.

A City to Philosophize In

The city and the houses to which philosophy descends, however, are not necessarily real locations or spaces; they are not urban centers with exact names. They themselves are philosophical constructions: *ideal* cities or families, inasmuch as they belong to postsensory operations of the soul that, according to medieval and early modern philosophers, occupy specific areas of the human brain. To these special parts of the brain where postsensory activities (imagination, fantasy, thought, memory, common sense) operate, medieval cognitivists gave the name of "cells," a word that in itself evokes a space that serves as a place for living, a chamber—they were also called *ventriculi*, or little wombs.[8] These are factitious spaces and therefore scientific fictions—that is, philosophical hypotheses for continuing critical work.

But these cities for philosophizing could also be spaces of genuine interchange, where flesh-and-blood people interact and philosophize together—possibly on several different levels, sometimes within a philosophy aligned with the Christian faith, and occasionally beyond it. The library is the city. This expression ("el centre de lectura és la ciutat mateixa"), which originates with Tomàs Cavallé, president of the reading center (Centro de Lectura) of Reus from 1915 to 1922, has been theorized by Aurélie Vialette in her work on intellectual philanthropy: she looks at how modes of association and of economic and social development adopt models of cultural construction and interaction in public spaces. In Vialette's view, it is within these library-cities or reading center–cities that debates about the democratization of culture arise.[9] Of course Vialette's work refers to the nineteenth century, but it makes us reflect on the model of the library, *studium*, and reading center as they were designed in aristocratic and bourgeois circles—a bourgeoisie that was professional, administrative, and basically composed of

---

8. As an example, see manuscript MS.55 of the Wellcome Collection, which contains the text by Peter Gerticz of Dresden known as *Parvulus philosophiae naturalis*. The image on folio 93r is a diagram of the human brain, divided into cells for postsensory operations.

9. Vialette, *Intellectual Philanthropy*, 111–36.

jurists. Some of these centers, like Santillana's library in Guadalajara, accumulate over the years the corpus of texts around which intellectuals and writers model themselves.[10]

A library is a space for a political philosophy based on what constitutes specific activities in times of peace. Manuscript MSS/10212 of Spain's Biblioteca Nacional belonged to Íñigo López de Mendoza, who acquired it shortly before becoming the Marquis of Santillana in 1445. The text it contains, which would have interested López de Mendoza very much, is the Castilian translation of the treatise *De Militia*, composed by Leonardo Bruni d'Arezzo in 1422 for Rinaldo Maso degli Albizi. By that date Bruni was in a sort of interregnum because he had ceased to be chancellor of the Republic of Florence and would not return to the post for several years; Paolo Viti says that Bruni at that time was a *semplice cittadino*—although it is very hard to imagine Bruni as a "mere citizen," given that he was writing treatises like *De Militia* that propose the transformation of republican power.[11]

At that same time Íñigo López de Mendoza was in an interregnum of his own. Bruni's treatise reached him sometime in 1443, and he had read it by 1444. In 1443 John of Navarre carried out the so-called "golpe de Rámaga," a coup in which he imprisoned King John II; from that point until the Battle of Olmedo in 1445, civil war pitted the forces of John II and his constable Álvaro de Luna (with whom Íñigo López de Mendoza was allied) against the princes of Navarre and Aragon.[12] López de Mendoza appears to have been totally taken up with his activities in war and diplomacy (which is war by other means). In 1445, emerging on the winning side, he was raised to the rank of marquis.[13] The end of the war and its political consequences had been detectable since the 1430s, and especially from 1439 onward many intellectuals, both knights and jurists, from the court of King John II of Castile conceived

---

10. Andrew Hui's book *The Study*, published after I completed this book, studies the study, that is the private libraries of humanists in urban centers or in their villas (or castles!), and the way in which those study rooms reorganized knowledge in lay environments.

11. Leonardo Bruni, *Opere letterarie e politiche*, esp. 649–701.

12. There is extensive bibliography on the civil war between the Castilian monarchy and the princes of Navarre and Aragon, most of it very traditional. See Castillo Cáceres, "¿Guerra o torneo?," 139–66. The battle itself is narrated in several contemporary chronicles such as Luna, *Crónica de don Álvaro de Luna*; and Carrillo de Huete, *Crónica del Halconero de Juan II*.

13. For a complete biography of Íñigo López de Mendoza (though often voluntarist or even providentialist, as is typical of the genre), see the four volumes from the exhibit *El Marqués de Santillana, 1398–1458*, edited by Yarza Luaces et al. The biography most consulted is that of Pérez Bustamante and Calderón Ortega, *Íñigo López de Mendoza*.

the kingdom's policies from the perspective of the republican political theories that prevailed in city-states such as Florence, which had also been theorized in other centers of power such as the Duchy of Burgundy from the time of Philip the Bold (r. 1363–1404).[14] Íñigo López de Mendoza was extremely interested in Bruni's book, translated especially for him (and not very well, we must admit), and in 1443 he sat down in his study to read it in silence. I know that he read it himself, and probably silently, because he left some marks of his reading in the margins that help us to understand what issues caught his attention, and even to establish a hierarchy of his concerns.[15] In short, he studied the text.

As soon as he finished reading it, on January 15, 1444, he wrote to the bishop of Burgos, Alonso de Cartagena, the spiritual and intellectual guide of the Castilian political elites in the first half of the fifteenth century. In his letter, Santillana speaks of the work he has just read and asks Cartagena about the possibility of receiving a knightly investiture in the style of the *ordo equestris* or Roman knightly order, instead of the feudal-monarchical one that then prevailed, ruled by the laws of Alfonso X and debated in several places.[16] Why does he care about this different kind of investiture? Why was the ritual important, and how does it relate to his reading of Bruni's text? I believe that this is why: while the two investitures resemble each other in their military obligations, they seem to differ radically in the mission they assign to the warrior in peacetime. And, as might be expected, Bruni wants to establish in detail the mission of the knight in peacetime because he himself is a jurist whose mission is the legislative, judicial, and executive construction of the republic; he is someone who seeks to suppress armed violence within the city.

Bruni offers a republican concept of the militia: it should remain outside the walls of the city and never enter its gates. If warriors wish to cross the threshold of the polis they must transform themselves, laying down their arms and assuming a different persona, whose public actions focus on politics, the judiciary, or rhetoric. This vision, described by Bruni in 1422, is what astonished López de Mendoza in

---

14. On republican politics in Burgundy and Florence, see Vanderjagt, *Qui sa vertu anoblist*; Schnerb, *L'État Bourguignon*; and Maire Vigueur, *Cavaliers et citoyens*.

15. I studied these marks and their consequences for cultural and political action in Rodríguez Velasco, "Santillana en su laberinto," 3–9.

16. See Rodríguez Velasco, *Ciudadanía*.

1443. And not only him: a few years later another translation of the same text was made for the aristocrat Rodrigo Manrique, signed by Pedro de la Panda, an Aragonese traveler and humanist. There is a single surviving manuscript of that translation, which passed from the Manrique family to the library of the Marquis of Laurencin and is now in the Biblioteca Nacional de España, MSS/23090.

The knight's mission in peacetime is connected to the universe of the city-library. It is the space of political philosophy, or, if you wish, of a different form of violence that appears in cultural activity and critical debate. Alonso de Cartagena, in his reply to Santillana, takes no account of that republican knighthood that has the knight exchange his armor for a robe so as to participate actively in the politics of the realm. For Cartagena and many others, that is a job for clerics with university degrees, not for intellectuals educated in private spaces that are more or less open to other actors, both religious and lay. This debate, repeated a thousand times, appears abundantly in the bibliography.

But that does not make the library-city less active. On the contrary, what we find is an increase in these spaces, and a greater variety of objects of study within them. One of Santillana's ancestors, Gómez Suárez de Figueroa, lord of Zafra, also had a library in the early fifteenth century that became a center for critical debate. Manuscript MSS/10289 of Spain's Biblioteca Nacional belonged to it, and transmits, with some glosses by the translator and others by a highly irritated anonymous reader, a Castilian translation of the Hebrew versions of Maimonides's *Guide for the Perplexed* (which we spoke of in chapter 2 of this book). The libraries of Gómez Suárez de Figueroa, Santillana, Rodrigo Manrique, Pedro Fernández de Velasco in Haro, and others all have at least a half-open door policy for research, creativity, and debate. The glosses of many manuscripts show that this interchange entered into the formation of intellectual networks whose activity in political theory and practice is revealed in microliteratures.

Glossed manuscripts, together with some commentaries that lack that microliterary corpus, are like connective tissue that joins intellectual networks between each of the centers of calculation that constitute it, especially the library-cities. The notion of the center of calculation comes from Bruno Latour and his sociological theory of the history of knowledge and science within networks. In his article "Ces réseaux que la raison ignore: Laboratoires, bibliothèques, collections," Latour sees the library not as an "isolated fortress" but as the "node of a vast network within which not signs, not subject matters, but subject matters that are becoming signs circulate."[17] In that library, a center of calculation that is a node in the network, these materials take shape and are shared, transformed into documents (such as glossed books) that also contain their own forms of expression and conceptual maps.

Manuscript books show the marks and underlinings, the variations in letter size, the abstract signs that unite the center with the margin, or link a treatise to a letter and its reply. In that way they create the language in which the very network expresses itself: its ideas, notions, and expressions for debate and discussion. The library, as a space for study, copying, interchange, and debate, stabilizes its modes of philosophical and critical life.

A Radical Artist

Female intellectuals, from their more marginal position, are obliged to disturb the foundations of the city that is a space for philosophizing. They need to confront the structures that support the library as a center of calculation, the intellectual networks, and, naturally, the very subject matters that will be converted into signs. They need to learn how to achieve this process of change involving a subject matter: its facts, its concepts, its historical observations—in other words, its signs. These women need to act in this way if they wish to leave their mark on how one philosophizes in this city, which must now be rebuilt.

Christine de Pizan, with whom I began this book even in its preface, is a radical artist. All her literary creations spring from her resolve to submit received knowledge to scrutiny. Scholars may emphasize that the sources Christine used for her work, like the *Book of the City of Women*, were traditional, or trapped in immovable notions of patriarchal society such as the Christian religion, chastity, the story of the Fall, or even assumptions about the minority of women. Christine's transformation into a man, as she narrates it in her *Book of the Mutability of Fortune*, can be read as a determination to become a speaking body rather than a categorized woman (here I am adapting Paul B. Preciado's idea from his *Countersexual Manifesto*). It can also be read as an acknowledgment that only one gender can be politically active, and that in order to participate in the universe of political theory and

---

17. "le noeud d'un vaste réseau où circulent non des signes, non des matières, mais des matières devenant signes." Latour, "Ces réseaux," 23.

practice one must adopt that gender, become it. Whether a champion of protofeminism or an appropriator of masculine discourse, Christine seems to move in a binary universe, but only in appearance. Christine arises from her confrontation with binarism: she can change her nature and her gender at will, writing either as a woman or after having turned herself into a man.[18]

In some manuscripts commissioned or created by inspiration from Christine's ideas, we see her in her professional library.[19] There are several images of such a scene, including some in which she is alone. In others she is debating men who seem clearly disoriented; sometimes she appears working in a scholarly library. In the manuscript of the *City of Women* that is in the Bibliothèque de Genève, Ms. fr. 180, folio 3v, Christine has a revolving bookcase that lets her consult several books at the same time, moving from one to the next, working with a variety of sources. This last shows not only an author's library but that of someone devoted to research.

What is she looking for? It is, in fact, a fully microliterary form of research: she wants books that can offer her just one or two lines, a comment, a glossary, or a history of several women from all over the world and any era who may have acted in some political capacity. Among them are queens, military leaders, religious leaders, martyrs. Christine will draw them all together to bear witness to her plan of building a city where discourse and political action would derive from those women's words and precedents. That would mean bringing philosophy down from the heaven of history and thought into this city and this house.

The manuscripts of the *City of Women*, which were finished in 1405, not only give us an idea of the histories of these women, carefully organized according to a political and historical plan; they also offer the reader *historiae*: a frame that is like a window designed precisely so as to observe figures, landscapes, gestures, movements, and all the other elements of the story being told. Just as in Leon Battista Alberti's *De Pictura* (written around 1435, just a little after Christine's work), what counts is the *historia*, that is the mathematical and optical rules that govern the stories, characters, and objects included in the frame-window and make

---

18. For a reading of Christine that is more radically trans, and that defends the use of masculine pronouns for her, see the fascinating study by Gutt, "Transgender Mutation," 451–58.

19. Bell, "Christine de Pizan."

it possible to convey their mental and emotional state.[20] In other words, the manuscripts contain not only a theoretical premise in words but also a map of visual concepts that constitutes the story: a sort of theater, a collection of miniatures, windows that we must look through.

These stories are poetic, and therefore qualify as philosophy. They narrate things as they might have been, not as they have been. Aristotle thought that poetry was more philosophical than history, or more precisely than what he calls ἱστορίας, the scientific disciplines.[21] Poetry is more philosophical because it is more universal, inasmuch as ἱστορίας are studies of the empirical aspects of the things and narratives that to enable us to communicate those ontological elements of thought. Poetry, by contrast, allows us to explain things as they might have been, within the limits of the verisimilar and the necessary.

Data mining is a complex process of extraction. The chief metaphor of Christine's work, that of architectural construction and cultural engineering, marries well with the program she has set herself as a researcher: to extract structural materials that will be used to build a city according to a new urban plan, even if those materials clearly carry the authority and majesty of earlier buildings in the public realm.

Yan Thomas, in his article on the ornaments of Rome, showed that majesty was carried by the *ornatum* of the city. Construction of new buildings depended on the reuse of materials that were recognizable as parts of the public pagan structures of ancient Rome.[22] Therefore construction materials were recycled not only because they were available, but above all because they retained signs of power—they had belonged to the politically marked spaces of the ancient regime. In another article Thomas showed that the inviolable nature of tombs also protected the buildings raised above them: to the extent that those buildings were sacralized by the power emanating from the corpses beneath them, they could no longer serve as objects of commercial exchange.[23]

We can think of this double framework (the reuse of materials that retain majesty, and the sacred aura of bodies beneath buildings) as a way of analyzing Christine's work. For her, extraction meant identifying materials through their ability to transfer their own majesty, their own

---

20. Alberti, *De pictura (1435)*, book 2, paragraphs 35–45, pp. 168–87.
21. "διὸ καὶ φιλοσοφώτερον καὶ σπουδαιότερον ποίησις ἱστορίας ἐστίν" (poetry is more philosophical and more noble than history). See Crane, *Greek Word Study Tool*, under ἱστορία (historía).
22. Thomas, "Les ornements," 44–75.
23. Thomas, "Corpus aut ossa aut cineres," 73–112.

agency, their own rights and presence, to the new edifice. The extraction of data is, therefore, a critical process in which those variables (sources, histories, characters, narratives, et cetera) play a significant role within the plan of the work. They are difficult to extract because all those elements, their *ornatus*, their *majesty*, must also be extracted—they cannot be forgotten or laid aside.

Now for the subjects that Christine transfers. First come the three ladies who form the conceptual foundations of this architectural work: *Raison* (Reason), *Droitture*, and *Justice*. *Droitture* is, strictly speaking, the direct connection to law, while Justice is the origin and purpose of law, and Reason is logical and argumentative discourse, often associated in the Middle Ages with rhetorical perfection. In other words, these three women determine the philosophical-legal conceptual map of Christine's politics. After them Christine presents the histories of more than 140 women in order to debate and question the male paradigms of war, cruelty, prophecy, and intellectual study, so as to oppose all forms of sexual dominance and rape culture; Christine invites into her city female saints, prostitutes (who became saints), and women who became men so as to live a transgender life. This immense necropolis will sacralize the construction and the edifices of the new city. They give the author not only the materials themselves but also the bodies, *speaking bodies* that form a cemetery over which the city, the new civil society, will also have unalienable rights—and that ultimately will remain there beyond any type of commerce.

Was Christine aware of the legalist debates about materials, things, human remains, reuse of construction materials, and so on? It is difficult to know, or rather, it would be desirable and interesting to investigate this particular question. One is tempted to answer it in the affirmative, especially because it was also debated by medieval jurists in the thirteenth, fourteenth, and fifteenth centuries and gave rise to theories, pronouncements, and commentaries: from the *persona ficta*, or artificial person, perfected by Sinibaldo de' Fieschi, to the debates about how the transformation of things changed the criteria of property and possession, such as the disputes about the ship of Theseus, which wonder whether his ship is still his ship once all its parts have been replaced because they had been damaged; or the question of the disappearing community, which asks whether the walls of a city can convey moral and legal personality when nobody lives inside them.[24]

---

24. Panizo Orallo, *Persona jurídica y ficción*; Thomas, *Les Opérations du droit*.

But mere nearness in time, in intellectual climate, and even in access to jurists and specialists in law do not allow us to state unequivocally that Christine knew about all this, without seeking proof. Whether she knew it or not is, in a way, secondary, because it matters more here to have a paradigm to think with, not a genealogy of precise sources. And within this paradigm it is fundamental to think about Christine's sources not only as mere literary debts but also as constructive elements that partake of majesty on the one hand and sacredness on the other.

Creating a metaphor implies that its creator must inhabit that metaphor for its literary or argumentative duration. It requires that person to be the subject of an action that is metaphorical. For example, if the metaphor is the construction of a city of women, then the one who deploys it must become an architect.

Adriana Cavarero, one of the most fascinating scholars of modernity, in her book *Nonostante Platone* (*In Spite of Plato*), writes that her research will concern "ancient female figures stolen [*rubate*, in the Italian original] from their contexts." The context is that of Platonic philosophy, in which the characters have been transmitted, but not their subjectivity. Cavarero is specifically wondering how to speak of the latter. Christine's project is far from being Cavarero's, but I think that she does belong to the philosophical and historiographical lineage of this type of research: she recognizes a series of female interlocutors whose name and social status have entered history within narratives that have, however, resisted identifying and examining their political subjectivity. Their whole moral personality depends on the masculine power structure to which they belong. And although Christine does not always want to extract her protagonists from the family structure that endows women with both moral and legal personhood, that does not prevent her from building a civil society in accordance with the political subjectivity of these more than 140 women.

Teresa's Voice

One of my PhD students from a few years back, Tamara Hache, wrote in a paper that the voice of Teresa de Cartagena was *acousmatic*: it can be heard, but it is impossible to identify its source. She comes to us as a disembodied voice, to which we are also forbidden to respond. Like Pythagoras's probationary pupils, we cannot see the teacher, whose tones reach our ears (which are now our eyes) in blurred form, marked by a strange musical note that is silence, or a pause. Christine de Pizan, for her part, tells the story of Novella d'Andrea, who in place of her father Giovanni d'Andrea (well-known to Castilian jurists) taught his classes in canon law in Bologna from behind a curtain.[25] Another acousmatic voice, this time a modern one.

Hearing (with our eyes) Teresa's voice, in this book, will be our final investigation of microliterature as a search for constructing a space in which to philosophize. As we shall see, it is also an exploration of the nodes and connective tissues that create and consolidate the spaces of critical thinking, that is, centers of calculation, libraries, laboratories.

But Teresa presents different challenges when we seek to understand the construction of these networks in which microliterary activity can circulate. To begin with, her center of calculation is the library of a cloistered convent. The cloister is certainly a space for meditation and thought, for study and criticism. Cloistered authors such as Hildegard of Bingen kept trying to communicate with the outside world and create their own city within the republic of letters, but they often met with the obstacle of confessors or other male figures who limited the potential reach of their works. It is also true that such obstacles sometimes could not silence these women's voices—again, both Hildegard and Teresa are good examples.

Further, Teresa is relatively invisible, and attempts to reconstruct her life story have not been easy. Her biography has become clearer only recently, through the work of Yonsoo Kim and her indefatigable research in convent libraries.[26] Even so, Teresa's voice is disembodied; to quote Tamara Hache again, it is acousmatic. And when the nature of her body is identified it turns out to be a sickly one, dominated both physically and discursively by an incapacity that was intolerable to her. Yonsoo Kim has studied and expressed better than anyone the physical, theological, and political conditions of this frail body that seeks a shady grove (*arboleda*) in which to rest and finds it necessary (though perhaps not surprising) to defend its right to speak. Teresa, nonetheless, is living proof (the Trojan War is happening right now) that disability is one of the forms of normativity, one of the ways in which central power, whether of the state or the church, assumes the right to decide which abilities are normal and acceptable and which are not.

---

25. Pizan, *Livre de la cité des dames*, 2.36.3.
26. Kim, *Between Desire and Passion*; Kim, *El saber femenino*.

178   CHAPTER 6

Cristina Morales, in *Lectura fácil*, has written an extraordinary critique of the criteria of ability and disability.[27]

Prudent Men

Teresa de Cartagena's treatise titled *Admiraçión operum Dei*, written sometime before 1481 (and in any case about two years after her first work, known as *Arboleda de los enfermos* [ca. 1473–79]) fulfills a promise.[28] Teresa (by means unknown to us) had assured Juana de Mendoza, the wife of Gómez Manrique (then *corregidor* or appellate judge of Toledo), that she would contact her, and she finally did so through this combined treatise and letter. As Juan Carlos Conde notes, it is possible, though not certain, that Juana de Mendoza was also the recipient of Teresa's first treatise, *La Arboleda de los enfermos*.[29] In any case, we have here the first problem: that first treatise and letter—for it is an essay written in the second person and addressed to a lady—ran up against an ill-defined group of men whom Teresa calls, nearly always, the prudent men—*prudentes varones*.

This is a well-known sequence of events. A woman composes a work, and a group of men expresses their (let's be generous) doubts about the contents of the work, the quality of the work, the chances that it was written by its ostensible author, and a long series of other reservations that it would be too boring to list. I think this is a good example of the English term *mansplaining*. Although Merriam-Webster defines mansplaining as "to explain something to a woman in a condescending way that assumes she has no knowledge about the topic," these *prudentes varones*, who don't have access to Teresa herself, assume that she has no knowledge either of the topic or the form she uses.[30]

---

27. Morales, *Lectura fácil*.

28. The manuscript in the library of the Monasterio de San Lorenzo del Escorial in San Lorenzo, h.III.24, is the only one that contains both of Teresa's works. It was copied by Pedro López del Trigo, who dated it on folio 79r in 1481. Both works were obviously composed earlier, but not much earlier. The date proposed by Juan Carlos Conde in the introduction to his forthcoming edition is the one mentioned in the text.

29. See note number 5 in Conde's edition of the *Arboleda*, which will appear in Cátedra's Letras Hispánicas series together with the *Admiraçión*. In an exchange of text messages on November 23, 2020 (I mention this only to record what may seem like an antique form of communication someday), Conde seemed perhaps more disposed to accept that the *Arboleda*, too, was meant for Juana de Mendoza: "no pondría la mano en el fuego, pero la acercaría bastante." (I would not put my hand in the fire, but I would get it close enough.)

30. As I wrote on December 31, 2020, the online edition of the *New York Times* reproduced a review from August of the same year of Nicole Tersigni's book *Men to Avoid in Art and Life*:

Both prudent historians of literature and female scholars of Teresa de Cartagena's text have had to face the fact that, as they search for the formation of a minimal intellectual network among fifteenth-century women in Castile, one of the people who set it in motion, Teresa, saw her work immediately minimized by this set of unnamed men. As Juan Carlos Conde points out, Teresa's work was read within a very narrow circle that was close to her life experience. Not until the modern editions, initiated by Lewis Joseph Hutton in 1967, was her work extracted from that circle to bring it closer to the Castilian literary canon.[31] Hutton, although he edited it, was dismissive: Teresa's works, for him, "do not belong to the highest category of literary creation." He does condescend to place them in that minor category of writing that is "an important reflection of the thought, and a good example of the prose, of the fifteenth century in Castile."[32]

For one thing, it is not clear that "the highest . . . literary creation" is a universal "category" (perhaps that was known in 1967, but I don't remember because I was only two). Besides, Teresa does not seem to have cared very much for the institution that some of her contemporaries, like Gómez Manrique himself, took part in—the one we call literature. She possesses the credentials, though she treats them ironically: she feels that the "few years" that she spent in the *estudio* of Salamanca should earn her a plenary indulgence (*remisyon plenaria*) rather than granting her "wisdom in those things I wish to say" (sabiduría en lo que dezir quiero).[33] Belonging to the institution of literature, or not, is an act of authority; granting it, or not, also means including or not including someone in the circle of persons who exert authority in turn. How can it be granted to someone whom the "prudent men" of the time seem to disdain? To someone who writes in an uncomfortable genre, transmitting in the vernacular doctrinal elements that form part

---

Gupta, "She Explains Mansplaining." I am very grateful to Marlyn Miller for her comments and I think she has taught me something I did not consider with full attention.

31. There are few published editions of Teresa's work. The first, and most important, is Hutton's edition of *Arboleda de los enfermos*. Anthony Cárdenas made a transcription for the electronic text of the Hispanic Seminar of Medieval Studies. Mercedes Vaquero, in 2000, directed the doctoral dissertation of Clara Esther Castro-Ponce ("Teresa de Cartagena"), which is unpublished. We therefore await Conde's edition from Cátedra.

32. "no pertenecen a la más alta categoría de la creación literaria . . . un importante reflejo del pensamiento y una buena muestra de la prosa del siglo XV en Castilla." Cartagena, *Arboleda de los enfermos*, ed. Hutton, 8.

33. I quote from Conde's edition, but see the same passage in Hutton's edition, 123, where he transcribes *estudié* (I studied) where the manuscript has *estude* (i.e., *estuve*, "I was").

of theological learning and its authorizing discipline? To someone who admits that she does not belong, even though the arguments in her treatises are based on many "authorities"?[34]

But Teresa does not write against the "prudent men"—she composes her work *with* them. Her intellectual intuition is not to write literature but to write microliterature. She studies the intellectual models of her critics, and places herself in a space of vulnerability that exceeds the limits of false modesty or *captatio benevolentiae*; what's more, she assures her hearers that she is harmless because she is a woman, she is sickly, she is cloistered.

Critics have not behaved very differently from those prudent men. Teresa is an enigmatic character because the only known elements of her persona come either from educated guesses or from what she tells us about herself in her works. Those educated guesses depend entirely on the fact that she was the granddaughter of Pablo de Santa María (1350–1435), born Solomon ha-Levi in Burgos; he was chief rabbi of the city before converting to Christianity in 1390, having undergone forced baptism. Pablo de Santa María, who formed part of the royal administration in Castile, became bishop of Burgos in 1415. He not only founded a clerical-intellectual dynasty that included Teresa, but also gave his name to a science of commentary. Pablo was also Paulus, who demolished Nicholas of Lyra's *Postillae* through his hundreds of *additiones*, often transmitted together with the commentaries of Nicholas and the Bible with its *glossa ordinaria*. Although everything distilled from Pablo's additions cannot be summarized in one sentence, we can establish his central thesis: that a literal interpretation of the biblical text is in the first place impossible, and furthermore undesirable. It is impossible because the text is subject to immense variations, many of which come from those who interpret it literally, both Jews and Christians; it is undesirable because very often a literal interpretation does not tell us either what we should believe ("nullam praestat cognitionem utilem in credendis") nor how we should act ("nec in agendis").[35] A fundamental article by Yosi Yisraeli shows that Pablo de Santa María's opposition to literal interpretation is a criticism not merely of Brother Nicholas but also of his most important source,

---

34. Teresa regularly refers to the authors she cites, and especially the quoted passages, as "authorities."

35. Genesis 8.

Rashi, the rabbi from Champagne.³⁶ Klaus Reinhardt and Horacio Santiago-Otero list twenty-six manuscripts of the *Additiones*, as well as more than twenty-five printed editions if we count only those that also include the *Postillae*; that leaves out editions that also include the *glossa ordinaria*, the prologues of Saint Jerome, and other works.³⁷ These serve as proof of the tremendous diffusion of Pablo de Santa María's work, and of how it fits into a tradition of reading and use of the Bible that crosses all frontiers.

After reading Yisraeli's contributions, I emailed him to ask his opinion on whether Teresa could have known, or taken into account, her grandfather's work in Latin. Since we have no textual proof for establishing this intellectual genealogy, it would mean introducing one more conjecture into research on Teresa de Cartagena. Yisraeli replied at once to say that the notion was not impossible, but that two factors inclined him to pessimism: first, that the textual history of Pablo's Latin work seemed to resonate more outside the Iberian Peninsula than within it; and second, that at the date of the *Arboleda*'s composition, later than 1470, it was unlikely that Pablo's ideas about exegesis would have held any sway. Obviously, Pablo's theories depended heavily on the Jewish intellectual tradition in Hebrew, which was under violent scrutiny in Castile in the last third of the fifteenth century.³⁸

Conjectures about Teresa and her lineage have not ceased with the passage of years. In a 2020 article Rica Amrán explores Teresa's debts to Jewish authors who wrote in Hebrew.³⁹ There is no doubt at all that Pablo knew the language, but whether any of his children, including Alonso de Cartagena, had philological competence in Hebrew remains to be demonstrated. And still in the realm of conjecture is whether Pablo's son Pedro, Teresa's father and principally a merchant, would have given his offspring a knowledge of the language that was both philological and theological—this in a political milieu marked by the

---

36. Yisraeli, "A Christianized Sephardic Critique," 118–41. Yosi Yisraeli has kindly sent me his doctoral dissertation, in which he treats Pablo de Santa María's whole theoretical system in greater detail: "Between Jewish and Christian Scholarship."

37. Reinhardt and Santiago-Otero, *Biblioteca bíblica ibérica medieval*, 241–44.

38. The email exchange between Yosi Yisraeli and I took place between November 24 and December 17, 2020, and it was one of the most delightful email exchanges about microliterary questions I have had.

39. Amrán, "Acerca de Teresa de Cartagena," 569–82.

proliferation of what David Nirenberg has called "communities of violence."[40]

All these speculations are useful because they convey some of the surprise and the impact that Teresa's work generates in the modern era. They establish a direct connection between the prudent men and contemporary research. But they also perpetuate the acousmatism of Teresa's voice, and consign her to invisibility.

I Am a Worm

And yet, Teresa is the builder of a civil society. She begins to write from a place that is not philosophical, an island to which she gives a name drawn from Psalm 22:6: "But I am a worm, and no man; a reproach of men, and despised of the people." She means that if she inhabits that island it is because she is a worm: as the Arragel translation has it, "¶ τ yo so gusano τ non homne verguença de omnes τ menospreciado de pueblos." The ordinary glosses of the Bible cite several different authorities on this point. The first is Augustine: a person who claims to have been conceived without the action of human semen commits the sin of pride. Next comes Cassiodorus, who notes that worms are born without prior coitus, and therefore without need of semen; someone claiming to have been born without semen or coitus is also saying that they were born without sin. Theodosius is the last authority, observing that worms in effect reproduce spontaneously, so that one calling himself a worm means that he or she was born of a virgin. The interlinear glosses, which also mention Augustine, leave no doubt: a worm is produced without concupiscence.

Karl Steel has analyzed the theory of the worm in the twelfth and thirteenth centuries. For the authors he studies, worms reproduce without exchanging fluids, in a nonhuman manner, while sharing in a heavenly virtue.[41] The ordinary gloss is much more radical in its conception: not content to theorize about the worm as an entity, it explicates the theological nature of the worm at the moment in which it comes into being in the doctrinal and legal text of Christianity. The worm is Adam, his nature is divine, and he is a messianic figure. Therefore the worm is not only death or the decay of the flesh—it is new life.

---

40. Nirenberg, *Communities of Violence*.
41. Steel, *How Not to Make a Human*.

Of course, the ordinary gloss is not just any resource; it is inscribed in the "Cartagena conjecture." But we can go even further: Juan Carlos Conde's research shows, I think convincingly, that most of Teresa's biblical references and the commentaries on them are related to the *glossa ordinaria* of the Bible.[42]

I am a worm, says Teresa. And while placing herself at the lowest level of existence, she also claims to be a virginal creation. Teresa comes from nowhere, but is spontaneously generated on this island where she lives apart from the world and from which she tries to recover a space of civilization, the *Arboleda de los enfermos*, a place designed expressly for thinking and philosophizing. She is a worm that, in generating herself, gives life.

A Silkworm

Perhaps the best metaphor is that of the silkworm. It not only can build the house in which its metamorphosis will take place, but it does so with threads that weave a net to contain that house or node. The main concern in Teresa's writings is to produce a space, to build a city in which to philosophize. Although Pedro del Trigo, the copyist of the Escorial manuscript that contains her works, presents them as treatises, it is equally true that the *Arboleda* and the *Admiración* seem like letters. These letters participate in the microliterary impulse to produce a space for writing within which to think alongside the founding authorities of Christian morality, and to do so as a woman. But just as important is the need—also microliterary—to create an intricate weaving of women with whom to think, inside the physical spaces of power. The network is that space. The network is, in the end, the name of the city to which one can bring down critical—and, frankly, feminist—thinking, and give it a home.

---

42. Conde, "La ortodoxia," 115-23.

Epilogue

Charles of Navarre, prince of Viana, had written a letter to be sent to all the "valiant scholars" (*valientes letrados*) of Spain (which would be a large number). In it he encouraged them (and us, in my opinion) to read and study Aristotle's *Ethics*. He had made a version of it himself, based on Leonardo Bruni's Latin translation, for Alfons V the Magnanimous of Aragon. The manuscript that contains the exemplar of this translation, with stitching where its parchment is worn, is in the British Library, Add. 21120. It contains 1294 glosses (if my count is correct) that constitute the conceptual system of ethics in Castilian, as Charles had set it down. His letter to the valiant scholars, as found in the codex now preserved in the Biblioteca Nacional de España, VITR/17/3, contains marginal glosses that allow us to establish a network of imaginary lines between the letter itself and the conceptual map in the translation, the *Ética*. The letter moves, it goes from place to place—or to many places, because it is directed to many people, like a circular letter is. It may even be a chain letter, the kind that warns you to send it on to your friends and not break the chain. And at the same time it is like an Advent calendar with little windows, behind each of which is a gift or a piece of candy. But here the windows are the tie marks for the glosses, and behind them is a vision of ethics sent out into the world as a circular letter. The letter encourages not only reading the *Ethics* but also losing oneself in its thicket of accompanying glosses, glosses newly made so as to construct a politics, a public life, for ethics.

Charles died too soon. His servant and friend Fernando de Bolea y Galloz decided to continue what the prince had begun, and wrote letters to the kings of Aragon, Castile, and Portugal (in that order in the manuscript preserved in the Biblioteca Nacional), before writing in his own name to the *valientes letrados* of Spain; his letter is placed before the one to them that Charles had signed. He urges them to have their subjects become serious students of the *Ethics*, naturally by using the prince's translation and conceptual scheme. Fernando thereby fulfills, we might say, the mission of producing a margin in which to write one's thoughts, and a set of networks through which to continue that process of thinking together, creating that city in which to philosophize.

The present book has moved between these two necessities. On the one hand the need to produce a margin, to control the art of the manuscript. On the other, to create a system of interchange in which to propagate the universe of critical thought that originates and is built in the margins. Microliteratures, as we have said from the beginning, are a way of writing, an activity, and a critical movement. This movement is a feature of the humanities, as they existed then and exist now: of the paper-and-pencil humanities and the digital ones, of the quantum humanities of the future (should they come to pass), and of whatever follows them; it will claim the right, if necessary, to write on a grain of rice, and then share it as part of a paella meant for twenty-five diners when eighty unexpected guests show up.

Microliteratures should not be underestimated, and we find them in many unexpected fields of research. They produce ideas that are worthy of consideration. Before Hernando de Talavera became Hernando de Talavera, when he was a mere bachelor of arts who was proud to have learned to write a neat scholastic hand under Vicente Panyella in Barcelona, he translated Petrarch's *Invective Against a Physician* as *Invectivas contra el médico rudo y parlero*. Aside from translating it he added an introduction and marginal glosses, all written in heavy, severe scholastic letters with subtitles, rubrics, and a whole system of signs that owes little to Petrarch. The contents of the glosses, however, can be seduced by the Petrarchan rhetoric of invective: criticism that combines theoretical precision, political argument, and acidulous personal insult. The key concept of the translator's foray into Petrarchism is *eutrapelia*: a relatively new term in Castilian, used before Talavera (as the *Corpus*

EPILOGUE

diacrónico del español informs us) only by El Tostado and Alfonso de la Torre. Talavera says in his prologue:

¶ In reading the books that can offer you not curiosities, but the perfection of the virtuous habits to which your fine mind naturally inclines you:: you seek, virtuous sir, in the time allowed, to relieve the fatigue that human understanding receives from the body's complaints, with light and playful lessons and polite jests. It is no small virtue, in my view, of eutrapelia, which people today call levity or urbanity/ in our vernacular, or benign and pleasant conversation.

(¶ Leyendo los libros que no curiosidad mas perfecçion de las virtuosas costunbres aque vuestro ylustre jngenio natural mente vos jnclina pueden prestar:: queres virtuoso señor la fatiga que el entendimiento humano por la pesadumbre del cuerpo resçibe releuar en los tienpos a ello conçessos con lecçiones donosas de juegos y burlas honestas. no es pequeño grado a mj ver de eutra-pellia virtud que los modernos ya llaman jocundidad o urbani-dad/ en nuestro [2v] vulgar benjgna y dulce conuersacion)

In his glosses, Talavera practices these forms of eutrapelia. He wants to enjoy himself and amuse his interlocutor, displaying a certain degree of vulgarity that is sometimes inherited from other glosses (like those in the Boethius translation made for Ruy López Dávalos, in which *scenicas meretriculas* are also called *putillas*—sluts), sometimes of his own inspiration. For instance, he glosses *culina* (for *cocina*, kitchen) by noting that it evokes the place from which filth is excreted (*culo*), and *caque* (which recalls *caca*—"poo poo," in the unforgettable words of Nancy Pelosi) with the remark that it sounds unfortunate but should be attributed to a "defect of our language." Obviously, before taking up eschatology, Talavera was interested in scatology. In his glosses he seeks to adopt the jesting, and also wounding, tone of invective. He is amusing his interlocutor (his uncle and mentor Fernán Álvarez), but at the same time he is testing his own style, imagining how far he might go in combining a knowledge of philosophy—how fictions can carry allegorical meaning; what is the value of Averroes's thought; how intellectual, rational knowledge differs from practical experience—with a eutrapelic form of writing. Eutrapelia is an epistemological artifact, and humor is as well.

The unknown glosser of manuscript MSS/6728 of Spain's Biblioteca Nacional, which contains Juan de Lucena's *Diálogo de vita beata*, understood the eutrapelian style. In Lucena's dialogue three serious individuals of the then recent intellectual history of Castile, Juan de Mena, Alonso de Cartagena, and the Marquis of Santillana, maintain a conversation. All three, at that time, were among the honored dead. Lucena has them roasting and insulting each other, while still displaying their ethical and intellectual values. The glosser annotates lavishly. Whether anonymous or not (different scholars register different opinions), the author is clearly writing his comments in Íñigo López de Mendoza's own library, which housed the books of the man who had died as the Marquis of Santillana. Some of the glosses can only refer, in an obviously parodic manner, to books from that collection, two of them by Pero Díaz de Toledo, whom we have met in the present volume. One is the *Diálogo y razonamiento en la muerte del marqués de Santillana*, and the other is the translation of Plato's *Phaedo*.[1] The first gloss in *De vita beata* repeats Díaz de Toledo's definition of *diálogo* (a new word in the fifteenth century): the *Diálogo y razonamiento* defines it as "speech between two [people], one who asks and another who answers" (fabla de dos, uno que pregunta e otro que responde), while also referring to the Platonic "*Phedrón*," which is none other than the translation of the *Phaedo* that Pero Díaz de Toledo called *Libro llamado Fedrón*. The glosser also reproduces (and misattributes) a sentence from Cicero's *Tusculanae Disputationes*. Eutrapelia in glossing is not only an epistemological artifact, but also reveals the intellectual networks that are created through microliterary glosses and commentaries.

It would be easy to keep following the trail of glossed manuscripts and their presence in libraries, including those of the bourgeoisie. Manuscript MSS/23123 of the Biblioteca Nacional de España (BNE), which contains a *Trevet castellano*, belonged to one Diego de Pastrana, an employee of Seville's mercantile exchange and the grandson of a jurist of that city—these were members of the comfortable professional class. Other glossed manuscripts may also come from bourgeois libraries, for instance BNE MSS/1518, which contains a Castilian translation of the Book of Maccabees. BNE MSS/3666, which is ugly and difficult to read, with glosses that would try the patience of a saint, may proceed from a middle-class library as well.

Microliterary artifacts—public, copied a thousand times, or sometimes secreted within a single manuscript—are ways of bringing us into

---

1. MSS/10226, Biblioteca Nacional de Madrid: Pero Díaz de Toledo, *Diálogo y razonamiento [en la muerte del Marqués de Santillana]*.

the conversations that take place inside those networks; sometimes they allow us to make critical, theoretical, or stylistic investigations. These searches take us into a shared intellectual space that is very hard to create, and therefore is of immense value.

Microliterature, as a form of writing, spreads through the narrow margins of what has already been written, modifying it and commenting on it. That is how it proclaims its wish to intervene in the production of contemporary thought, and to not let the past stay exclusively in the past. Microliterature, lacking any method, moves through the labyrinths of what people think they know. It speaks, attempts, lies, interrupts. Sometimes it pauses to participate, from its uncomfortable perch, in the discussion of themes and problems that have occupied this world since it began and are part of its structure and system. Microliteratures are constrained by their lack of space, by the number of characters, by abbreviations, labels, and marks. They seek out corners where they can express themselves, blank spaces where they declare: "I can write here." They need to produce that space (because it was not meant for them), appropriate it, and turn it into a platform from which to jump off into the world; and from there to weave the fabric of voices both anonymous and known, invented and genuine, that can speak without asking permission. And so this book wants to say, with Horace (and with respect): What are you laughing at? This fable is about you.

Acknowledgments

At several points throughout this book, I have referred to personal communications, letters, text messages. All of them, no matter how academic, have been the fruit of conversations, exchanges of ideas, and unexpected inspirations. In fact, this work originated in an exchange of letters in the fall of 1992. I was a young doctoral student in Paris, and a French academic journal had asked me to review Julian Weiss's book *The Poet's Art*, published in 1990. In my enthusiasm for the book I sent Professor Weiss a letter through the mail. A few weeks later his answer arrived in my tiny room at the École Normale Supérieure, and a fairly long correspondence between us began. I told him of my recent acquaintance with glossed manuscripts, which I had begun to study on the side during the research that would lead to my doctoral dissertation, which I defended in May 1995. Julian Weiss was, and continues to be, a model both intellectually and ethically, and I haven't enough words to thank him for his generosity. He sent me a photocopy of his typed provisional catalogue of glossed manuscripts, which he would publish in a much improved version in 2013, in two parts, one devoted to Castilian authors and the other to translations. This early exchange, and my many conversations with Julian Weiss over the years at different points on the globe, have guided my work, have made me ever more demanding, and have also freed me enormously: if there is anything that distinguishes Julian Weiss's teaching it is the intellectual freedom he inspires. I hope that this book will reflect even a shadow of that freedom.

I won't need to recount here every detail of this volume's genealogy, but just a few details will not go amiss. For a long time, I thought I would be unable to write it at all, because I always came up against the impenetrable wall of trying to be exhaustive. I have had to abandon that wish before concluding that the book is really one chapter in a series of pieces I have been writing and publishing over the years, and perhaps will keep writing in the future. Finishing it has been like following a course of treatment and could happen only after a series of events that I will recall here. On March 16, 2020, New York City's public schools were shut down by the COVID-19 pandemic, so that our son, who was then four years old, remained at home, full of joy and energy; from then on all his schooling took place online. I didn't return to the classroom either—that semester, and the academic year 2020-21, were conducted virtually. On April 17, 2020, our daughter was born at Mount Sinai hospital in Midtown Manhattan. New York's streets and great avenues, totally deserted but dotted with field hospitals, marked another historic moment in which we are still living as I send this book to the Spanish press. Thanks to Kaela Pierce, with her matchless professionalism and warmth, from September 2020 we were able to carve out some work time beyond classes and administrative tasks, and it was then that I decided to put the book together—it was now or never. One early winter day I finally had the finished manuscript in my hands, and after I had reread it, made corrections, and put the final version into the computer, my son asked me, "Can we throw the manuscript in the fireplace?" And since I can't deny him anything, that's what we did—he had seen me do it with an earlier book, *Dead Voice* (University of Pennsylvania Press, 2020). I hope that by the time this book is published we'll have returned to some kind of normal life, and that our families in Spain and France will have been able to meet our little girl (nota bene: they did). Every text has its gloss, it seems.

Aurélie Vialette, who lived through all that with me, has had time to give birth to our daughter, write a few research articles, finish a book, write a furious critique of the lack of maternity leave in the State of New York, play with both children, direct her department's graduate program, being awarded for the latter, and read my manuscript with a careful and critical eye. I could only thank her for all this if I borrowed one of the multisyllabic words that our son likes to invent.

Several generations of students at the universities of Salamanca, Berkeley, Columbia, and Yale have been patient enough to study and discuss with me several aspects of the research that gave rise to this book. I thank them all for their incredible intellectual generosity. Especial thanks to Esteban Crespo Jaramillo, who helped me enormously in revising and formatting the bibliography, no easy task. I am equally grateful to Ana Fernández-Blázquez, who reviewed the English version.

Noel Blanco Mourelle, Laura Fernández Fernández, Rachel Stein, and my three sisters, Blanca, Margarita, and Mariajosé Rodríguez Velasco, have read and critiqued drafts of this book. My brothers Javier and Juanjo have had to put up with my long-distance calls at all hours. What can I say about the family that I haven't already told them?

Over the years Pedro Cátedra, Patricia Dailey, Enrique Gavilán, Michael Gerli, Carlos Heusch, Yonsoo Kim, Claudio Lomnitz, Georges Martin, Natalia Morozova, and Selby Wynn Schwartz have read and commented on passages or ideas that have ended up between these covers. Conversations with Juan Carlos Conde and Yosi Yisraeli have been very important for me. The director of my doctoral thesis in law, Emanuele Conte (EHESS, Paris, and Roma Tre, Giurisprudenza), has made queries and offered comments that proved extremely helpful. As I said in the preface, Mia Ruyter, both meaning to and not meaning to, showed me a path that I was unaware of before then. The influence of my friend Bernard Harcourt, in many theoretical aspects and in a form of intellectual searching, has been, I believe, fundamental. My gratitude goes also to many people I do not name here but do remember, who have helped me in many ways throughout these years in France, Spain, the United States, Great Britain, Germany, Italy, and Argentina. I owe a special debt to the libraries and librarians of several countries who have made this work possible with their great professionalism, kindness, and above all intellectual generosity. All of them deserve my admiration and thanks. Any errors, of which there are probably many, are mine alone.

I am grateful to Josune García López for his belief in me in first publishing the book. Since childhood I had dreamed of publishing with Editorial Cátedra, and it is gratifying and dizzying to see that dream fulfilled.

My gratitude is now extended to the wonderful enthusiasm of Cecilia Gaposchkin, Anne Lester, and Mahinder Kingra, who have been so kind as to host this book as part of their wonderful catalog. Hussein Fancy and Jerry Singerman also need to be thanked for their continued encouragement. The splendid team at Cornell University Press and the extraordinary copy editor Marlyn Miller, a historian, are now in my pantheon of heroes.

Julie Stone Peters, friend, coconspirator, intellectual partner, and much more, has been instrumental for the production of the English translation, and my gratitude cannot be measured in words. Julie also found the perfect translator for this task, my dear and admired colleague Consuelo López-Morillas, an extraordinary academic, now professor emerita at Indiana University, Bloomington.

ACKNOWLEDGMENTS

This book would never have come into being without the intellectual support, the devoted reading, and the criticisms of my true model in this life, my companion of the last twenty-three years (and counting), Aurélie Vialette, together with our children, Miguel and Simone. For them, always, everything.

Bibliography

Manuscript Sources

Beinecke Rare Book and Manuscript Library, Yale University.

Marston MS 2. *Canticum Canticorum, cum Glossa Ordinaria.*

Biblioteca de la Fundación Bartolomé March, Palma de Mallorca.

B95-V3-27. Aegidius Romanus, arzobispo de Bourges. *Regimiento de príncipes.*

Biblioteca de Menéndez Pelayo, Santander.

M-94. *Libro de Vegecio de la caballería y del arte de las batallas.*

Biblioteca General Histórica de la Universidad de Salamanca, Salamanca.

MS. 2709. Aegidius Romanus, arzobispo de Bourges. *Regimiento de príncipes.* Translated by Juan García de Castrojeriz, ca. 1345.

Biblioteca Histórica de la Universidad Complutense, Madrid.

BH MSS 84. Pero Díaz de Toledo. *Enchiridión.*

Biblioteca Nacional de España, Madrid.

MSS.FACS/622-23. Arragel, Moses, and Jeremy Schonfield. *La Biblia de Alba: An Illustrated Manuscript Bible in Castilian; Commissioned in 1422 by Don Luis de Guzmán and Now in the Library of the Palacio de Liria, Madrid.* 2 vols. Facsimile. Madrid: Fundación Amigos de Sefarad, 1992.

MSS/1341. *Obras de Mosen Diego de Valera.*

MSS/1518. *Historia de los macabeos.*

MSS/3666. *Tratados varios.*

MSS/3694. Pedro de Portugal, 4. condestável de Portugal. *Coplas de contemptu mundi.*

MSS/4023. Pedro de Portugal, 4. condestável de Portugal. *Sátira de Felice e Infelice vida.*

MSS/6728. Juan de Lucena, protonotario. *Diálogo de vita beata.*

MSS/9220. Quintus Curtius Rufus. *Historia de Alejandro Magno (III–XII).*

MSS/10220. Boecio [Boethius]. *Consolación de filosofía.*

MSS/10226. Pero Díaz de Toledo. *Diálogo y razonamiento [en la muerte del marqués de Santillana].*

MSS/10289. *El More en Castellano traducido por el Maestro Pedro de Toledo.*

MSS/17975. Enrique de Villena. *Carta; Comentario a Virgilio; Publius Vergilius Maro, Eneida.* Translated by Enrique de Aragón, marqués de Villena, 9/28/1427–10/10/1428.

MSS/19344. *Vida y memorias del licenciado Gregorio de Tovar, caballero natural de Valladolid, fiscal y oidor que fue de esta Chancillería, de la Audiencia de La Coruña y del Real Consejo de Ordenes.*

MSS/23090. Pedro de la Panda. *Letra al muy ilustre conde don Rodrigo Manrique [conde de Paredes].*

MSS/23123. Boecio [Boethius]. *Consolación de filosofía.* With commentary by Trevet.

RES/35. *Historia de los reyes de España y otras cosas.*

VITR/15/7. Alfonso XI, rey de Castilla y León. *Ordenamiento de Alcalá de Henares de 1348 (era 1386).*

VITR/17/3. Carlos de Aragón, príncipe de Viana. *Epístola del serenísimo y virtuoso príncipe don Carlos, primogénito de Aragón etc. de inmortal memoria, enderezada a todos los valientes letrados de la España exhortando y requiriéndoles que den obra y fin a lo que por ella podrán ser informados.*

VITR/17/3. Fernando de Bolea y Galloz. *La carta que Fernando de Bolea y Galloz hace a los valientes letrados de la España pidiéndoles de gracia que cumplan lo que exhortado y requerido les es por su señor, el muy esclarecido príncipe don Carlos de inmortal memoria, por una epístola que bajo de la presente hallaréis.*

VITR/17/4. Pero Diaz de Toledo. *Plato: Libro llamado Fedrón.*

Bibliothèque de Genève

Ms. Fr. 180. Christine de Pizan, *Livre de la cité des dames.* https://www.e-codices.ch/en/list/one/bge/fr0180

Bibliothèque de l'Arsenal, Paris.

Ms-3172. Christine de Pizan. *Livre de la Mutation de Fortune.*

Bibliothèque Nationale de France, Paris.

Ms Fonds Espagnol 211. *Libro de Vegecio de la caballería y del arte de las batallas.*

Ms Fonds Espagnol 295. *Libro de Vegecio de la caballería y del arte de las batallas.*

Ms Fonds Francais 137. *Ovide Moralisé.*

Pizan, Christine de. *Livre de la cité des dames.* Gallica. https://gallica.bnf.fr/html/und/manuscrits/manuscrits-de-christine-de-pizan?mode=desktop.

British Library, London.

Add. 20787. *Alfonso X, rey de Castilla y León. Siete partidas (1).*
Add. 21120 (ff. 1r–235v.). Aristoteles. *Ética de Aristóteles.*

Harley 4431. Christine de Pizan. *The Book of the Queen.*

British Museum, London.

Royal MS 17 E IV. *Ovide Moralisé.*

Hispanic Society of America

HC 371/173. Boecio. *Consolación de filosofía.*

Real Biblioteca del Monasterio de San Lorenzo de El Escorial, San Lorenzo.

de El Escorial. h.III.24. Teresa de Cartagena. *Arboleda de los enfermos; Admiración operum Dei.*

Real Biblioteca del Palacio Real de Madrid, Madrid.

II/215. *Imago Mundi.* Spanish ed.
II/569. *Libro de Vegecio de la caballería y del arte de las batallas.*

Victoria and Albert Museum, London.

KRP.D.13. Gil de Roma and Juan García de Castrojeriz. *Regimiento de príncipes.*

Wellcome Collection of the University of London, London.

MS.55 (fols. 94r-99v). Peter Gerticz of Dresden. *Parvulus philosophiae naturalis.*

Works Cited

Accorsi, Federica. "Estudio del *Espejo de verdadera nobleza* de Diego de Valera: Con edición crítica de la obra." PhD diss. Università di Pisa, 2011.

Adorno, Rolena. *The Polemics of Possession in Spanish American Narrative.* New Haven, CT: Yale University Press, 2007.

Aegidius Romanus [Giles of Rome]. *De regimine principum libri tres.* Rome: Bartolomeo Zanetti, 1607.

Aegidius Romanus [Gil de Roma], and Juan García de Castrojeriz. *Regimiento de Príncipes.* Seville: Meinardo Ungut and Stanislao Polono, 1494.

Aers, David. *Medieval Literature: Criticism, Ideology, and History.* New York: St. Martin's, 1986.

Agamben, Giorgio. "What Is the Contemporary?" In *What Is an Apparatus? And Other Essays*, 39–54. Stanford, CA: Stanford University Press, 2009.

Agnew, Michael. "The 'Comedieta' of the *Sátira*: Dom Pedro of Portugal's 'Monkeys in the Margins.' " Hispanic issue, *MLN* 118, no. 2 (2003): 298–317.

Agúndez Fernández, Antonio. *La doctrina jurídica de Gregorio López en la defensa de los derechos humanos de los indios.* Mérida: Editora Regional de Extremadura, 1992.

Agustín [Saint Augustine]. *La ciudad de Dios.* Vols. 16–17 of *Obras completas de san Agustín.* Federación Agustiniana Española. Edited by Pío de Luis

BIBLIOGRAPHY

Vizcaíno, María Teresa Iniesta, Miguel Fuertes Lanero, et al. Translated by Santos Santamarta del Río and Miguel Fuertes Lanero. Bilingual ed. Madrid: Biblioteca de Autores Cristianos, 1988.

Agustín. [Saint Augustine]. *Las confesiones*. Vol. 2 of *Obras completas de san Agustín*. Bilingual ed. Madrid: Biblioteca de Autores Cristianos, 1991.

Alberti, Leon Battista. *De pictura (1435); De la peinture*. Edited by Jean Louis Schefer, translated by Cecil Grayson. Latin ed. Paris: Macula, 1992.

Albertus Magnus. *Ethicorum libri X*. Vol. 7 of *Beati Alberti Magni ratisbonensis episcopi, ordinis praedicatorum, Opera omnia*. Edited by Auguste Borgnet. Paris: Louis Vivès, 1891.

Alfonso X. *Las Siete Partidas del sabio rey don Alonso el Nono*. Edited by Gregorio López. Salamanca: Andrea de Portonariis, 1555. Reprint, Madrid: Boletín Oficial del Estado, 1985.

Alighieri, Dante. *Il convivio*. Edited by Giovanni Busnelli, Giuseppe Vandelli, Michele Barbi, and Antonio E. Quaglio. Florence: F. Le Monnier, 1964.

Alighieri, Pietro. *Pietro Alighieri, Comentum Super Poema "Comedie" Dantis: A Critical Edition of the Third and Final Draft of Pietro Alighieri's Commentary on Dante's "The Divine Commedy."* Edited by Massimiliano Chiamenti. Tempe, AZ: Arizona Center for Medieval and Renaissance Studies, 2002.

Amrán, Rica. "Acerca de Teresa de Cartagena y *La arboleda de los enfermos*: Algunas puntualizaciones, preguntas e hipótesis." In *Pasados y presente: Estudios para el profesor Ricardo García Cárcel*, edited by Rosa María Alabrús Iglesias, José Luis Beltrán Moya, Francisco Javier Burgos Rincón, Bernat Hernández, Doris Moreno, and Manuel Peña, 569–82. Barcelona: Universitat Autònoma de Barcelona, 2020.

Anderson, Benedict, and Richard O'Gorman. *Imagined Communities: Reflections on the Origin and Spread of Nationalism*. Rev. ed. London: Verso, 2006.

Apter, Emily. *Against World Literature: On the Politics of Untranslatability*. London: Verso, 2013.

Archer, Robert. *The Problem of Woman in Late-Medieval Hispanic Literature*. Woodbridge, Suffolk, UK: Tamesis, 2005.

Arcipreste de Hita. *Libro de buen amor*. Edited by Alberto Blecua. Madrid: Cátedra, 2006.

Arias Bonet, Juan Antonio. *Alfonso X. Primera Partida: Según el manuscrito Add. 20.787 del British Museum*. Valladolid: Universidad de Valladolid, 1975.

Aristotle. *Aristotelous peri poietikes; Aristotelis ars poetica; Poetica de Aristóteles*. Edited by Valentín García Yebra. Trilingual ed. Madrid: Editorial Gredos, 1974.

Aristotle. *Categories; On Interpretation; Prior Analytics*. Translated by H. P. Cooke and Hugh Tredennick. Cambridge, MA: Harvard University Press, 1938.

Aristotle. *"Ética" a Nicómaco*. Edited by María Araujo and Julián Marías. Madrid: Centro de Estudios Constitucionales, 1989.

Aristotle. *Politics*. Translated by H. Rackham. London: Heinemann, 1932.

ARLIMA: Archives de littérature du Moyen Âge. Accessed December 3, 2024. http://www.arlima.net.

Asad, Talal. *Genealogies of Religion: Discipline and Reasons of Power in Christianity and Islam*. Baltimore, MD: Johns Hopkins University Press, 1993.

Auerbach, Erich. "Figura." In *Scenes from the Drama of European Literature*, 11–76. Minneapolis: University of Minnesota Press, 1984.
Augustine. *Confessions*. Edited by Carolyn J. B. Hammond. Cambridge, MA: Harvard University Press, Loeb Classical Library, 2014.
Baets, Antoon de. *Responsible History*. Oxford: Berghahn, 2009.
Baker, Denise N., ed. *Inscribing the Hundred Years' War in French and English Cultures*. Albany: State University of New York Press, 2000.
Baldissera, Andrea. "La *Exhortación de la Paz* di Diego de Valera (edizione critica)." In *Guerra e pace nel pensiero del Rinascimento*, edited by Luisa Secchi Tarugi, 467–91. Florence: Franco Cesati, 2005.
Barthes, Roland. *Camera lucida*. New York: Hill and Wang, 1981.
Bartolo da Sassoferrato. [*De dignitatibus*]. "Ad xij libr. Cod. De dignitatibus." In *Commentaria in tres libris Codicis*, 45v–48v. Lyon: Compagnie des Libraires de Lyon, 1555.
Bartolo da Sassoferrato. *De insigniis et armis*. In *A Grammar of Signs: Bartolo da Sassoferrato's "Tract on Insignia and Coats of Arms,"* edited by Osvaldo Cavallar, Susanne Degenring, and Julius Kirschner, 42–84. Berkeley: University of California Press, 1994.
Bartolo da Sassoferrato. *De insula*. Translated by Prometeo Cerezo de Diego. Madrid: Centro de Estudios Constitucionales, 1979.
Bartolo da Sassoferrato. "Sobre las enseñas y cotas de armas." Edited by Jesús Rodríguez Velasco. "El *Tractatus de insigniis et armis* de Bartolo y su influencia en Europa (con la edición de una traducción castellana cuatrocentista)." *Emblemata* 2 (1996): 52–70.
Bataille, Georges. *Inner Experience*. Translated and with an introduction by Stuart Kendall. Albany: State University of New York Press, 2014.
Bataille, Georges. *L'Experiénce intérieure*. Paris: Gallimard, 1943.
Bautista, Francisco. *La Estoria de España en época de Sancho IV: Sobre los reyes de Asturias*. London: University of London, 2006.
Bautista, Francisco. "La idea de nobleza en conflicto." Lecture, "Theorica" Seminar. Lyon: École Normale Supérieure de Lyon, December 5, 2013. Video, 56 min., 30 sec. http://cle.ens-lyon.fr/espagnol/ojal/traces-huellas/theorica-2013.
Baxandall, Michael. *Giotto and the Orators: Humanist Observers of Painting in Italy and the Discovery of Pictorial Composition, 1350–1450*. Oxford: Oxford University Press, 1986.
Behm, Nicolas, Sherry Rankins-Robertson, and Duane Roen. "The Case for Academics as Public Intellectuals." *Academe* 100, no. 1 (January–February 2014). https://www.aaup.org/article/case-academics-public-intellectuals#.YK150JP0nOQ.
Bell, Fleming L., and Leona B. LeBlanc. "The Language of Glosses in L2 Reading on Computer: Learners' Preferences." *Hispania* 83, no. 2 (May 2000): 274–85.
Bell, Susan Groag. "Christine de Pizan in Her Study." *Cahiers de recherches médiévales et humanistes*. June 10, 2008. https://doi.org/10.4000/crm.3212.
Bellomo, Manlio. *L'Europa del diritto comune: La memoria e la storia*. Rome: Galileo Galilei, 1989.

Benjamin, Walter. *Crítica de la violencia*. Edited by Eduardo Maura Zorita. Madrid: Biblioteca Nueva, 2010.
Benjamin, Walter. *Toward the Critique of Violence: A Critical Edition*. Edited by Peter Fenves and Julia Ng. Stanford, CA: Stanford University Press, 2021.
Beresford, Andrew M., Louise M. Haywood, and Julian Weiss, ed. *Medieval Hispanic Studies in Memory of Alan Deyermond*. Woodbridge, Suffolk, UK: Tamesis, 2013.
Bluhme, Friedrich, ed. *Leges Burgundionum*. Monumenta Germaniae Historiae 3. Hanover: Aulicus Hahnianus, 1863.
Boccaccio, Giovanni. *Famous Women*. Edited and translated by Virginia Brown. I Tatti Renaissance Library 1. Cambridge, MA: Harvard University Press, 2001.
Boccaccio, Giovanni. *Genealogia deorum gentilium libri XV*. Edited by Vincenzo Romano. Bari: Laterza, 1951.
Boccaccio, Giovanni. *Il corbaccio*. Edited by Tauno Nurmela. Helsinki: Suomalainen Tiedakatemian Toimituksia-Annales Academiae Fennicae, 1968.
Bourdieu, Pierre. *Homo academicus*. Paris: Éditions de Minuit, 1984.
Bourdieu, Pierre. *La Distinction: Critique sociale du jugement*. Paris: Éditions de Minuit, 1979.
Bourdieu, Pierre. *La Noblesse d'État: Grandes écoles et esprit de corps*. Paris: Éditions de Minuit, 1989.
Boureau, Alain. *Des Vagues individus: La condition humaine dans la pensée scolastique*. La Raison scolastique III. Paris: Les Belles Lettres, 2008.
Boureau, Alain. *La Réligion de l'État: La construction de la République "étatique" dans le discours théologique de l'Occident médiéval, 1250–1350*. La Raison scolastique I. Paris: Les Belles Lettres, 2006.
Boureau, Alain. *Le Feu des manuscrits: Lecteurs et scribes des textes médiévaux*. Paris: Les Belles Lettres, 2018.
Boureau, Alain. *L'empire du livre: Pour une histoire du savoir scolastique, 1200–1380*. La Raison scolastique II. Paris: Les Belles Lettres, 2007.
Boureau, Alain. *L'Errance des normes: Éléments d'éthique scolastique (1220–1320)*. La Raison scolastique IV. Paris: Les Belles Lettres, 2016.
Boureau, Alain. "Peut-on parler d'auteurs scholastiques?" In *Auctor et Auctoritas: Invention et conformisme dans l'écriture médiévale; Actes du colloque tenu à l'Université de Versailles-Saint-Quentin-en-Yvelines, 14–16 juin 1999*, edited by Michel Zimmermann, 267–79. Paris: École des Chartes, 2001.
Boynton, Susan, and Diane J. Reilly, eds. *The Practice of the Bible in the Middle Ages: Production, Reception, and Performance in Western Christianity*. New York: Columbia University Press, 2011.
Brabant, Siger of. *Siger de Brabant: Écrits de logique, de morale, et de physique*. Edited by Bernardo Bazán. Louvain: Publications universitaries, 1974.
Breaugh, Martin. *L'Expérience plébéienne: Une histoire discontinue de la liberté politique*. Paris: Payot & Rivages, 2007.
Brownlee, Marina Scordilis. *The Severed Word: Ovid's "Heroides" and the Novela Sentimental*. Princeton, NJ: Princeton University Press, 1990.

Bruni, Leonardo. *Opere letterarie e politiche di Leonardo Bruni*. Edited by Paolo Viti. Turin: UTET, 1996.
Butler, Judith. *Giving an Account of Oneself.* New York: Fordham University Press, 2005.
Cabañas González, María Dolores. *La caballería popular en Cuenca durante la baja Edad Media*. Madrid: Prensa Española, 1980.
Cahn, Walter. *Romanesque Bible Illumination*. Ithaca, NY: Cornell University Press, 1982.
Camille, Michael. Review of *The Craft of Thought: Mediation, Rhetoric, and the Making of Images, 400–1200*, by Mary Carruthers. *Modern Philology* 98, no. 1 (2000): 3–6.
Canales, Jimena. *Bedeviled: A Shadow History of Demons in Science*. Princeton, NJ: Princeton University Press, 2020.
Cappelli, Guido. *El humanismo italiano: Un capítulo de la cultura europea entre Petrarca y Valla*. Madrid: Alianza, 2007.
Carrillo de Huete, Pedro. *Crónica del Halconero de Juan II, Pedro Carrillo de Huete*. Edited by Juan de Mata Carriazo. Madrid: Espasa-Calpe, 1946.
Carruthers, Mary. *The Book of Memory: A Study of Memory in Medieval Culture*. Cambridge: Cambridge University Press, 1990.
Carruthers, Mary. *The Craft of Thought: Meditation, Rhetoric, and the Making of Images, 400–1200*. Cambridge: Cambridge University Press, 1998.
Carruthers, Mary, and Jan M. Ziolkowski. *The Medieval Craft of Memory: An Anthology of Texts and Pictures*. Philadelphia: University of Pennsylvania Press, 2002.
Cartagena, Alonso de. *Discurso sobre la precedencia del rey Católico*. Vol. 1 of *Prosistas españoles del siglo XV*, edited by Mario Penna, 205–33. Biblioteca de Autores Españoles 116. Madrid: Ediciones Atlas, 1959.
Cartagena, Alonso de. *Título de la amistança: Traducción de Alonso de Cartagena sobre la "Tabulatio et expositio Senecae" de Luca Mannelli*. Edited by Georgina Olivetto. San Millán de la Cogolla: Cilengua, 2011.
Cartagena, Teresa de. *Arboleda de los enfermos; Admiraçion operum Dei*. Edited by Juan Carlos Conde. Madrid: Cátedra, forthcoming.
Cartagena, Teresa de. *Arboleda de los enfermos y Admiraçion operum Dey*. Edited by Lewis Joseph Hutton. Madrid: Aguirre, 1967.
Cassin, Barbara, ed. *Vocabulaire européen des philosophies: Dictionnaire des intraduisibles*. Paris: Seuil, Le Robert, 2004.
Castilla Urbano, Francisco. *El pensamiento de Francisco de Vitoria: Filosofía política e indio americano*. 1st ed. Barcelona: Anthropos-Universidad Autónoma Metropolitana, Unidad Iztapalapa, 1992.
Castillo Cáceres, Fernando. "¿Guerra o torneo? La Batalla de Olmedo, modelo de enfrentamiento caballeresco." *En la España Medieval* 32 (2009): 139–66.
Castro-Ponce, Clara Esther. "Teresa de Cartagena, *Arboleda de los enfermos; Admiraçión operum Dey*, Edición crítica singular." PhD diss., Brown University, 2001.
Cátedra, Pedro M., ed. *Enrique de Villena: Traducción y glosas de la Eneida*. Salamanca: Biblioteca Española del Siglo XV, 1989.

Cátedra, Pedro M. "Enrique de Villena y algunos humanistas." In *Nebrija y la introducción del Renacimiento en España: Actas de la III Academia Literaria Renacentista, Universidad de Salamanca, 9, 10 y 11 de diciembre, 1981*, 187–203. Salamanca: Universidad de Salamanca, 1983.

Cátedra, Pedro M. *Exégesis, ciencia, literatura: La exposición del salmo "Quoniam videbo" de Enrique de Villena*. Madrid: El Crotalón, 1985.

Cátedra, Pedro M. *Liturgia, poesía y teatro en la Edad Media: Estudios sobre prácticas culturales y literarias*. Madrid: Gredos, 2005.

Cátedra, Pedro M., ed. *Obras completas de Enrique de Villena*. 3 vols. Madrid: Turner, 1994–2000.

Cavarero, Adriana. *Tu che mi guardi, tu che mi racconti: Filosofia della narrazione*. Milan: Feltrinelli, 1997.

Chartier, Roger. *Inscrire et effacer: Culture écrite et littérature (XIe–XVIIIe siècles)*. Paris: Gallimard, Seuil, 2005.

Chartier, Roger. "Jack Cade, the Skin of a Dead Lamb, and Hatred of the Written Word." *Shakespeare Studies* 34 (2006): 77–89.

Chenu, Marie-Dominique. *Introduction a l'étude de saint Thomas d'Aquin*. Paris: Vrin, 1993.

Cicero. *On Invention; The Best Kind of Orator; Topics*. Edited by H. M. Hubbell. Cambridge, MA: Harvard University Press, 1949.

Claraval, Bernardo de [Bernard of Clairvaux]. *Liber de gradibus humilitatis et superbiae*. Vol. 1 of *Obras completas de san Bernardo*, edited by Monjes Cistercienses de España, 126–209. Madrid: Biblioteca de Autores Cristianos, 1983.

Colunga Cueto, Alberto, and Lorenzo Turrado, eds. *Biblia sacra iuxta Vulgatam Clementinam*. Madrid: Biblioteca de Autores Cristianos, 1999.

Compagnon, Antoine. *La Seconde main, ou le Travail de la Citation*. Paris: Seuil, 1979.

Conde, Juan Carlos. "La ortodoxia de una heterodoxa: Teresa de Cartagena y la Biblia." *Hispania Sacra* 72, no. 145 (2020): 115–23.

Conte, Emanuele. "L'istituzione del testo giuridico tra XII e XIII secolo." In *Tavolarotonda 1: Conversazioni di storia delle istituzioni politiche e giuridiche dell'Europa mediterranea*, 51–88. Milan: Giuffre, 2004.

Conte, Emanuele. *Tres libri Codicis: La ricomparsa del testo e l'esegesi scolastica prima di Accursio*. Frankfurt am Main: Klostermann, 1990.

Cortes de los antiguos reinos de León y de Castilla. 5 vols. Real Academia de la Historia. Madrid: M. Rivadeneyra, 1861–66; Sucesores de Rivadeneyra, 1882–1903.

Cortijo Ocaña, Antonio, and Teresa Jiménez Calvente, eds. "Salió buen latino: Los ideales de la cultura española tardomedieval y protorrenacentista." Special issue, *La Corónica* 37, no. 1 (2008).

Craddock, Jerry R. "La Cronología de las obras legislativas de Alfonso X." *Anuario de historia del derecho español* 51 (1981): 365–418.

Craddock, Jerry R. *The Legislative Works of Alfonso X, El Sabio: A Critical Bibliography*. London: Grant & Cutler, 1986.

Craddock, Jerry R., and Jesús Rodríguez Velasco. *Alfonso X, Siete Partidas 2.21, "De los caballeros."* Berkeley: University of California, 2008. https://escholarship.org/uc/item/1cg57404.
Crane, Gregory R., ed. *Greek Word Study Tool*. Perseus Digital Library. Accessed December 3, 2024. https://www.perseus.tufts.edu/hopper/morph.
Culler, Jonathan D. *The Literary in Theory*. Stanford, CA: Stanford University Press, 2007.
Dagenais, John. *The Ethics of Reading in Manuscript Culture: Glossing the "Libro de Buen Amor."* Princeton, NJ: Princeton University Press, 1994.
Dahan, Gilbert. *Études d'exégèse médiévale: Ancien Testament*. Strasbourg: Presses universitaires de Strasbourg, 2017.
Dahan, Gilbert. *Lire la Bible au Moyen Âge: Essais d'herméneutique médiévale*. Geneva: Droz, 2009.
Dahan, Gilbert. *L'Occident médiéval, lecteur de l'Écriture*. Paris: Éditions du Cerf, 2001.
Daniel, Arnaut. *Poesías*. Edited by Martín de Riquer. Barcelona: Quaderns Crema, 1994.
Davis, Kathleen. *Periodization and Sovereignty: How Ideas of Feudalism and Secularization Govern the Politics of Time*. Philadelphia: University of Pennsylvania Press, 2008.
De Certeau, Michel. *Arts de faire*. Vol. 1 of *L'Invention du quotidien*. Paris: Gallimard, 1980.
De Certeau, Michel. *La Fable mystique: XVIe–XVIIe siècle*. Vol. 2. Edited by Luce Giard. Paris: Gallimard, 2013.
De Hamel, Christopher. *Glossed Books of the Bible and the Origins of the Paris Booktrade*. Woodbridge, Suffolk, UK: D. S. Brewer, 1984.
Deleuze, Gilles. *Nietzsche et la philosophie*. Paris: Presses universitaires de France, 1962.
Deleuze, Gilles. *Nietzsche*. Paris: Presses Universitaires de France, 1965.
Deleuze, Gilles, and Félix Guattari. *Kafka: Pour une littérature mineure*. Paris: Éditions de Minuit, 1975.
Deleuze, Gilles, and Félix Guattari. *Qu'est-ce que la philosophie?* Paris: Éditions de Minuit, 1991.
De Lubac, Henri. *Exégèse médiévale: Les quatre sens de l'Écriture*. 4 vols. Paris: Aubier, 1959–64.
Del Valle, Carlos. "El comentario de Abraham ibn Ezra al Cantar de los Cantares, sus análisis filológicos." *Fortunatae* 22 (2011): 329–36.
Derrida, Jacques. *De la grammatologie*. Paris: Éditions de Minuit, 1967.
Derrida, Jacques. *Mal d'archive: Une Impression Freudienne*. Paris: Galilée, 1995.
Derrida, Jacques. *Marges de la philosophie*. Paris: Éditions de Minuit, 1972.
Desmond, Marilynn, and Pamela Sheingorn. *Myth, Montage, and Visuality in Late Medieval Manuscript Culture: Christine de Pizan's "Epistre Othea."* Ann Arbor: University of Michigan Press, 2003.
Díaz de Games, Gutierre. *El Victorial*. Edited by Rafael Beltrán Llavador. Madrid: Taurus, 1994.

Díaz de Montalvo, Alonso. *Copilación de las leyes del reino*. Huete: Álvaro de Castro, 1484.
Díaz de Toledo, Pero. *Libro llamado Fedron: Plato's "Phaedo" translated by Pedro Díaz de Toledo*. Edited by Nicholas G. Round. London: Tamesis, 1993.
Di Camillo, Ottavio. *El humanismo castellano del siglo XV*. Valencia: Fernando Torres, 1976.
Díez Garretas, María Jesús. "Recursos estructurales y argumentos de autoridad, ejemplificación y paremiología en el *Gobernamiento de príncipes* de Gil de Roma." *Revista de poética medieval* 23 (2009): 151-96.
Díez Garretas, María Jesús, José Manuel Fradejas-Rueda, and Isabel Acero-Durántez. "Las versiones A y B de la traducción castellana del *De regimine principum* de Gil de Roma." In *Actas del IX Congreso Internacional de la Asociación Hispánica de literatura medieval, a Coruña, 18-22 de septiembre de 2001*, edited by Mercedes Pampín Barral and Carmen Parrilla García, 1:227-33. La Coruña: Toxosoutos Editorial, 2005.
Díez Garretas, María Jesús, José Manuel Fradejas-Rueda, and Isabel Acero-Durántez. *Los manuscritos de la versión castellana del "De Regimine Principum" de Gil de Roma*. Tordesillas: Instituto de Estudios de Iberoamérica y Portugal, Seminario de Filología Medieval, Universidad de Valladolid, 2003.
Dingledy, Frederick W. "The *Corpus Juris Civilis*: A Guide to Its History and Use." *Legal Reference Services Quarterly* 35, no. 4 (2016): 231-55. https://doi.org/10.1080/0270319X.2016.1239484.
Dolezalek, Gero Rudolf. "La *pecia* e la preparazione dei libri giuridici nei secoli XII-XIII." In *Luoghi e metodi di insegnamento nell'Italia medioevale: Atti del convegno internazionale di studi, Lecce-Otranto 6-8 Ottobre 1986*, edited by Luciano Gargan and Oronzo Limone, 201-17. Lecce: Congedo editore, 1986.
Dolezalek, Gero Rudolf. "Taking Inventory of Juridical Manuscripts: Survey of Tasks Achieved, and Tasks to Do." In *Proceedings of the Fourteenth International Congress of Medieval Canon Law, Toronto 5-11 August 2012*, edited by Joseph Goering, Stephan Dusil, and Andreas Thier, 275-87. Vatican City: Biblioteca Apostolica Vaticana, 2016.
Doñas Beleña, Antonio. "Bibliographia Boethiana I." *Memorabilia: Boletín de Literatura Sapiencial* 13 (2011): 285-334.
Doñas Beleña, Antonio. "Bibliographia Boethiana II." *Memorabilia: Boletín de Literatura Sapiencial* 14 (2012): 161-92.
Doñas Beleña, Antonio. "Bibliographia Boethiana III." *Memorabilia: Boletín de Literatura Sapiencial* 15 (2013): 255-60.
Doñas Beleña, Antonio. "Versiones hispánicas de la *Consolatio Philosophiae* de Boecio: Testimonios." *Revista de Literatura Medieval* 19 (2007): 295-312.
Dondaine, Antoine. *Secrétaires de Saint Thomas*. 2 vols. Rome: Editori di S. Tommaso, 1956.
Dove, Mary, ed. *Glossa ordinaria in "Canticum canticorum": Pars 22*. Turnhout, Belgium: Brepols, 1997.
Dove, Mary, trans. *The "Glossa Ordinaria" on the Song of Songs*. Kalamazoo: TEAMS, Western Michigan University, 2004.
Drimmer, Sonja. *The Art of Allusion: Illuminators and the Making of English Literature, 1403-1476*. Philadelphia: University of Pennsylvania Press, 2018.

Dutton, Brian, and Stephen Fleming. *Catálogo-índice de la poesía cancioneril del siglo XV*. Madison, WI: Hispanic Seminary of Medieval Studies, 1982.

Eden, Kathy. "Poetry and Equity: Aristotle's Defense of Fiction." *Traditio* 38 (1982): 17–43.

Fabian, Johannes. *Time and the Other: How Anthropology Makes Its Object*. New York: Columbia University Press, 2014.

Faulhaber, Charles. *Libros y bibliotecas en la España medieval: Una bibliografía de fuentes impresas*. London: Grant & Cutler, 1987.

Fenster, Thelma S., and Clare A. Lees, eds. *Gender in Debate from the Early Middle Ages to the Renaissance*. New York: Palgrave, 2002.

Fernández Fernández, Laura. "Folios reutilizados y proyectos en curso: Imagen histórica e imagen jurídica en el proyecto político alfonsí." In *Alfonso el Sabio y la conceptualización jurídica de la monarquía en las "Siete Partidas,"* edited by Mechthild Albert, Ulrike Becker, and Elmar Schmidt, 73–114. Bonn: Veröffentlichungen der Bonn University Press, 2021.

Fernández López, José Antonio. "An Intertextual Argument Between Two Translators in Pedro de Toledo's Translation of the *Guide of the Perplexed*." *Yod* 22 (2019): 79–106.

Fernández López, José Antonio, ed. *Mostrador e enseñador de los turbados: Traducción cuatrocentista de Pedro de Toledo*. Zaragoza: Certeza Riopiedras, 2016.

Fingernagel, Andreas, and Christian Gastgeber. *The Most Beautiful Bibles*. Hong Kong: National Library of Austria-Taschen, 2008.

Fischer, Bobby. *Bobby Fischer Teaches Chess*. Stamford, CT: Learning International, 1966.

Fish, Stanley Eugene. *Is There a Text in This Class? The Authority of Interpretive Communities*. Cambridge, MA: Harvard University Press, 1980.

Foronda, François, ed. *Avant le contrat social: Le Contrat politique dans l'Occident médiéval, XIIIe–XVe siècles; Actes du Colloque international de Madrid, Casa de Velázquez, 2008*. Paris: Éditions de la Sorbonne, 2019.

Foucault, Michel. *Le Courage de la vérité*. Vol. 2 of *Le Gouvernement de soi et des autres: Cours au Collège de France, 1984*. Paris: Seuil, Gallimard/EHESS, 2009.

Foucault, Michel. *Qu'est-ce que la critique? Suivi de la culture de soi*. Edited by Henri-Paul Fruchaud and Daniele Lorenzini. Paris: Vrin, 2015.

Foucault, Michel. "Qu'est-ce qu'un auteur?" *Bulletin de la Société Française de Philosophie* 63, no. 3 (1969): 73–104.

Foucault, Michel. *Surveiller et punir: Naissance de la prison*. Paris: Gallimard, 1975.

Fradejas Rueda, José Manuel, ed. "7 Partidas Digital: Edición crítica digital de las *Siete Partidas*." Universidad de Valladolid, 2019. http://7partidas.hypotheses.org.

Fradejas-Rueda, José Manuel, María Jesús Díez Garretas, and Isabel Acero-Durántez. "La transmisión textual de la versión castellana del *De regimine principum* de Gil de Roma: Estado de la cuestión y conclusiones." In *Proceedings of the Twelfth Colloquium*, edited by Alan Deyermond and Jane Whetnall, 31–38. Papers of the Medieval Hispanic Research Seminar 34. London: Queen Mary College, University of London, 2003.

France, Marie de. *Lais de Marie de France*. Edited by Karl Warnke and Laurence Harf-Lancner. Paris: Librairie Générale Française, 1990.

Froehlich, Karlfried, and Margaret T. Gibson, eds. *Biblia Latina cum Glossa ordinaria: Facsimile Reprint of the Editio Princeps Adolph Rusch of Strassburg 1480/81*. 4 vols. Turnhout, Belgium: Brepols, 1992.

Gaffiot, Félix. *Dictionnaire illustré latin-français*. Paris: Hachette, 1934.

Gally, Michèle. *L'Intelligence de l'amour d'Ovide à Dante: Arts d'aimer et poésie au Moyen-Âge*. Paris: CNRS, 2005.

Galvez, Marisa. *The Subject of Crusade: Lyric, Romance, and Materials, 1150 to 1500*. Chicago, IL: University of Chicago Press, 2020.

García-Gallo, Alfonso. "El *Libro de las leyes* de Alfonso el Sabio: Del *Espéculo* a las *Partidas*." *Anuario de historia del derecho español* 21–22 (1951–52): 345–528.

García-Gallo, Alfonso. "Nuevas observaciones sobre la obra legislativa de Alfonso X." *Anuario de historia del derecho español* 46 (1976): 609–70.

Gavilán, Enrique. "The Gnostic Imprint on Parsifal, An Illumination of Ruins." Translated by Monique Dascha Inciarte. *Romanic Review* 103, no. 1–2 (2012): 133–53. https://doi.org/10.1215/26885220-103.1-2.133.

Gentry, Howard S., Marc Mittleman, and Peter R. McCrohan. "Introduction of Chia and Gum Tragacanth in the U.S." In *Advances in New Crops*, edited by Jules Janick and James E. Simon, 252–56. Portland, OR: Timber Press, 1990.

Gherardi, S. "The Fluid Affective Space of Organizational Practices." *Qualitative Research in Organizations and Management* 18, no. 5 (2023): 1–19.

Gibert y Sánchez de la Vega, Rafael. "La Glosa de Gregorio López." In *Historia de la literatura jurídica en la España del Antiguo Régimen*, edited by Javier Alvarado Planas, 1:423–72. Madrid: Marcial Pons, 2000.

Gil Fernández, Luis. *Panorama social del humanismo español (1500–1800)*. Madrid: Alhambra, 1981.

Gille Levenson, Matthias. "L'évolution du *Regimiento de los prínçipes* (1345–1494), conditionnée par le pouvoir politique?" In *"Écritures" du Pouvoir*. Vol. 2 of *Les cultures politiques dans la péninsule Ibérique et au Maghreb, VIIIe–XVe siècles*, edited by Véronique Lamazou-Duplan, 137–48. Bordeaux: Ausonius, 2019.

Gilli, Patrick. *La Noblesse du Droit: Débats et controverses sur la culture juridique et le rôle des juristes dans l'Italie médiévale (XIIe–XVe siècles)*. Paris: Honoré Champion, 2003.

Gilli, Patrick, Jacques Verger, and Daniel Le Blévec. *Les Universités et la ville au Moyen Âge: Cohabitation et tension*. Leiden: Brill, 2007.

Gleave, Robert. *Islam and Literalism: Literal Meaning and Interpretation in Islamic Legal Theory*. Edinburgh: Edinburgh University Press, 2012.

The *Glossa ordinaria*. The Lollard Society. Accessed December 3, 2024. https://lollardsociety.org/?page_id=409.

González Jiménez, Manuel. *Alfonso X El Sabio*. Barcelona: Ariel, 2004.

González Rolán, Tomás, Antonio Moreno Hernández, and Pilar Saquero Suárez-Somonte. *Humanismo y teoría de la traducción en España e Italia en la primera mitad del siglo XV: Edición y estudio de la Controversia Alphonsiana (Alfonso de Cartagena vs. L. Bruni y P. Candido Decembrio)*. Madrid: Ediciones Clásicas, 2000.

González-Vázquez, Sara. "Représentation et théorisation de la noblesse dans les traités castillans du XVe siècle: Une édition du *Nobiliario Vero* de Ferrán Mexía." PhD diss., École Normale Supérieure de Lyon, 2013.
Graeber, David, and Marshall Sahlins. *On Kings*. Chicago, IL: Hau Books, 2017.
Grafton, Anthony. *The Footnote: A Curious History*. Cambridge, MA: Harvard University Press, 1999.
Green, William M. "Hugh of Saint-Victor: *De tribus maximis circumstantiis gestorum*." *Speculum* 18, no. 4 (1943): 484–93.
Greenblatt, Stephen. *Renaissance Self-Fashioning: From More to Shakespeare*. Chicago, IL: University of Chicago Press, 1980.
Guilarte, Alfonso. "Capítulos de concierto para la primera edición de las *Partidas*, con la glosa de Gregorio López." *Anuario de historia del derecho español* 16 (1945): 670–75.
Gumbrecht, Hans Ulrich. *The Powers of Philology: Dynamics of Textual Scholarship*. Urbana: University of Illinois Press, 2003.
Gumbrecht, Hans Ulrich. *Production of Presence: What Meaning Cannot Convey*. Stanford, CA: Stanford University Press, 2004.
Gupta, Alisa Haridasani. "She Explains Mansplaining with Help from 17th-Century Art." *New York Times*, August 10, 2020.
Gutt, Blake. "Transgender Mutation and the Canon: Christine de Pizan's *Livre de la Mutacion de Fortune*." *Postmedieval* 11, no. 4 (2020): 451–58. https://doi.org/10.1057/s41280-020-00197-2.
Harkins, Franklin T., and Frans A. van Liere, eds. *Interpretation of Scripture: Theory; A Selection of Works of Hugh, Andrew, Richard and Godfrey of St Victor, and Robert of Melun*. Victorine Texts in Translation 3. Turnhout, Belgium: Brepols, 2012.
Harrison, Chris. "Bible Cross-References." Christharrison.net. Accessed December 3, 2024. https://www.chrisharrison.net/index.php/Visualizations/BibleViz.
Hauptmann, Robert. *Documentation: A History and Critique of Attribution, Commentary, Glosses, Marginalia, Notes, Bibliographies, Works-Cited Lists, and Citation Indexing and Analysis*. Jefferson, NC: McFarland, 2008.
Hay, David J. *The Military Leadership of Matilda of Canossa, 1046–1115*. Manchester: Manchester University Press, 2008.
Heller, Marvin J. Review of *The Book of Hebrew Script*, by Ada Yardeni. *The Papers of the Bibliographical Society of America* 98, no. 2 (2004): 246–48.
Hernández, Francisco J. *Los hombres del rey y la transición de Alfonso X el Sabio a Sancho IV*. Salamanca: Universidad de Salamanca, 2021.
Herrero Prado, José Luis. "El *Enchiridión* de Pedro Díaz de Toledo." *Epos* 9 (1993): 571–77.
Herrero Prado, José Luis. "Pero Díaz de Toledo, Señor de Olmedilla." *Revista de Literatura Medieval* 10 (1998): 101–15.
Hinojo Andrés, Gregorio. "Οἱ βασιλεῖσ τῇ Ἐγκυκλοπαιδείᾳ αὐτη τοίς βασιλεῦσι" [Oí basileîs te enkyklopaideía aúte toís basileûsi]. In *Munus Quaesitvm Meritis: Homenaje a Carmen Codoñer*, edited by Gregorio Hinojo Andrés and José Carlos Fernández Corte, 463–72. Salamanca: Universidad de Salamanca, 2007.

Holtz, Louis. "Glosse e commenti." In *Lo spazio letterario del Medioevo 1: Il Medioevo Latino*. Vol. 3: *La ricezione del testo*, edited by Guglielmo Cavallo, Claudio Leonardi, and Enrico Menestò, 59–105. Rome: Salerno, 1995.
Hui, Andrew. *The Study: The Inner Life of Renaissance Libraries*. Princeton, NJ: Princeton University Press, 2024.
Illich, Ivan. *In the Vineyard of the Text: A Commentary to Hugh's "Didascalicon."* Chicago, IL: University of Chicago Press, 1993.
Ingham, Patricia C. *The Medieval New: Ambivalence in an Age of Innovation*. Philadelphia: University of Pennsylvania Press, 2015.
Innocent IV. *[Super libros quinque Decretalium] Commentaria innocentii quarti pont: Maximi super libros quinque decretalium; Cum indice peculiari nunc recens collecto, novisque insuper summariis additis, et Margarita baldi de ubaldis perusini*. Frankfurt am Main: Sigismundus Feiereabend, 1570.
Jara Fuente, José Antonio. *Concejo, poder y élites: La clase dominante de Cuenca en el siglo XV*. Madrid: Consejo Superior de Investigaciones Científicas, 2000.
Jed, Stephanie. *Chaste Thinking: The Rape of Lucretia and the Birth of Humanism*. Bloomington: Indiana University Press, 1989.
Justinian. *Corpus Iuris Civili s Ivstinianei, cvm commentariis Accvrsii, scholiis Contii, et D. Gothofredi Lvcvblationibvs ad Accvrsivm, in quibus Glossae obscuuriores explicantur, similes & contrariae afferuntur, vitiosa notantur*. 6 vols. Lyon: Andrea et Jacobus Prost, Barlet, 1627. http://digi.ub.uni-heidelberg.de/diglit/justinian1627ga.
Kabatek, Johannes. *Die Bolognesische Renaissance und der Ausbau romanischer Sprachen: Juristische Diskurstraditionen und Sprachentwicklung in Südfrankreich und Spanien im 12. und 13. Jahrhundert*. Tübingen: Niemeyer, 2005.
Kantorowicz, Hermann, William Warwick Buchland, and British Museum Department of Manuscripts. *Studies in the Glossators of the Roman Law: Newly Discovered Writings of the Twelfth Century*. Cambridge: Cambridge University Press, 1938.
Kasoy, Anna. "Arabic and Islamic Reception of the *Nicomachean Ethics*." In *The Reception of Aristotelian Ethics*, edited by Jon Miller, 85–106. Cambridge: Cambridge University Press, 2013.
Kim, Yonsoo. *Between Desire and Passion: Teresa de Cartagena*. Leiden: Brill, 2012.
Kim, Yonsoo. *El saber femenino y el sufrimiento corporal de la temprana Edad Moderna*. Córdoba: Universidad de Córdoba, 2008.
Ko, Myong Hee. "Glosses, Comprehension, and Strategy Use." *Reading in a Foreign Language* 17, no. 2 (2005): 125–43.
König-Pralong, Catherine. *Le bon usage des savoirs: Scolastique, philosophie et politique culturelle*. Paris: Vrin, 2011.
König-Pralong, Catherine, and Ruedi Imbach. *Le Défi laïque: Existe-t-il une philosophie de laïcs au Moyen Âge?* Paris: Vrin, 2013.
Koselleck, Reinhart. *Vergangene Zukunft: Zur Semantik geschichtlicher Zeiten*. Frankfurt am Main: Suhrkamp, 1979.
La Biblia, que es, los sacros libros del Viejo y Nuevo Testamento, Trasladada en español: La palabra del Dios nuestro permanece para siempre. Translated by Casiodoro de Reina. Basel: Samuel Apiarius, 1569.

Lacarra, Eukene. "Los discursos científico y amoroso en la *Sátira de Felice e Infelice vida* del Condestable D. Pedro de Portugal." In *"Never-Ending Adventure": Studies in Medieval and Early Modern Spanish Literature in Honor of Peter N. Dunn*, edited by Edward H. Friedman and Harlan Sturm, 109–28. Newark, DE: Juan de la Cuesta, 2002.

Latour, Bruno. "Ces réseaux que la raison ignore: Laboratoires, bibliothèques, collections." In *Le Pouvoir des bibliothèques: La Mémoire des livres en Occident*, edited by Christian Jacob and Marc Baratin, 23–46. Paris: Albin Michel, 1996.

Lawrance, Jeremy. "Humanism in the Iberian Peninsula." In *The Impact of Humanism on Western Europe*, edited by Anthony Goodman and Angus MacKay, 220–58. London: Longman, 1990.

Lawrance, Jeremy. "On Fifteenth-Century Spanish Vernacular Humanism." In *Medieval and Renaissance Studies in Honour of Robert Brian Tate*, edited by Ian Michael and Richard A. Cardwell, 63–79. Oxford: Dolphin, 1986.

Leiris, Michel. *Biffures*. Vol. 1 of *La Regle du jeu*. Paris: Gallimard, 1948.

Lewis, Charlton T., Charles Short, and E. A. Andrews, eds. *A Latin Dictionary: Founded on Andrews' Edition of Freund's Latin Dictionary*. Oxford: Clarendon, 1879. https://www.perseus.tufts.edu/hopper/text?doc=Perseus:text:1999.04.0059.

Libera, Alain de. *L'Archéologie philosophique: Séminaire du Collège de France, 2013–2014*. Paris: Vrin, 2016.

Libera, Alain de. *Penser au Moyen Âge*. Paris: Seuil, 1991.

Lipking, Lawrence. "The Marginal Gloss." *Critical Inquiry* 3, no. 4 (1977): 609–55.

López Nevot, José Antonio. "Las ediciones de las *Partidas* en el siglo XVI." *e-Spania: Revue interdisciplinaire d'études hispaniques medievales et modernes* 36 (2020): 1–31. https://doi.org/10.4000/e-spania.35041.

Löwy, Albert, ed. *Miscellany of Hebrew Literature*. London: N. Trübner, 1872.

Lucena, Juan de. *De vita felici*. Edited by Olga Perotti. Pavia: Ibis, 2004.

Lucena, Juan de. *Diálogo sobre la vida feliz: Epístola exhortatoria a las letras*. Edited by Jerónimo de Miguel. Madrid: Real Academia Española, Centro para la Edición de los Clásicos Españoles, 2014.

Lucena, Luis Ramírez de. *Repeticion de amores y arte de ajedrez*. Salamanca: Leonardo Hutz y Lope Sanz, 1496.

Luna, Álvaro de. *Crónica de don Álvaro de Luna, condestable de Castilla, Maestro de Santiago*. Edited by Juan de Mata Carriazo. Madrid: Espasa-Calpe, 1940.

Luna, Álvaro de. *Libro de las virtuosas e claras mugeres*. Edited by Julio Vélez-Sainz. Madrid: Cátedra, 2009.

Luna, Álvaro de. *Virtuosas y claras mujeres*. Edited by Lola Pons. Burgos: Instituto Castellano y Leonés de la Lengua, 2008.

Madero, Marta. "Façons de croire: Les Témoins et le juge dans l'oeuvre juridique d'Alphonse X le sage, roi de Castille." *Annales: Histoire, Sciences Sociales* 54, no. 1 (1999): 197–218.

Madrigal, Alonso de. "El Tostado." In *Brevyloquyo de amor e amiçiçia*. Edited by Nuria Belloso. Pamplona: Universidad de Navarra, 2000.

Maire Vigueur, Jean-Claude. *Cavaliers et citoyens: Guerre, conflits et société dans l'Italie communale, XII–XIII siècles*. Paris: EHESS, 2003.
Mannetter, Terrence A., ed. *Text and Concordance of the "Leyes del estilo," Escorial Ms. Z.III.11*. Madison, WI: Hispanic Seminary of Medieval Studies, 1990. Microfilm.
Mannetter, Terrence A., ed. *Text and Concordance of the "Leyes del estilo," Ms. 5764, Biblioteca Nacional, Madrid*. Madison, WI: Hispanic Seminary of Medieval Studies, 1989. Microfilm.
Manrique, Gómez. *Cancionero*. Edited by Francisco Vidal González. Madrid: Cátedra, 2003.
Marichal, Juan. *La voluntad de estilo*. Madrid: Alianza Universidad, 1984.
Marino, Nancy. "La Relación entre historia y poesía: El caso de *La Esclamación e querella de la gouernación* de Gómez Manrique." In *Propuestas teórico-metodológicas para el estudio de la literatura hispánica medieval*, edited by Lillian von der Walde Moheno, 211–25. Mexico City: Universidad Nacional Autónoma de México, 2003.
Marmursztejn, Elsa. *L'Autorité des maîtres: Scolastique, normes et société au XIIIe siècle*. Paris: Belles Lettres, 2007.
Martin, Georges. "Alphonse X maudit son fils." *Atalaya: Revue française d'études médiévales romanes* 5 (1994): 153–78.
Martin, Georges. "Alphonse X ou la science politique: *Septénaire*, 1–11." *Cahiers de Linguistique Hispanique Médiévale* 20 (1995): 7–33.
Martínez, H. Salvador. *Alfonso X, el Sabio: Una biografía*. Madrid: Ediciones Polifemo, 2003.
Martorell, Joannot. *Tirant lo Blanch*. Edited by Albert Hauf. Valencia: Clàssics Valencians, Conselleria de Cultura, Educació i ciència de la Generalitat Valenciana, 1990.
Marx, Karl. "Revolutionary Spain: IV." In *Revolution in Spain* by Karl Marx and Friedrich Engels, 42–50. New York: International Publishers, 1939.
Marx, Karl. "Revolutionary Spain: Fourth Article." *New York Daily Tribune*, October 27, 1854.
Matteis, F. D. *Affective Spaces: Architecture and the Living Body*. 1st ed. London: Routledge, 2020.
Mbembe, Achille. *Critique of Black Reason*. Durham, NC: Duke University Press, 2017.
McKenzie, Donald F. *Bibliography and the Sociology of Texts*. London: British Library, 1986.
Mena, Juan de. *Coronación del Marqués de Santillana*. Seville: Ladislao Polono, 1499.
Mena, Juan de. *Coronación del Marqués de Santillana*. Seville: Meinardo Ungut y Stanislao Polono, 1499.
Mena, Juan de. *Coronación del Marqués de Santillana*. Seville: Cromberger, 1512.
Mena, Juan de. *La coronación*. Edited by Maximiliaan P. A. M. Kerkhof. Madrid: Consejo Superior de Invesigationes Científicas, 2009.
Mena, Juan de. *Las Trescientas*. Seville: Meinardo Ungut y Estanislao Polono, 1496.

Mena, Juan de. *Las Trescientas*. Seville: Tres compañeros alemanes (Pegnitzer, Thomas y Magno), 1499.
Mena, Juan de. *Las Trescientas*. Granada: Juan Varela de Salamanca, 1505.
Mena, Juan de. *Las Trescientas*. Zaragoza: Jorge Coci, 1509.
Mena, Juan de, and Francisco Sánchez de las Brozas. *Obras de Juan de Mena*. Salamanca: Lucas de Junta, 1582.
Menéndez Pelayo, Marcelino. *Antología de poetas líricos*. Vol. 2. Madrid: Bailly-Baillière, 1944.
Meschonnic, Henri. *Poétique du traduire*. Lagrasse: Éditions Verdier, 1999.
Mignolo, Walter. *The Darker Side of Western Modernity: Global Futures, Decolonial Options*. Durham, NC: Duke University Press, 2011.
Miguel-Prendes, Sol. *El espejo y el piélago: La "Eneida" castellana de Enrique de Villena*. Kassel: Reichenberger, 1998.
Mombello, Gianni. *La tradizione manoscritta dell' "Epistre Othea" di Christine de Pizan: Prolegomeni all'edizione del testo; Memoria*. Turin: Accademia delle Scienze, 1967.
Montaner, Alberto. "De los márgenes al centro: Edición y compaginación de las glosas." In *Regards croisés sur la glose au Moyen Âge: Colloque international*. Lyon: École Normale Supérieure-LSH, 2006.
Moore, Robert I. *La formación de una sociedad represora (900–1250)*. Barcelona: Crítica, 1984.
Morales, Cristina. *Lectura fácil*. Barcelona: Anagrama, 2018.
Morard, Martin, and Fabio Gibiino, et al., eds. *Glossa ordinaria*. Glossae Sacrae Scripturae electronicae. Paris: CNRS-IRHT, 2016–17. http://gloss-e.irht.cnrs.fr.
Morrás, María. "Coluccio Salutati en España: La versión romance de las *Declamationes Lucretiae*." *La corónica* 39, no. 1 (2010): 209–48.
Murano, Giovanna. *Copisti a Bologna (1265–1270)*. Turnhout, Belgium: Brepols, 2006.
Nabokov, Vladimir. *Pale Fire: A Novel*. New York: Putnam, 1962.
Nelson, Jinty, and Damien Kempf. *Reading the Bible in the Middle Ages*. New York: Bloomsbury, 2015.
Nieto Soria, José Manuel. *Sancho IV: 1284–1295*. Palencia: La Olmeda, Diputación Provincial de Palencia, 1994.
Nirenberg, David. *Communities of Violence: Persecution of Minorities in the Middle Ages*. Princeton, NJ: Princeton University Press, 1996.
Nirenberg, David. *Neighboring Faiths: Christianity, Islam, and Judaism in the Middle Ages and Today*. Chicago, IL: University of Chicago Press, 2014.
O'Brien, Flann. "Buchhandlung." In *The Best of Myles: A Selection from Cruiskeen Lawn*, 17–22. New York: Walker, 1968.
Olivetto, Georgina. "Política y sermón en el Concilio de Basilea." In *Aspectos actuales del hispanismo mundial: Literatura, cultura, lengua*, edited by Christopher Strosetzki, 2:222–31. Berlin: De Gruyter, 2019.
Oluo, Ijeoma. *So You Want to Talk About Race*. New York: Seal Press, 2018.
Opitz, Michael, and Erdmut Wizisla. *Benjamins Begriffe*. 2 vols. Frankfurt am Main: Suhrkamp, 2000.

Orellana Calderón, Raúl. "'Contra los de dentro tortizeros e sobervios': Los otros 'defensores,' jurisdicción y poder en el proyecto político alfonsí." *e-Spania: Revue interdisciplinaire d'études hispaniques medievales et modernes* 1 (June 2006). https://doi.org/10.4000/e-spania.331.

Orellana Calderón, Raúl. "Hacia una edición crítica de la *Tercera Partida* de Alfonso X el Sabio: Testimonios y fuentes." In *Campus Stellae: Haciendo camino en la investigación literaria; Studia in honorem Alan Deyermond*, edited by Dolores Fernández López, Mónica Domínguez Pérez, and Fernando Rodríguez-Gallego López, 1:184–92. Santiago de Compostela: Universidad de Santiago de Compostela, 2006.

Ots y Capdequí, José María. *Historia del derecho español en América y del derecho indiano*. Madrid: Aguilar, 1969.

Palencia, Alfonso de. *Universal Vocabulario en latín y en romance: Reproducción facsimilar de la edición de Sevilla, 1490*. Madrid: Comisión Permanente de la Asociación de Academias de la Lengua Española, 1967.

Panizo Orallo, Santiago. *Persona jurídica y ficción: Estudio de la obra de Sinibaldo de Fieschi*. Pamplona: Universidad de Navarra, 1975.

Passagieri, Rolandino de'. *Summa totius artis notariae Rolandini Rodulphini Bononiensis*. Venice: Giunta, 1546. Anastatic reprint, Bologna: Consiglio Nazionale del Notariato, A. Forni, 1977.

Paz y Meliá, Antonio, ed. *Biblia (Antiguo Testamento) Traducida del hebreo al castellano por Rabí Mosé Arragel de Guadalfajara (1422–1433) y publicada por el Duque de Berwick y de Alba*. 2 vols. Madrid: Imprenta Artística, 1920–22.

Pedro de Portugal. *Coplas del contempto del mundo*. Zaragoza: Pablo Hurus, 1490.

Pedro de Portugal. *Sátira de Infelice e Felice vida*. Edited by Guillermo Serés. Alcalá de Henares: Centro de Estudios Cervantinos, 2008.

Penna, Mario, ed. *Prosistas españoles del siglo XV*. Vol. 1. Biblioteca de Autores Españoles 116. Madrid: Atlas, 1959.

Perec, Georges. *La vie, mode d'emploi*. Paris: Hachette, 1978.

Pérez Bustamante, Rogelio, and José Manuel Calderón Ortega. *Íñigo López de Mendoza, Marqués de Santillana (1398–1458): Biografía y documentación*. Madrid: Taurus, 1983.

Pérez de la Canal, Miguel Ángel. "La pragmática de Juan II, de 8 de febrero de 1427." *Anuario de Historia del Derecho Español* 26 (1956): 659–68.

Pérez Martín, Antonio. "El aparato de Glosas a las *Siete Partidas* de Gregorio López de Valenzuela." *Glossae* 13 (2016): 486–534.

Pérez-Prendes y Muñoz de Arracó, José Manuel. *Curso de historia del derecho español*. Madrid: Universidad Complutense de Madrid, Facultad de Derecho, 1984.

Pizan, Christine de. *Debate of the "Romance of the Rose."* Edited by David F. Hult. Chicago, IL: University of Chicago Press, 2010.

Pizan, Christine de. *Epistre Othéa*. Edited by Gabriella Parussa. Geneva: Droz, 1999.

Poe, Edgar Allen. *Fragments des "Marginalia."* Translated by Paul Valéry. Montpellier: Fata Morgana, 1980.

Poe, Edgar Allen. "Marginalia." *The Democratic Review* 15, no. 77, November 1844.

Powitz, Gerhardt. "Textus cum commento." *Codices Manuscripti: Zeitschrift für Handschriftenkunde* 5, no. 3 (1979): 80–89.
Preciado, Paul B. "Déclarer la grève des utérus." *Libération*, January 17, 2014. https://www.liberation.fr.
Preciado, Paul B. *Countersexual Manifesto*. Translated by Kevin Gerry Dunn, foreword by Jack Halberstam. New York: Columbia University Press, 2018.
Preciado, Paul B. *Manifiesto contrasexual*. Barcelona: Opera Prima, 2002.
Pulgar, Fernando del. *Crónica de los Reyes Católicos*. Edited by Juan de Mata Carriazo. Madrid: Espasa-Calpe, 1943.
Quaglioni, Diego. *La giustizia nel medioevo e nella prima età moderna*. Bologna: Il Mulino, 2004.
Quintilian. *The Instituto oratoria of Quintilian, with an English translation*. Translated by H. E. Butler. Cambridge, MA: Harvard University Press, 1920.
Rabasa, José. *Writing Violence on the Northern Frontier: The Historiography of Sixteenth-Century New Mexico and Florida and the Legacy of Conquest*. Durham, NC: Duke University Press, 2000.
Rashdall, Hastings. *The Universities of Europe in the Middle Ages*. 2 vols. in 3 parts. Oxford: Clarendon Press, 1895. Reprint, Cambridge: Cambridge University Press, 2010.
Real Academia Española. Database CORDE: *Corpus diacrónico del español*. Accessed December 3, 2024. http://www.rae.es/cordenet.html.
Real Academia Española. *Diccionario de autoridades*. Real Academia Española. https://apps2.rae.es/DA.html. Originally published Madrid, 1726–39.
"Real Decreto-ley 1/2015, de 27 de febrero, de mecanismo de segunda oportunidad, reducción de carga financiera y otras medidas de orden social." Jefatura del Estado, Ref: BOE-A-2015-2109. *Boletín Oficial del Estado* 51, February 28, 2015, 19058–19101. http://www.boe.es/boe/dias/2015/02/28/pdfs/BOE-A-2015-2109.pdf.
Recio Ferreras, Eloy. *Gómez Manrique, hombre de armas y de letras (siglo XV)*. Hato Rey, PR: Publicaciones Puertorriqueñas, 2005.
Reinhardt, Klaus, and Horacio Santiago-Otero. *Biblioteca bíblica ibérica medieval*. Madrid: Consejo Superior de Investiaciones Científicas, 1986.
Riché, Pierre, and Guy Lobrichon, eds. *Le Moyen Âge et la Bible*. Paris: Beauchesne, 1984.
Rodríguez del Padrón, Juan. "Triumpho de las donas." In *Obras completas*, edited by César Hernández Alonso, 209–58. Madrid: Editora Nacional, 1982.
Rodríguez Velasco, Jesús. "Autoglosa: Diego de Valera y su *Tratado en defensa de virtuosas mujeres*." *Romance Philology* 61, no. 1 (2007): 25–47.
Rodríguez Velasco, Jesús. *Ciudadanía, soberanía monárquica y caballería: Poética del orden de caballería*. Madrid: Akal, 2009.
Rodríguez Velasco, Jesús. "Diego de Valera, artista microliterario." In *Mosén Diego de Valera: Entre las armas y las letras*, edited by Cristina Moya García, 81–102. Woodbridge, Suffolk, UK: Tamesis, 2014.
Rodríguez Velasco, Jesús. *El debate sobre la caballería en el siglo XV: La tratadística caballeresca castellana en su marco europeo*. Valladolid: Junta de Castilla y León, Consejería de Educación y Cultura, 1996.

Rodríguez Velasco, Jesús. "El *Tractatus de insigniis et armis* de Bartolo y su influencia en Europa (con la edición de una traducción castellana cuatrocentista)." *Emblemata* 2 (1996): 35-70.

Rodríguez Velasco, Jesús. "La 'Bibliotheca' y los márgenes: Ensayo teórico sobre la glosa en el ámbito cortesano del siglo XV en Castilla; I: Códice, dialéctica y autoridad." *eHumanista: Journal of Iberian Studies* 1 (2001): 119-34.

Rodríguez Velasco, Jesús. "La producción del margen." *La Corónica* 39, no. 1 (2010): 249-72.

Rodríguez Velasco, Jesús. "Microbiographies." *New Literary History* 50, no. 3 (2019): 473-81.

Rodríguez Velasco, Jesús. *Order and Chivalry: Knighthood and Citizenship in Late Medieval Castile*. Translated by Eunice Rodríguez Ferguson. Philadelphia: University of Pennsylvania Press, 2010.

Rodríguez Velasco, Jesús. *Plebeyos márgenes: Ficción, industria del derecho y ciencia literaria, siglos XIII–XIV*. Salamanca: Seminario de Estudios Medievales y Renacentistas, 2011.

Rodríguez Velasco, Jesús. "Political Idiots and Ignorant Clients: Vernacular Legal Language in Thirteenth-Century Iberian Culture." *Digital Philology* 2, no. 1 (2013): 86-112.

Rodríguez Velasco, Jesús. "Santillana en su laberinto de lecturas." *Insula* 666 (2002): 3-7.

Rodríguez Velasco, Jesús. "Theorizing the Language of Law." *Diacritics* 36, no. 3-4 (2006): 64-86.

Roma, Gil de. See Aegidius Romanus.

Rojas, Fernando de. *La Celestina*. Edited by Francisco J. Lobera, Guillermo Serés, Paloma Díaz-Mas, Carlos Mota e Íñigo Ruiz Arzálluz, and Francisco Rico. Madrid: Real Academia Española, 2011.

Rorty, Richard. "The Contingency of Language." In *Contingency, Irony, and Solidarity*, 3-22. Cambridge: Cambridge University Press, 1989.

Round, Nicholas G. "Gómez Manrique's *Exclamación e querella de la governación*: Poem and Commentary." In Beresford et al., *Medieval Hispanic Studies*, 149-74.

Russo, Sara. "Aproximación a la tradición textual de Gómez Manrique, S. XV–XVI." Master's thesis, Universidad Complutense Madrid, 2012. https://eprints.ucm.es/17359/1/SaraRusso_TFM_MULE_2012.pdf.

Ruzzier, Chiara, and Xavier Hermand, eds. *Comment le Livre s'est fait livre: La fabrication des manuscrits bibliques (IVe–XVe siècle); Bilan, résultats, perspectives de recherche; Actes du colloque international organisé à l'Université de Namur du 23 au 25 mai 2012*. Turnhout, Belgium: Brepols, 2015.

Saenger, Paul. "Lire aux derniers siècles du Moyen Âge." In *Histoire de la lecture dans le monde occidental*, edited by Guiglielmo Cavallo and Roger Chartier, 147-74. Paris: Seuil, 2001.

Saenger, Paul. *Space Between Words: The Origins of Silent Reading*. Stanford, CA: Stanford University Press, 1997.

Saint-Victor, Hugh of. *De tribus maximis circumstantiis gestorum*. Edited by William M. Green. Cambridge, MA: Mediaeval Academy of America, 1943.

Saint-Victor, Hugh of. *Didascalicon of Hugh of St. Victor: A Medieval Guide to the Arts*. Edited by Jerome Taylor. New York: Columbia University Press, 1961.

Saint-Victor, Hugh of. *Hugonis de Sancto Victore, Didascalicon: De Studio Legendi*. Edited by Henry Buttimer. Washington, DC: Catholic University Press, 1939.

Salomon, David A. *An Introduction to the "Glossa Ordinaria" as Medieval Hypertext*. Cardiff: University of Wales Press, 2012.

Sánchez-Prieto Borja, Pedro, ed. "Carta de juramento de 1436. *Documentos del Archivo municipal de Guadalajara (a 1200–a 1492)*. Madrid: Universidad de Alcalá, 1999.

San Cristóbal, Alfonso de, and Flavio Vegecio Renato. *La versión castellana medieval de la "Epitoma rei militaris" de Flavio Vegecio Renato*. Edited by José Manuel Fradejas Rueda. San Millán de la Cogolla: Cilengua, 2014.

Santaella, Rodrigo de. *Vocabulario Eclesiástico*. Real Academia Española, Database CORDE: "Corpus diacrónico del español." Accessed December 3, 2024. http://www.rae.es/cordenet.html.

Saussure, Ferdinand de. *Cours de linguistique générale*. Edition by Charles Bally and Albert Sechehaye. Paris: Payot, 1971.

Schmitt, Jean-Claude. *La Conversion d'Hermann le juif: Autobiographie, histoire et fiction*. Paris: Seuil, 2003.

Schnerb, Bertrand. *L'État Bourguignon: 1363–1427*. Paris: Perrin, 1999.

Scott, James Brown. *The Spanish Origin of International Law: Lectures on Francisco de Vitoria (1480–1546) and Francisco Suárez (1548–1617)*. Washington, DC: The School of Foreign Service, Georgetown University, 1928.

Shklovsky, Victor. "El arte como artificio." In *Teoría de la literatura de los formalistas rusos*, edited by Tzvetan Todorov, translated by Tzvetan Todorov and Ana María Nethol, 127–46. Mexico City: Siglo XXI Editores, 1980.

Simonds, Roger T. *Philosophy and Legal Traditions: Reflections on the Jurisprudence of the Glossators; An Inaugural Lecture Delivered Before the American University on April 10, 1973*. Washington, DC: American University, 1973.

Smalley, Beryl. *The Study of the Bible in the Middle Ages*. Oxford: Blackwell, 1952.

Smith, Ali. *How to Be Both*. New York: Pantheon Books, 2014.

Smith, Lesley. *The "Glossa Ordinaria": The Making of a Medieval Bible Commentary*. Leiden: Brill, 2009.

Soetermeer, Frank. *Utrumque ius in peciis: Aspetti della produzione libraria a Bologna fra Due e Trecento*. Milan: Giuffrè Editore, 1997.

Spearing, A. C. *Medieval Autographies: The "I" of the Text*. Notre Dame, IN: University of Notre Dame Press, 2012. https://doi.org/10.2307/j.ctvpg859b.

Spijker, Ineke van 't, ed. *The Multiple Meaning of Scripture: The Role of Exegesis in Early-Christian and Medieval Culture*. Leiden: Brill, 2009.

Steel, Karl. *How Not to Make a Human: Pets, Feral Children, Worms, Sky Burial, Oysters*. Minneapolis: University of Minnesota Press, 2019.

Steinová, Evina. *Notam Superponere Studui: The Use of Annotation Symbols in the Early Middle Ages*. Turnhout, Belgium: Brepols, 2019.

Stern, Josef. "The Maimonidean Parable, the Arabic *Poetics*, and the Garden of Eden." *Midwest Studies in Philosophy* 33, no. 1 (2009): 209–47.

Stewart, Roger A., and Tracy L. Cross. "A Field Test of Five Forms of Marginal Gloss Study Guide: An Ecological Study." *Reading Psychology* 14, no. 2 (1993): 113–39.

Stock, Brian. *The Implications of Literacy: Written Language and Models of Interpretation in the Eleventh and Twelfth Centuries*. Princeton, NJ: Princeton University Press, 1983.

Stock, Brian. *Listening for the Text: On the Uses of the Past*. Baltimore, MD: Johns Hopkins University Press, 1990.

Talmy, Leonard. *Toward a Cognitive Semantics*. Vol. 1, *Concept Structuring Systems*. Cambridge, MA: MIT Press, 2000.

Tarradach, Madeleine, and Joan Ferrer. "El comentario de Rashi al *Cantar de los Cantares*: Edición y traducción del ms. 50h de la Bibliothèque de l'Alliance Israélite Universelle de París." *Miscelánea de Estudios Árabes y Hebraicos, Sección Hebreo* 53 (2004): 407–39.

Tate, Robert Brian. Review of *El humanismo castellano*, by Ottavio di Camillo. *Modern Language Review* 73, no. 2 (1978): 444–47.

Teissier-Ensminger, Anne. "La loi au figuré: Trois illustrateurs du Code pénal français." *Sociétés & Représentations* 2, no. 18 (2004): 277–91.

Tersigni, Nicole. *Men to Avoid in Art and Life*. San Francisco: Chronicle Books, 2020.

Thomas Aquinas. *Corpus Thomisticum*, edited by Enrique Alarcón. Pamplona: Universidad de Pamplona-Fundación Tomás de Aquino, 2000–2019. https://www.corpusthomisticum.org.

Thomas Aquinas. *Opera fratris Thome de Aquino quorum exempla sunt Parisius*, edited by Martin Grabmann and Enrique Alarcón. Pamplona: Universidad de Pamplona-Fundación Tomás de Aquino, 2000–2019. http://www.corpusthomisticum.org/.

Thomas Aquinas. *Sententia libri Ethicorum*. Latin and English translation. Accessed December 3, 2024. https://aquinas.cc/la/en/~Eth.

Thomas, Yan. "Corpus aut ossa aut cineres: La chose réligieuse et le commerce." *Micrologus* 7 (1999): 73–112.

Thomas, Yan. *Les opérations du droit*. Edited by Marie-Angèle Hermitte and Paolo Napoli. Paris: Gallimard/EHESS, Seuil, 2011.

Thomas, Yan. "Les ornements, la cité, le patrimoine." In *Images romaines: Actes de la table ronde organisée à l'École normale supérieure (24–26 octobre 1996)*, edited by Clara Auvray-Assayas, 44–75. Paris: Presses de l'École normale supérieure, 1998.

Thomas, Yan. "L'Extrême de l'ordinaire: Remarques sur le cas médiéval de la communauté disparue." In Thomas, *Les Opérations du droit*, 207–37.

Tribunal Constitucional. "Sentencia del Tribunal Supremo de 27 de marzo de 1860." *Colección legislativa* 71 (1860).

Tura, Adolfo. "Essai sur les *marginalia* en tant que pratique et documents." In *Scientia in margine: Études sur les Marginalia dans les manuscrits scientifiques du Moyen Âge à la Renaissance*, edited by Danielle Jacquart and Charles Burnett, 261–387. Geneva: Droz, 2005.

Valdés, Juan de. *Diálogo de la lengua*. Edited by Cristina Barbolani. Madrid: Cátedra, 1990.

Valera, Diego de. *Crónica Valeriana*. In *Edición y estudio de la "Valeriana" ("Crónica abreviada de España" de Mosén Diego de Valera)*, edited by Cristina Moya García. Madrid: Fundación Universitaria Española, 2009.
Valera, Diego de. *Defensa de virtuosas mujeres*. Edited by Federica Accorsi. Pisa: ETS, 2009.
Valera, Diego de. *Espejo de verdadera nobleza*. Edited by Federica Accorsi. Pisa: Università di Pisa, 2011.
Valera, Diego de. *Tratado de las epístolas*. In *Prosistas castellanos del siglo XV*, edited by Mario Penna, 3–51. Biblioteca de Autores Españoles 116. Madrid: Atlas, 1959.
Vanderjagt, Arjo. *Qui sa vertu anoblist: The Concepts of 'Noblesse' and 'Chose Publique' in Burgundian Political Thought*. Groningen: Jean Miélot, 1981.
Van Liere, Frans A. *An Introduction to the Medieval Bible*. Cambridge: Cambridge University Press, 2014.
Van Liere, Frans A., and Franklin T. Harkins, eds. and trans. *Interpretation of Scripture: Practice; A Selection of Works of Hugh, Andrew and Richard of St Victor, Peter Comestor, Robert of Melun, Maurice of Sully and Leonius of Paris*. Turnhout, Belgium: Brepols, 2015.
Vega, Garcilaso de la, and Fernando de Herrera. *Obras de Garcilasso de la Vega con anotaciones de Fernando de Herrera*. Seville: Alonso de la Barrera, 1580.
Velasco, Jesús R. *Dead Voice: Law, Philosophy, and Fiction in the Iberian Middle Ages*. Philadelphia: University of Pennsylvania Press, 2020.
Vélez Sáinz, Julio. *"De amor, de honor e de donas": Mujer e ideales corteses en la Castilla de Juan II (1406–1454)*. Madrid: Universidad Complutense, 2013.
Verger, Jacques. *Les Gens de savoir dans l'Europe de la fin du Moyen Âge*. Paris: Presses universitaires de France, 1997.
Verger, Jacques. *Les Universités au Moyen Âge*. Paris: Presses universitaires de France, 1973.
Vialette, Aurélie. *Intellectual Philanthropy: The Seduction of the Masses*. West Lafayette, IN: Purdue University Press, 2018.
Villena, Enrique de. *La primera versión castellana de "La Eneida" de Virgilio: Los libros I–III traducidos y comentados por Enrique de Villena (1384–1434)*. Edited by Ramón Santiago Lacuesta. Madrid: Real Academia Española, 1976.
Villena, Enrique de. *Traducción y glosas de la "Eneida," libros I–III*. Vol. 2 of *Obras completas de Enrique de Villena*. Edited by Pedro M. Cátedra. Madrid: Turner-Biblioteca Castro, 1994.
Virgil. *Omnia opera diligenti castigatione exculta aptissimisque ornata figuris, commentantibus Servio, Donato, Probo, Domitio, Landino, Antonioque Mancinello viris clarissimis, additis insuper in Servium multis quae deerant Graecisque dictionibus et versibus quam plurimis, qui passim corrupte legebantur, in pristinum decorem restitutis*. Venice: Bartolomeo Zanneto, 1514.
Vírseda Bravo, Marta. "La biblioteca de los Velasco en el hospital de la Vera Cruz: Arte y cultura escrita." PhD diss., Universidad Complutense Madrid, 2019.
Vismann, Cornelia. *Files: Law and Media Technology*. Translated by Geoffrey Winthrop-Young. Stanford, CA: Stanford University Press, 2008.

Vitoria, Francisco de. *Political Writings*. Edited by Anthony Pagden and Jeremy Lawrance. Cambridge: Cambridge University Press, 1991.

Vitoria, Francisco de. *Relecciones jurídicas y teológicas*. 2 vols. Edited by Antonio Osuna Fernández-Lago and Jesús Cordero Pando. Salamanca: San Esteban, 2017.

Vonnegut, Kurt. *Slaughterhouse-Five, or, The Children's Crusade: A Duty-Dance with Death*. Delacorte Press, 1969. Reprint, New York: Dial Press, 2009.

Walser, Robert. *Microscripts*. Translated by Susan Bernofsky, afterword by Walter Benjamin. New York: New Directions-Christine Burgin Gallery, 2010.

Ward, John O. *Ciceronian Rhetoric in Treatise, Scholion, and Commentary*. Turnhout, Belgium: Brepols, 1995.

Wei, Ian P. *Intellectual Culture in Medieval Paris: Theologians and the University, c. 1100–1320*. Cambridge: Cambridge University Press, 2012.

Weiss, Julian. "Juan de Mena's *Coronación*: Satire or *sátira*?" *Journal of Hispanic Philology* 6, no. 2 (Winter 1982): 113–38.

Weiss, Julian. "Las fermosas e peregrinas ystorias: Sobre la glosa ornamental cuatrocentista." *Revista de literatura medieval* 2 (1990): 103–12.

Weiss, Julian. "'¿Qué demandamos de las mugeres?': Forming the Debate About Women in Late Medieval Spain (with a Baroque response)." In Fenster and Lees, *Gender in Debate*, 237–81.

Weiss, Julian. "Vernacular Commentaries and Glosses in Late Medieval Castile, I: A Checklist of Castilian Authors." In *Text, Manuscript and Print in Medieval and Modern Iberia: Studies in Honour of David Hook*, edited by Barry Taylor, Geoffrey West, and Jane Whetnall, 199–243. New York: Hispanic Society of America, 2013.

Weiss, Julian. "Vernacular Commentaries and Glosses in Late Medieval Castile, II: A Checklist of Classical Texts in Translation." In Beresford et al., *Medieval Hispanic Studies*, 237–71.

Weissberger, Barbara. "'Deceitful Sects': The Debate About Women in the Age of Isabel the Catholic." In Fenster and Lees, *Gender in Debate*, 207–35.

Weissberger, Barbara. *Isabel Rules: Constructing Queenship, Wielding Power*. Minneapolis: University of Minnesota Press, 2003.

Wesseling, Klaus-Gunther. "Walafrid Strabo." In *Biographisch-Bibliographisches Kirchenlexikon*, edited by Friedrich-Wilhelm Bautz, 13:169–76. Herzberg: Bautz, 1998.

Winroth, Anders. *The Making of Gratian's "Decretum."* Cambridge: Cambridge University Press, 2000.

Woerther, Frédérique. "The Arabic Tradition: Averroes' *Middle Commentary* on Aristotle's *Nicomachean Ethics*." In *Phantasia in Aristotle's Ethics: Reception in the Arabic, Greek, Hebrew, and Latin Traditions*, edited by J. L. Fink, 37–64. London: Bloomsbury, 2019.

Yardeni, Ada. *The Book of Hebrew Script: History, Paleography, Script Styles, Calligraphy, and Design*. Jerusalem: Carta, 2010.

Yarza Luaces, Joaquín, Nicasio Salvador Miguel, Ángel Gómez Moreno, et al. *El Marqués de Santillana, 1398–1458: Los albores de la España Moderna*. 4 vols. Hondarribia: Nerea, 2001.

Yisraeli, Yosi. "Between Jewish and Christian Scholarship in the Fifteenth Century: The Consolidation of a *'Converso* Doctrine' in the Theological Writings of Pablo de Santa María." PhD diss., Tel Aviv University, 2014.

Yisraeli, Yosi. "A Christianized Sephardic Critique of Rashi's Peshaṭ in Pablo de Santa Maria's *Additiones ad Postillam Nicolai de Lyra*." In *Medieval Exegesis and Religious Difference*, edited by Ryan Szpiech, 118–41. New York: Fordham University Press, 2015.

Young, Robert J. C. "Postcolonial Remains." *New Literary History* 43, no. 1 (2012): 19–42.

Zakai, Avihu, and David Weinstein. "Erich Auerbach and his 'Figura': An Apology for the Old Testament in an Age of Aryan Philology." *Religions* 3, no. 2 (2012): 320–38.

Zysow, Aron. *The Economy of Certainty: An Introduction to the Typology of Islamic Legal Theory*. Atlanta, GA: Lockwood Press, 2013.

Index

Page numbers followed by letter "f" refer to figures.

academic disciplines: renewal and invention in medieval era, 19, 23n6, 24, 38–42. *See also ordo disciplinae*
Accorsi, Federica, 115, 116, 121
Accursio, Francesco: and *Corpus Iuris Civilis*, glosses on, 4, 28, 49, 79, 94; *Magna Glossa*, 17; and manuscript production, 54; *statio* (workshop) of, 79–80
activism: definition of, 107–8; microliterature and, 13–14, 104–5; poetry and, 125–26, 136; process of constructing a subject and, 139; public intellectuals and, 102–3, 106; radical, 136. *See also* microliterary artist(s)/activist(s)
Admiraçion operum Dei (Cartagena), 105, 178, 183
Adorno, Rolena, 96
Aegidius Romanus (Giles of Rome), 38; *De regimine principum*, 41; figured approach of, 41–42; *Glosa castellana al Regimiento de príncipes*, 5; on jurists, 135
Aeneid (Virgil), Villena's translation of/glosses on, 7, 8f, 17
Aers, David, 43, 44, 45
affective space: exegesis as, 31, 32; margins as, 12; notion of, 31n26
Afonso V (King of Portugal), 151, 154–55
Agamben, Giorgio, 9
Agnew, Michael, 146
Agúndez Fernández, Antonio, 97
Ailly, Pierre d', *Imago Mundi*, 59–61, 63
Alberti, Leon Battista, *De Pictura*, 173–74
Albertus Magnus: on *pertransitum*, 42; on *scientia perfecta*, 23n6; *Tractatus I: De Delectatione*, 41
Alexander the Great: glosses on, in Pedro's *Coplas*, 151–56, 160; narratives about, role in medieval history and political theory, 151
Alfons V the Magnanimous (King of Aragon), 184
Alfonso X the Wise (King of Castile): and editorial history of *Las Siete Partidas*, 12, 87; and transformation of academic disciplines, 23n6. *See also Las Siete Partidas*
Alfonso XI (King of Castile), and *Ordenamiento de Alcalá*, 87–88
Alighieri, Pietro, glosses on Dante's *Commedia*, 81
America, conquest of: López's gloss related to political debate on, 13, 96–97, 99; Thomas Aquinas's work and, 79
Amrán, Rica, 181
anagogy, 30
Andrea, Giovanni, 94, 177
Andrea, Novella d', 177
Anselm of Liège, 81n11
Arboleda de los enfermos (Cartagena), 105, 178, 183
Archer, Robert, 116
Archimedes, 37
Argos (Pedro de Portugal), 142–44
Aristotle: *Peri Hermeneias*, 36; on philosophical approach to history, 137; *Poetics*, 40; on poetry vs. history, 174; *Politics*, 135, 167; *On the Soul*, 167. *See also Nichomachean Ethics*
Arragel, Moshé, 46
Aryan philology, Auerbach's rejection of, 33–34
assemblage, epistemological device of, 139–40, 149; Pedro de Portugal and, 139–40, 149, 152, 153, 163; and perspectivism, 152
Auerbach, Erich, 33–34

INDEX

Augustine, Saint: conception of time, 106, 131, 132; and *contuitu*, theory of, 132, 136; *De Civitate Dei/La ciudad de Dios*, 95, 106–7, 130; on perpetual peace, 113; and theodicy, theory of, 130, 133, 134; on three ways of life, 106–7
authority, gloss and economy of, 81
autoglossing, 5, 64, 104; Mena and, 81, 141; Pedro de Portugal and, 141–44, 145, 146, 150–60, 161–62; Pizan and, 5, 141, 141n11; poetry and, 81; as source of pleasure, 144, 145; Valera and, 5, 117–19, 121; Villena and, 5, 17
Averroes, Middle Commentary on Aristotle's *Ethics*, 40
Azo of Bologna, 80, 94

Baets, Antoon de, 155
Baker, Denise, 104n3
Baldo de Ubaldis, 24, 94, 98
Barrero García, Ana Maria, 97–98
Barthes, Roland, 65n19
Bartolo da Sassoferrato, 24–25, 109n13; on chivalry, 63, 108; *De dignitatibus*, 123, 141, 141n12; *De insula*, 17, 25n9; and tradition of marginal glossing, 94; Valera's interpretation and commentary on, 109, 121, 122, 123
Bataille, Georges, 140
Bautista, Francisco, 109n13
Baxandall, Michael, 119
Benahatín, prophecies of, 113
Benedict XIII (antipope), 164
Ben Ezra, Abraham, 45
Ben Judah, Joseph, 56
Bentham, Jeremy, 144–45
Bernard of Clairvaux, Saint, 45; influence of, 78–79; *retractiones* by, 78
Bernofsky, Susan, 2, 78n1
Bible: *figura* in, 33–34; *glossa ordinaria* of, 22, 24, 25–26, 28–29, 44–45, 79, 183; Nicholas of Lyra's glosses on, Santa María's *additiones* to, 58, 180–81; production of different editions of, 26–27; strabismic reading of, 26; ultimate command of, 47. *See also* Song of Songs
Biffures (Leiris), 15
Boccaccio, and *querelle des femmes*, 116
Boethius, *De consolatione philosophiae*, 62; glossed manuscripts of, 56–58, 186
Bolea y Galloz, Fernando de, 185
Bologna, Azo of, 80, 94
Boltanski, Luc, 16

Book of the City of Women (Pizan), 116n24, 172, 173–77
Book of Hours, 4
Book of the Mutability of Fortune (Pizan), 172
Book of the Queen (Pizan), xiii–xiv
Borbón, Juan Carlos de, 91
Boulogne, Mathieu de, 116
Bourdieu, Pierre, 80–82
Boureau, Alain, 24n7, 38
Brownlee, Marina, 140
Bruni d'Arezzo, Leonardo: Cartagena's friendly debate with, 66; *De militia*, 132, 169–70; Latin translation of Aristotle's *Ethics*, 184; Latin translation of Plato's *Phaedo*, 164

Camille, Michael, 53n3
canon law, 50; and Castilian law, 90; glosses in books of, 79; Gratian and, 81n11; Roman, study of, 84
Carrillo, Alonso, 126, 127
Carruthers, Mary, 53n3, 165
Cartagena, Alonso de, 66–67, 127, 167, 170, 171; address to Council of Basel, 123, 141n12; intellectual lineage of, 181; *Libro de las Sesiones*, 115; in Lucena's *Diálogo de vita beata*, 187; and Mannelli's *Tabulatio et Expositio Senecae*, glossed and expanded translation of, 167; in network of civil interchange, 167; Santillana's correspondence with, 170, 171; Valera on, 109n13
Cartagena, Teresa de, 103, 177; *acousmatic* voice of, 176, 177, 182; *Admiraçion operum Dei*, 105, 178, 183; *Arboleda de los enfermos*, 105, 178, 183; biblical references by, 182–83; fate of works of, 12, 105, 178–79, 182; husband of, 125; intellectual genealogy of, 180–82; as microliterary artist, 105, 180, 183; *prudentes varones'* (prudent men's) response to work of, 178–80
case *(casus):* Díaz de Toledo's definition of, 129; as *exemplum*, 153–54; and interpretation of politics, 134–35; in margins of legal manuscripts, 154
Castilian language: anxiety about translating in, 69, 73; legal codes produced in, 83–84; Pedro de Portugal's glosses in, 161; Pedro de Toledo's translation of Maimonides's *Guide* in, 68–75, 68f, 70f, 171; San Cristóbal's translation of Vegetius's

Epitoma rei militaris in, 62–64; translation of Aristotle's *Ethics* in, 184–85; translation of Bruni's *De militia* in, 169; translation of d'Ailly's *Imago Mundi* in, 59–61; translation of Petrarch's *Invective against a Physician* in, 185–86

Castilian law: under Alfonso X, 83–84; under Alfonso XI, 87–88; under Sancho IV, 84; *Siete Partidas* within, 88, 89–90

Catherine of Lancaster (Queen of Castile), 68

Cavallé, Tomàs, 168

central text, 3; gloss's relationship to, 17–18, 32, 67, 79, 100–101; marginal writing compared to, 4; non-glosses proposing disappearance of, 72–75; as translation of marginal writing, 151

Charles II (King of Navarre), 7

Charles of Navarre (Prince of Viana), 184–85

Charles V (Holy Roman Emperor), 82, 90n37

Chartier, Roger, 48n53

chastity: politicization of, 119, 119n34; writings about, 119–20

chivalry. See knight(s)/knighthood

Cicero: *On Friendship*, Mannelli's gloss drawing on, 167; on philosophy's move from heaven to city/home, 164, 165, 166, 168; *Tusculanae Disputationes*, 164; on verisimilitude, 39, 40

cinematic reading, 157–60

cities: ideal, 168; philosophy's move from heaven to, 164, 165, 166–68; as spaces for philosophizing: Charles of Navarre's mission to create, 184–85; female intellectuals and, 172

La ciudad de Dios (Augustine), 95, 106–7, 130

civic life, manuscript book as space of, 67–68

civil law: ordinary glosses on, 24; production of texts of, 53–54; Roman, study of, 84; tradition of marginal glossing in, 9, 94. See also *Corpus Iuris Civilis*

De Civitate Dei (Augustine), 95, 106–7, 130

Codex Iustiniani, glosses on, 25

coetaneity, 8–9

cognitive processing, glossed texts and, 52–53

cognitive semantics, concept of satellite in, 64–65

Coleridge, Samuel Taylor, 15

Collines, Simon, 81n12

colonization: López's gloss on war and, 100, 101. See also America, conquest of

Columbia University, social justice program of, xiii

Commedia (Dante), glosses on, 81

common law *(ius commune)*, 90

communities of violence, 33, 182

Conde, Juan Carlos, 178, 179, 183

contemporary issues: glosses' engagement with, 65–67, 92, 101; microliteratures and, 8, 9, 10, 11–12, 13, 188; and politics of translation, 105n5; Valera's writings and, 105–6, 105n5, 115, 124

contuitu, Augustine's theory of, 132, 136

convent libraries, 177

Il convivio (Dante), 141

Copilación de las leyes del reyno, 89

Coplas de contempto del mundo (Pedro de Portugal), 148–60, 152f, 158f; glosses in, 150–60; prologue to, 151; radical montage in, 157–59; rubrics in, 150; thousand verses of, 149–50

La Coronación (Mena), 117, 141; glosses on, 81; narrative series in, 149

Corpus Iuris Civilis: glosses on, 4, 17, 25, 28, 79; production of, 79–80; tradition of, 94; recovery and systematization of, 81

critical thinking: vs. exhaustiveness, 6; microliterature and, 6, 9, 21, 177; public intellectuals and, 103

Crónica Abreviada de España (Valera), 106

Dagenais, John, 3n6, 146, 165

Dahan, Gilbert, 30

Daniel, Arnaut, 61

Dante Alighieri: *Commedia*, Pietro Alighieri's glosses on, 81; *Il convivio*, 141

Davis, Kathleen, 103–4

debate(s): gloss as space for, 67; microliterary artists participating in, 94–101, 104–5; on women *(querelle des femmes)*, 116–20

Decembrio, Pier Candido, 153n26

de Certeau, Michel, 37, 104n3

Decio, Filippo, 94

De consolatione philosophiae (Boethius), 62; glossed manuscripts of, 56–58, 186

Decretales (Gregory IX), 79

INDEX

Decretum (Gratian), 81
De dignitatibus (Bartolo da Sassoferrato), 123, 141, 141n12
De insula (Bartolo da Sassoferrato), 17
delectation, as part of ethics, 41
Deleuze, Gilles, 110n14
de Lubac, Henri, 29–30
De militia (Bruni), 132, 169–70; Santillana's interest in, 169–71
De Pictura (Alberti), 173–74
De Re militari (Vegetius). See *Epitoma rei militaris* (Vegetius)
Derrida, Jacques: *Marges de la philosophie*, 14–15, 16; on *supplément*, 3n6, 122
Diálogo de vita beata (Lucena), glosses on, 128n50, 186–87
Diálogo y razonamiento en la muerte del marqués de Santillana (Díaz de Toledo), 187
Díaz de Games, Gutierre, *El Victorial*, 113n20
Díaz de Montalvo, Alonso. *See* Montalvo, Alonso Díaz de
Díaz de Toledo, Fernán, 132n60, 166n3
Díaz de Toledo, Pero: as converso, 132n60; *Diálogo y razonamiento en la muerte del marqués de Santillana*, 187; *Enchiridion*, 128–29; gloss on Manrique's *Exclamación y Querella de la Governaçión*, 125n45, 127–28, 129–36; as microliterary activist, 13, 14; in network of civil interchange, 167; on philosophy's move from heaven to cities, 164, 165, 166, 168; as public intellectual/activist, 129, 132–33, 134, 136; translation of Plato's *Phaedo*, 164–65, 165f, 187; translation of Plato's *Phaedrus*, 128n50
disability: Cartagena's, 177; criteria for, central power and, 177–78
Dove, Mary, 35n34, 37n37, 43, 44–45
Drimmer, Sonja, 86
Dyson, Michael Eric, 7n17

ecclesiastical law, marginal glossing in, 9
Eden, Kathy, 123
effect d'inscription, 104n3
Eiximenis, Francesc, 109
Enchiridion (Díaz de Toledo), 128–29
epiphonetic glosses, 153n26
epistolary microliteratures, 111–14
Epistre Othea (Pizan), xiv, 141; epistemological device in, 141n11; narrative series in, 149

Epistula ad Pisones (Horace), 61
Epitoma rei militaris/De Re militari (Vegetius), 62; San Cristóbal's translation of, 62–64; removal of marginal writing from, 4–5
Espejo de Verdadera Nobleza (Valera), 121–24
essay genre: microliteratures as manifestation of, 6, 122; treatise *(tratado)* as category of, 120
ethics, new discipline of, 42; Giles of Rome on, 41; Thomas Aquinas on, 38–39, 40–41
Ethics (Aristotle). See *Nichomachean Ethics* (Aristotle)
eutrapelia: concept of, 185–86; as glossing style, 186–87
exclamación, as rhetorical concept, 129
Exclamación y Querella de la Governaçión (Manrique), 125–26, 131; Díaz de Toledo's gloss on, 125n45, 127–28, 129–36
exegesis, medieval: as affective space, 31, 32; and creation of "lawscape," 47; historical/literal reading vs. spiritual/allegorical reading in, 30; as mode of interpretation, 31, 32; on Song of Songs, 45–46; studies of, 29–30; theoretical structure in, 31
exempla, in legal texts, 122
Exhortación a la Paz (Valera), 114, 115

Fabian, Johannes, 9
Fernández de Velasco, Pedro (count of Haro), library of, 7, 171
Fernández Fernández, Laura, 4n8
Ferreras, Eloy Recio, 126
Fieschi, Sinibaldo de', 175
figura, 21–22, 33; as artifact for theory of history, 37–38; Auerbach on, 33–34; ethical manifestation of, 47–48; as hermeneutic device, 36; as heuristic device, 37; as literal device, 37; as nucleus of interpretation, 35–36; and *ordo disciplinae*, 34, 38, 42; as synonym of verisimilitude, 39, 40; Thomas Aquinas on, 38–39
figuraliter et typo, perspective of, 42
Fischer, Bobby, 56
florilegia, vs. serial reading, 148
footnote(s), marginal writing distinguished from, 15–16
Foucault, Michel, 9, 38, 50, 113
France, Marie de, 3n6

INDEX   223

Franco, Francisco, 91
Fuero Real, 84, 87

Gaffiot, Félix, 20n1
Galvez, Marisa, 79
Garcés, Julián, 97
Gherardi, S., 31n26
Gibert y Sánchez de la Vega, Rafael, 100
Gilli, Patrick, 49
Ginés de Sepúlveda, Juan, 95, 96
Glosa castellana al Regimiento de príncipes (Aegidius Romanus), 5
gloss(es)/glossing: as act of discourse, 94; as allegorical interpretation, 44; and central text, relationship to, 17–18, 32, 67, 79; centripetal force exerted by, 100–101; and contemporary issues, engagement with, 65–67, 92, 101; definitions of, 20n1, 66; as deliberative and argumentative spaces, 67; and economy of authority, 81; effect on perception, 75; epiphonetic, 153n26; eutrapelian style of, 186–87; flexibility associated with, 101; images functioning as, 85, 86, 87; industry of, 77; institution of, 21; interlinear, 20n1, 21; and learning, 52–53, 80–82; literal, 118; as metamorphic agent, 21, 49, 67; and novelty, 140–42; one-hundred-eyed Argos compared to, 143–44, 145, 146, 149; ordinary, 21, 22–25; *ordo disciplinae* and, 28–29, 49–50, 65, 77; power of, 49; public role of, 22; purpose of, 79; as "strange things," 20–22. *See also* interlinear glosses; legal glosses; marginal writing; ordinary glosses
glossa ordinaria. See ordinary glosses
glossators/glossers: activists, 102; as apprentice jurists, 50–51; appropriation of space of page by, 72–75; becoming intellectuals, 65–66; courage of, 51; epistemological project of, misunderstanding of, 140; Romanistic tradition of, 94
glossed manuscript(s): and intellectual networks, 171–72; lexical hierarchy in, 59, 62–64; production of space on pages of, 54–61, 64; relationship between center and margin in, 59
Gómez, Alonso (of Seville), 90
Grafton, Anthony, 15
Gratian, *Decretum,* 81
Greenblatt, Stephen, 65

Gregory IX, Pope, *Decretales (Liber Extra),* 79
Grotius, Hugo, 112
Guattari, Félix, 110n14
The Guide for the Perplexed (Maimonides), 56; Hebrew translation of, 69n23, 71, 74; Pedro de Toledo's translation of, 68–75, 68f, 70f, 171; prologue to, 73; second glosser's comments on, 70–75
Guillén de Segovia, Pedro, 126, 127
Guzmán, Luis de, 46

Hache, Tamara, 176, 177
Harizi, Yehuda al-, 71
Haro, count of (Pedro Fernández de Velasco), library of, 7, 171
Hauptman, Robert, 16
Henry II (King of Castile and León), 113
Henry VI (Shakespeare), 48
Henry of Segusio/Susa (Hostiensis), 99
Herbert, Lynley Anne, 4
Herman the German, 40
hermeneutics, 36
hieratism, glosses and, 81
Hildegard of Bingen, 177
historiography, first vernacular work printed in Iberian Peninsula, 106
history: philosophical approach to, 137–38; vs. poetry, Aristotle on, 174; of Rome, Díaz de Toledo's gloss on, 131–34; theory of, *figura* as artifact for, 37–38
Horace, 61, 188
Hostiensis (Henry of Segusio/Susa), 99
How to Be Both (Smith), 138
Hult, David, 116n24
Hutton, Lewis Joseph, 179
hypertext, marginal gloss and, 16–17

ibn Tibbon, Samuel ben Jehudah, 69n23, 71, 74
images/miniatures: as glosses, 85, 86, 87; jurisgraphisms, 86–87; in *Libro del Fuero de las Leyes* (Alfonso X), 85–86, 85f; in manuscripts containing *Las Siete Partidas* (Alfonso X), 87
Imago Mundi (Ailly), translation into Castilian, 59–61, 63
Imola, Giovanni da, 94
impossibilium, 137
incommoditas (uncommodity): Bibles with *glossa ordinaria* as, 27; definition of, 27–28
Innocent IV, Pope, 48n53, 100

Innocent VII, Pope, 164
inscription effect, 104n3
intellectual networks, microliteratures and, 9, 12, 165–67, 187–88
interlinear glosses, 20n1, 21; as corrections to translation, 71, 74; in Pedro de Toledo's translation of Maimonides's *Guide*, 68f, 69–70, 70f, 71, 74; process of normalizing, 28
interpretive communities, 32
Irnerius, 94; and recovery and systematization of *Corpus Iuris Civilis*, 81
Isabella (Queen of Castile), 89, 117
ius commune (common law), 90
Ius Gentium (Law of nations), 95
Ivo of Chartres, 81n11

Jed, Stephanie, 119
Joanna of Austria (Princess of Portugal), 82
John I (King of Castile), 88
John II (King of Castile): books produced in court of, 7, 94; civil war and, 169; Valera's letters addressed to, 111–13, 115
John of Navarre, 169
John the Teutonic: glosses compiled by, 26, 28, 79; Valera on, 109
Juana (Queen of Portugal), 158
jurisgraphisms, 86–87
jurists: growing antagonism toward, 48–49; marginal comments by, 49
Justinian law code. See *Corpus Iuris Civilis*

Kant, Immanuel, 112
Kim, Yonsoo, 177
knight(s)/knighthood: Bartolo da Sassoferrato on, 63, 108; mission in peacetime, Santillani's interest in, 170–71; political theology and, 62–63; Valera's position on, 108
Koselleck, Reinhart, 3n6

las Casas, Bartolomé de, 95, 96, 98
Latour, Bruno, 171–72
law: emergence and development of disciplinary order in, 19; letter vs. spirit of, 43; medieval and early modern, concern with civil and religious life, 50; and monarchs' legitimacy, 88–89; Roman and Castilian, glosses establishing connections between, 90. *See also* canon law; Castilian law; civil law; common law; legal glosses; legal text(s); Roman law
legal glosses: ambition to overtake central text, 17, 79, 100–101; Italian style of *(mos italicus)*, 120–21, 122; marginal glosses in relation to, 49–50; Romanistic tradition of, 94; and Valera's writings, 118, 120–21
legal text(s): under Alfonso X, 83–84; under Alfonso XI, 87–88; in Castilian, study of, 88; disciplinary order of gloss in relation to, 43, 47–48; *exempla* in, 122; in Latin, study of, 84; marginal commentary in, 17, 22, 49–51, 79, 84, 94, 100–101; margins of, difficult task of reading, 20; miniatures as interpretation of, 85–87, 85f; ordinary glosses *(glossa ordinaria)* of, 24, 28, 54, 79; under Sancho IV, 84; Song of Songs as, 46; violence within, *figura* and, 33, 34
Leibniz, Gottfried Wilhelm, 130
Leiris, Michel, *Biffures*, 15
Leo XIII, Pope, 22
Lewis, Charlton T., 20n1
Leyes del Estilo, 84
Libera, Alain de, 23
liberal thought, modern, 144–45
Liber de gradibus humilitatis et superbiae (Bernard of Clairvaux), *retractatio* included in, 78n3
Liber Extra (Gregory IX), 79
libraries, medieval Iberian, 168–69; Christine de Pizan and, 173; and intellectual networks, 169, 171–72; and microliterary glosses, 7; and poetics of reading, 157; Santillana's, 7, 132, 169, 187; Teresa de Cartagena and, 177; Zafra's, 7, 72, 171
Libro de las Sesiones (Cartagena), 115
Libro del Fuero de las Leyes (Alfonso X), 84–86, 85f
Lipking, Lawrence, 15–16
literacy, discovery of power of, 65, 66
literal gloss, 118
Livre de la cité des dames (Pizan). See *Book of the City of Women* (Pizan)
Livre de Paix/de la Paix (Pizan), 114–15
Llull, Ramon, 23n6
Longinus, Saint, 125

López, Fernández, 69n23
López, Gregorio, 13, 82, 91; as editor of *Las Siete Partidas,* 91–93; educational background of, 95; gloss deployed as legal artifact by, 101; glosses on *Las Siete Partidas,* 12, 13, 48n53, 82, 87, 93–101; gloss on war, 13, 82, 95–100, 101; political role of, 95; position of privilege, 102; practice of verisimilitude, 42
López Dávalos, Ruy, 55–56; anonymous correspondent of, and marginal glosses on *De consolatione philosophiae* (Boethius), 56–58, 186
López de Ayala, Pero, 113
López de Mendoza, Íñigo. *See* Santillana, Marquis of
López de Tovar, Gregorio, 93
Lucena, Juan de, 127; *Diálogo de vita beata,* glosses on, 128n50, 186–87
Lucena, Luis de, 118n30
Luhman, Niklas, 110
Luna, Álvaro de, 116, 169

Madrigal, Alonso de ("el Tostado"), 113
Magna Glossa (Accursio), 17
Maimonides, *The Guide for the Perplexed,* 56; Hebrew translation of, 69n23, 71, 74; Pedro de Toledo's translation of, 68–75, 68f, 70f, 171; purpose of, 56; second glosser's comments on, 70–75
Mannelli, Luca, *Tabulatio et expositio Senecae,* Cartagena's glossed and expanded translation of, 167
Manrique, Gómez: *Exclamación y Querella de la Governaçión,* 125–26, 131; Díaz de Toledo's gloss on, 125n45, 127–28, 129–36; position as *regidor* (city governor), 134; wife of, 178, 179
Manrique, Rodrigo, 171
manuscript book(s): copied together with marginal commentary, 7; *pecia* system of copying, 38, 39n40, 80; as radical experience of montage, 157–60; as space of civic life, 67–68; in vernacular, hierarchy of texts in, 74–75, 76. *See also* glossed manuscript(s)
Manuzio, Aldo, 81n12
Marges de la philosophie (Derrida), 14–15, 16

margin(s): as affective space, 12; importance in textual study, 52–54; as institution, 54; made ordinary, 22; and microliterary impulse, 1–2; ornamental motifs in, 4, 68, 68f; production of, 12–13, 75–76; as space for reflection and theorizing, 166; usefulness of, 1
"Marginalia" (Poe), 1n2, 4, 15, 144–45
marginal writing/commentary: ambition to overtake center, 17–18; central text as translation of, 151; Derridean influence on criticism and creation of, 14–15, 16; erasure of, 4–5; expansive nature of, 2–3; *figura* and, 21–22; vs. footnote, 15–16; forms of, 21; *glossa ordinaria* as models of, 79; and hypertext, 16–17; in legal texts, 17, 22, 49–51, 79, 84, 94, 100–101; manuscript books copied together with, 7; in *Partidas* editions, 90; and philosophy, 15, 18; process of normalizing, 28; prohibitions on/ removal of, 3–5; and rhythm of reading, 145–46; scholarship on, 15–17; signs used to indicate, 2, 2n5, 61, 72, 146; as source of pleasure, 144, 145; tradition in law and theology, 9; typology and, 21; in vernacular, 54, 75. *See also* gloss(es)/glossing
Marino, Nancy, 126
Martínez de Toledo, Alfonso, 116
Martorell, Joanot, *Tirant lo Blanch,* 48–49
Marx, Karl, 110n14
Mary of Aragon (Queen of Castile), 116, 117
Maso degli Albizi, Rinaldo, 169
material text: as epistemological device, 138–39; and lived experience, 161
Matilda of Canossa, 81
Matteis, F. D., 31n26
McKenzie, D. F., 53n3
Mejía, Ferrán, 109n13
Mena, Juan de, 6n16; *La Coronación,* 81, 117, 141, 149; in Lucena's *Diálogo de vita beata,* 187; narrative series in glossed works of, 149; *querelle des femmes* and, 116; *Las Trescientas,* 4
Mendoza, Juana de, 178
mens (workshop), 38
Meun, Jean de, 116

INDEX

microliterary artist(s)/activist(s), 13–14, 104–5; contemporaneity of, 105–6; Díaz de Toledo as, 129, 132–33, 134, 136; Teresa de Cartagena as, 105, 180, 183; Valera as, 13–14, 105, 106, 108–10, 112, 114, 115; women as, 183

microliterary attitude, 11; Valera's, 115, 117, 118, 121

microliterature(s): and activism, 13–14; and contemporary issues, 8, 9, 10, 11–12, 13, 188; created in prison, xiii–xvi; as critical movement, 185; and critical thought, 6, 9, 21, 177; definition of, 3, 5; epistolary, 111–14; essay genre and, 6; as humanistic activity performed in public sphere, 6; and intellectual networks, 9, 12, 165–67, 187–88; margins and impulse for, 1–2; study of, 5; synchronization/non-chronological nature of, 11–12; as *thinking with*, 5–6; verisimilitude in, 42

Mignolo, Walter, 105n4

Miguel, Jerónimo, 128n50

Miguel-Prendes, Sol, 146

Mill, John Stuart, 144–45

Minaya, Bernardino de, 97

miniatures. *See* images

montage, manuscript as radical experience of, 157–60, 163

Montalvo, Alonso Díaz de, 89; edition of *Las Siete Partidas,* 87, 89–91, 93

Montoro, Antón de, 126, 127

Moore, Robert I., 33

Morales, Cristina, 178

narrative series: in Pedro de Portugal's glossed works, 149, 151–56, 163; and perspectivism, 152

Native Americans, Gregorio López's gloss on, 97, 99, 100

Nicholas of Lyra, *Postillae* (glosses on the Bible), Pablo de Santa María's *additiones* to, 58, 180–81

Nichomachean Ethics (Aristotle): Castilian translation and glosses on, 184–85; Giles of Rome's commentary on, 41; new discipline based on, 40; Thomas Aquinas's commentary on, 38–39, 40

Nirenberg, David, 33, 182

nobility, concept of, Valera on, 122–24

nomadic thought, notion of, 110n14

non-glosses, 72–75

novelty, glossing experience and, 140–42

O'Brien, Flann, 61

Olivetto, Georgina, 167

On Friendship (Cicero), Mannelli's gloss drawing on, 167

On the Soul (Aristotle), 167

orality: Valera's written reaction to, 121–22; writing as subproduct of, 122

ordinary glosses *(glossa ordinaria),* 21, 22–25; of Bible, 22, 24, 25–26, 28–29, 44–45, 79, 183; industry devoted to creation of, 28–29; of legal texts, 22, 24, 28, 54, 79; and *ordo disciplinae,* 28–29; perpendicular nature of, 25; reading techniques for, 44; of sacred texts, 54; on Song of Songs, 21, 35, 36f, 43–47; status of, 78, 79; use as reference, 45; workshops establishing, privileged position of, 102

ordo disciplinae (disciplinary order), 23; in co-laboratory, 38; *figura* and, 34, 38, 42; *glossa ordinaria* and, 28–29, 49–50, 65, 77

Padrón, Juan Rodríguez del, 109n13, 116

Palencia, Alfonso de, 105

Panda, Pedro de la, 171

Panyella, Vicente, 185

Parisian theology, 38

Partidas. See Las Siete Partidas

Passagieri, Rolandino de', 153

past future, concept of, 3n6

Pastrana, Diego de, 187

Paul, Saint, 30

Paul III, Pope, 97, 100

Paz y Melia, Antonio, 46n51

peace: permanent/perpetual, concept of, 112, 113, 113n20; Pizan's writings on, 114–15; Valera's writings on, 111–15

pecia system, of book copying, 38, 39n40, 80

pedagogy, 80; glosses and, 80–82

Pedro de Portugal (Pedro de Avis), 138; *Argos,* 142–44; and assemblage, epistemological device of, 139–40, 149, 152, 153, 163; autoglossing by, 141–44, 145, 146, 150–60, 161–62; *Coplas de contempto del mundo,* 148–60, 152f, 158f; manuscripts of, as epistemological artifacts, 14, 138–39; narrative series in glossed works of,

149, 151–56, 163; in network of civil interchange, 167; phenomenology of "I" in glossed works of, 160–63; Pizan's writings and, 114n22; pleasure derived from writing, 144, 145, 161–62; and poetics of reading/montage, 157–60, 163; radical literary art of, 142–44, 146, 148, 157–60; *Sátira de Infelice e Felice vida*, 4, 141–44, 145, 146, 147f–148f, 149
Pedro de Toledo: anxiety about process of translation, 69, 73; translation of Maimonides's *Guide for the Perplexed*, 68–75, 68f, 70f; prologue to, 73; second glosser's comments on, 70–75
Pelayo, Menéndez, 136
Penna, Lucas de, 98
Perec, Georges, *La vie, mode d'emploi*, 163
Pérez de Guzmán, Fernán, 130–31
Peri Hermeneias (Aristotle), 36
Perotti, Olga, 128n50
perspectivism, serial narration/assemblage and, 152
pertransitum, 42
peshat system of commentary, 58
Peter I (King of Castile and León), 113
Petrarch, *Invective against a Physician*, Talavera's translation of, 185–86
Phaedo (Plato), Díaz de Toledo's translation of/glosses on, 164–65, 165f, 187; in network of civil interchange, 167, 187
Phaedrus (Plato), Díaz de Toledo's translation of/glosses on, 128n50
Philip II (King of Spain), 82
Philip IV the Fair (King of France and Navarre), 41
Philippopoulos-Mihalopoulos, Andreas, 47
philosophy: Cartagena's gloss on, 167; and civil life, 127–28; marginal writing and, 15, 18; move from heaven to city/home, 164, 165, 166–68; poetry and, 40
Pius XII, Pope, 22
Pizan, Christine de, 103; autoglossing by, 5, 141, 141n11; *Book of the City of Women* (*Livre de la cité des dames*), 116n24, 172, 173–77; *Book of the Mutability of Fortune*, 172; *Book of the Queen*, xiii–xiv; construction and balancing of manuscripts of, xiv, 10; *Epistre Othéa*, xiv, 141, 149; and Iberian authors, resonances with works of, 114n22; *Livre de Paix/de la Paix*, 114–15; metamorphoses of, 10, 10n23, 172–73; as microliterary artist, 105; narrative series in glossed works of, 149; practice of verisimilitude, 42; prison seminar on, xiii–xvi; and *querelle des femmes*, 116; as radical artist, 172; research by, 173, 174–75; sources of, 172, 176; workshop of, 7
Plato: *Phaedo*, Díaz de Toledo's translation and glosses on, 164–65, 165f, 187; *Phaedrus*, Díaz de Toledo's translation and glosses on, 128n50; represented as errant philosopher, 164
pleasure: marginal writing as source of, 144, 145, 161–62; modern liberal thought and, 144–45
Plutarch, 153
Poe, Edgar Allan: "Marginalia"/theory of marginality, 1n2, 4, 15, 144–45; obsessive reading and note-taking by, 1
Poetics (Aristotle), 40
poetics of subjectivity, 139
poetry: and activism, 125–26, 136; autoglossing in, 81; Díaz de Toledo on, 128–31; vs. history, Aristotle on, 174; and philosophy, 40; and political activism, gloss demonstrating link between, 14
political conflicts, emerging, marginal notes related to, 9
political economy: liberal philosophy in, 144–45; of pleasure, 144, 145
political philosophy, medieval library as space of, 171
political science, new discipline of, 41, 42
Politics (Aristotle), 135; Mannelli's gloss drawing on, 167
politics of invisibility, 105
politics of the plebeian, Valera and, 123–24
Pons, Lola, 116
Portonariis, Andrea de, 91
Portuguese language, in Pedro de Portugal's *Sátira*, 161
Postillae (Nicholas of Lyra), Pablo de Santa María's *additiones* to, 58, 180–81
Preciado, Paul B., 119, 172
printing press, and *Siete Partidas* editions, 89–90, 91, 93
prison, seminar/workshop in, xiii–xvi

INDEX

providence, Díaz de Toledo's discourse on, 133
public intellectual(s), 102–3, 107; Díaz de Toledo as, 129, 132–33, 134, 136; microliterary artists as, 104–5; Valera as, 112, 115, 122
Pythagoras, probationary pupils of, 176

Quaestio de Magistro (Thomas Aquinas), 45
querelle des femmes, 116–20
Quevedo, Francisco de, 121
Quintilian, on interlinear glosses, 21
Quintus Curtius Rufus, 153

Rashi (Shlomo ben Itzak), 45, 54; and *peshat* system, 58; Santa María's criticism of, 181
Raymond of Penyafort, 79; *Summa de Penitentia et Matrimonio,* 120
reading: cinematic, 157–60; poetics of, Pedro de Portugal's exploration of, 157–60; rhythm of, marginal writing and, 145–46; serial, 148–49, 151–56, 163; strabismic, 13, 20, 26, 44
Reinhardt, Klaus, 181
Relectiones (Vitoria), 96
Rodríguez del Padrón, Juan, 109n13, 116
Rojas, Fernando de, 61
Roma, Gil de. *See* Aegidius Romanus
Roman law: and Castilian law, glosses establishing connections between, 90; study of, 84
Rome: construction materials recycled in, 174; history of, Díaz de Toledo's gloss on, 131–34
Rome, Giles of. *See* Aegidius Romanus
Round, Nicholas, 126, 136, 164
Russo, Sara, 125n45, 126
Rychner, Max, 2n3

Saenger, Paul K., 53n3
Saint-Victor, Hugh of, 30, 55
Saliceto, Bartolomeo da, 94
Salomon, David, 16
Salutati, Coluccio, 132
Sancho IV (King of Castile), 83, 84
San Cristóbal, Alonso de, 62–63; translation of Vegetius's *De Re militari,* 4–5, 62–64
Santaella, Rodrigo de, 105, 105n5
Santa María, Pablo de, 58, 180–81

Santiago-Otero, Horacio, 181
Santillana, Marquis of (Íñigo López de Mendoza): activities in war and diplomacy, 169; Bruni's *De militia* and, 169–71; correspondence with Cartagena, 170, 171; Díaz de Toledo's gloss including, 131; library of, 7, 132, 169, 187; in Lucena's *Diálogo de vita beata,* 187; Mena's glosses and, 81
Sassoferrato. *See* Bartolo da Sassoferrato
satellite, concept in cognitive semantics, 64–65
Sátira de Infelice e Felice vida (Pedro de Portugal), 142, 145, 147f–148f; glosses on, 4, 141–44, 145, 146, 149, 161–62; languages used in, 161, 162; Mena's *Coronación* and, 141n11; in network of civil interchange, 167; prologue to, 141; as radical literary art, 142
satire, 15th-century, 117
Saussure, Ferdinand de, 163
Schmitt, Carl, 130
Segusio (Susa), Henry of (Hostiensis), 99
self-gloss. *See* autoglossing
Sententia Ethicorum (Thomas Aquinas), 38–39, 40–41
serial reading, 148–49, 151; of Pedro de Portugal's glossed works, 151–56, 163. *See also* narrative series
sermons, glosses used in preparation of, 22, 45
Servius, glosses on Virgil's works, 81
Shakespeare, William, *Henry VI,* 48
Short, Charles, 20n1
Las Siete Partidas (Alfonso X): authenticity of, López's glosses and, 91, 93; contemporaneity of, López's glosses and, 91; earliest marginal commentary in, 87, 89; editorial history of, 82, 87–90; extant manuscripts of, 83, 84, 87, 88; historical background to publication of, 82; importance of, 13, 25, 88; *Libro del Fuero de las Leyes,* 84–86, 85f; López's edition of, 91–93; López's glosses on, 12, 13, 48n53, 82, 87, 93–101; monarchical overreach of, 83; Montalvo's edition of, 87, 89–91, 93; *Ordenamiento de Alcalá* and, 87–88; on price of different scripts, 39n40; printing press and, 89–90, 91, 93; prohibition on commentary on, 3

Siger of Brabant, 137
signs/marks, in glossed manuscript, 2, 2n5, 61, 72, 146; as instrument of cognition, 73; and organization of page space, 57–59, 73
Slaughterhouse-Five, or The Children's Crusade (Vonnegut), 11n24
Smith, Ali, *How to Be Both,* 138
social justice: Columbia University program of, xiii; microliteratures and critical thinking about, 8, 9, 82; process of constructing a subject and, 139. *See also* activism
Song of Songs: allegorical reading of, 43–47; Aristotelian reading of, 46; as erotic poem, debates on, 43, 45; exegesis on, 45–46; *glossa ordinaria* on, 35, 36f, 43–47; metamorphic agency of, 21; as legal text, 46
Spijker, Ineke van 't, 30
stationes (workshops), production of texts of civil law in, 53–54, 79–80
Steel, Karl, 182
Stern, Josef, 70
strabismic order, of glossed page, 25, 151
strabismic reading, 13, 20, 26, 44
Strabo, Walafrid, 25, 26
Suárez, Rodrigo, 94
Suárez de Figueroa, Gómez. *See* Zafra, lord of
subject: assemblage/construction of, 139–40; fragmentation of, narrative series and, 153
Summa de Penitentia et Matrimonio (Raymond of Penyafort), 120
Summa Theologiae (Thomas Aquinas), 62
supplément, Derrida on, 3n6, 122
surplus, marginal writing perceived as, 3n6
Susa (Segusio), Henry of (Hostiensis), 99
synchronization, microliteratures and, 11–12

Tabulatio et expositio Senecae (Mannelli), Cartagena's glossed and expanded translation of, 167
Talavera, Hernando de, 185–86
Talmud, marginal commentary in, 54
Teissier-Ensminger, Anne, 86n24
Tertullian, on *figura,* 33–34

theodicy: Augustine's theory of, 130, 133, 134; Díaz de Toledo's discourse about, 133
theology, tradition of glossing in, 9
Thévenot, Laurent, 16
Thomas, Yan, 174
Thomas Aquinas, 38; influence on public life of Christendom, 78–79; lines of debate with, López's edition of *Las Siete Partidas* and, 94, 98; *Quaestio de Magistro,* 45; *Sententia Ethicorum,* 38–39, 40–41; *Summa Theologiae,* 62; *Super libri ethycorum,* 41n44; writing style of, 78
time: Augustine's conception of, 106, 131, 132; past future, concept of, 3n6
Tirant lo Blanch (Martorell), 48–49
Torah, marginal commentary in, 54
Torroella, Pere, 116
Toti, Enrique (of Salamanca), 90
Traducción y glosas de la Eneida (Villena), 7, 8f, 17
translation: *ad sententiam,* 69n23; anxiety about, 69, 73; central text as, 151; contemporary issues and, 105n5; criticism of, by second glosser/reader, 71–75; literal *(de verbo ad verbum),* 69. *See also under* Castilian language
Tratado en defensa de virtuosas mujeres (Valera), 115, 116–19, 120, 121
treatise *(tratado),* as category of essay genre, 120
Las Trescientas (Mena), marginal glosses removed from, 4
Trevet, Nicholas, and glosses on Boethius's *De consolatione philosophiae,* 55–56, 58
Trigo, Pedro del, 183
tropology, 30
Tusculanae Disputationes (Cicero), 164
tutor text: use of term, 79. *See also* central text
typology, 22; and marginal glosses, 21

Ubaldis, Baldo de, 24, 94, 98
universitas, meaning of, 28n18
universities: and construction of kingdom/state, 90; corporations of theologians/lawyers and, 28; and legal commentary, 84; study of *Las Siete Partidas* in, 88, 90
University of Salamanca, 90n37

Valdés, Juan de, 5
Valera, Diego de, 103, 108; autoglossing by, 5, 117–19, 121; and contemporary issues, 105–6, 105n5, 115, 124; *Crónica Abreviada de España (Valeriana)*, 106; epistolary microliteratures, 111–14; *Espejo de Verdadera Nobleza*, 121–24; essays on political theory, 120–24; ethical and political experience of reading, 124–25; *Exhortación a la Paz*, 114, 115; as microliterary activist, 13–14, 105, 106, 108–10, 112, 114, 115; microliterary attitude of, 115, 117, 118, 121; nomadism of, 110, 110n14; personalities deployed in treatises of, 108–9; Pizan's writings and, 114, 114n22; and politics of the plebeian, 123–24; practice of verisimilitude, 42; as public intellectual, 112, 115, 122; sources of, 110–11; *Tratado en defensa de virtuosas mujeres*, 115, 116–19, 120, 121; writings about peace, 111–15; writing style of, 124

Valeriana, 106
Valéry, Paul, 15
van Liere, Frans, 30
Vegetius, Flavius Renatus, *De Re militari (Epitoma rei militaris)*, 62; San Cristóbal's translation of, 4–5, 62–64
Vélez, Julio, 116
verisimilitude: concept of, 39–40; in microliterary texts, 42
vernacular humanism, 138
vernacular language(s): historiography in, first in Iberian Peninsula, 106; marginal commentary/glosses in, 54, 75. See also Castilian language
vernacular media, production of margin in, 13
Vialette, Aurélie, 168
Vicente, Gil, 37
El Victorial (Díaz de Games), 113n20
Vidal, Francisco, 128
La vie, mode d'emploi (Perec), 163
Villena, Enrique de, 6n16; autoglossing by, 5, 17; on *exclamación*, 129; exegetical structure used by, 31; translation and glosses on *Aeneid* (*Traducción y glosas de la Eneida*), 7, 8f, 17
violence: communities of, 33, 182; gloss's desire for material coexistence and, 77; in legal texts, *figura* and, 33, 34; microliterary artists' response to, 104–5; preservation of law through acts of, López's gloss on, 100, 101
Virgil: *Aeneid*, Villena's translation and glosses on, 7, 8f, 17; glosses on works of, 81
Virseda Bravo, Marta, 7n18
Vismann, Cornelia, 154
Viti, Paolo, 169
Vitoria, Francisco de, 79n5, 91; lines of debate with, López's edition of *Las Siete Partidas* and, 94, 95–96, 99, 100; *Relectiones de Indis*, 96, 99
Vonnegut, Kurt, 11n24

Walser, Robert, microscripts of, 2, 11, 78
war, López's gloss on, 13, 82, 95–100, 101
Weinstein, David, 33
Weiss, Julian, 6n16, 116, 117, 118–19, 120
Weissberger, Barbara, 116
Wheel of Fortune, narrative of, 153, 154
women: imprisoned, microliteratures created by, xiv–xvi; intellectuals, cities as spaces for philosophizing and, 172; literary debate about *(querelle des femmes)*, 116–20; metamorphoses of, 10, 10n23, 172–73; microliterary artists, xiii–xiv, 5, 10, 105, 180, 183; minimization of work of, 178–80; nobility in, Valera on, 122; Pizan's writings on, 116, 172, 173–77; Valera's writings on, 115, 116–19; voices of, 176–77

Yisraeli, Yoshi, 58, 180, 181
Young, Robert J. C., 105n4

Zafra, lord of (Gómez Suárez de Figueroa): library of, 7, 72, 171; translation of Maimonides's *Guide for the Perplexed* for, 68
Zakai, Avihu, 33
Zúñiga, Alonso de, 89

www.ingramcontent.com/pod-product-compliance
Lightning Source LLC
Chambersburg PA
CBHW030540230426
43665CB00010B/970